VOX POPULI: ESSAYS IN THE HISTORY OF AN IDEA

SEMINARS IN THE HISTORY OF IDEAS

The Reaper. From the *Hortus Deliciarum* of the
Abbess of Herrad von Landsberg. Photograph by
The Milton S. Eisenhower Library, The Johns
Hopkins University.

VOX POPULI:
ESSAYS IN THE HISTORY OF AN IDEA

GEORGE BOAS

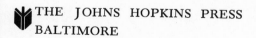 THE JOHNS HOPKINS PRESS
BALTIMORE

To the Librarian of
The Johns Hopkins University
and
His Staff

CONTENTS

ILLUSTRATIONS

PUBLISHER'S NOTE

The history of ideas as a form of scholarly inquiry took shape at The Johns Hopkins University in the first half of the century. The man chiefly responsible was Arthur O. Lovejoy, whose twenty-eight years as professor of philosophy were spent promoting the historiography of the intellect. With two colleagues, George Boas and Gilbert Chinard, he founded the History of Ideas Club, where, in an atmosphere at once congenial and critical, visiting scholars might offer their interpretations of the development of the great ideas that have influenced civilization. Lovejoy was instrumental in founding the *Journal of the History of Ideas* in pursuit of the same end. And in his own writings he persistently and patiently charted the transformations which a seminal idea might undergo— over time, across disciplines, or within the intellectual development of an individual thinker.

When, with Carnegie Corporation support, The Johns Hopkins University inaugurated an imaginatively new program of adult education in 1962, it was a happy inspiration to build it around a set of graduate seminars in the history of ideas; for the History of Ideas Club itself had long before been described as "a sort of seminar where mature men and women learned new and valuable lessons." To be sure, this evening program has followed Lovejoy's spirit of inquiry rather than his own actual practice. Not all the seminars are concerned to pursue in detail the transformations of a single unit-idea. Rather, there is a shared view that no theory— at any time, in any field—is simply self-generated, but that it springs by extension or opposition from earlier theories advanced in the field, or is borrowed from theories in cognate fields, or is derived from the blending of hitherto separate fields into one. To pursue the unfolding of any theory in these terms (so the teachers in the seminars believe) allows a sophisticated and rigorous discussion of contemporary scholarship with an audience lacking previous specified knowledge. These notions are an extension, not an abuse, of Lovejoy's concern; he had never wasted effort on being unduly prescriptive except to call, hopefully, for cooperative scholarship in a venture so clearly beyond the reasonable capabilities of a single scholar.

This series of books, *Seminars in the History of Ideas*, is intended to provide a wider audience with a chance to participate in "a sort of seminar" similar to those in the University's program. Just as the teaching seminars themselves draw on the spirit rather than merely the letter of Lovejoy's original enterprise, so this published series extends beyond those topics already offered in the University's program. But all, nonetheless, reflect that intent with which Lovejoy so long persisted in his own work: "the endeavor to investigate the history, and thereby, it may be hoped, to understand better the nature, of the workings of the human mind."

APOLOGIA

The problem which the essays in this book try to illuminate is the history of a famous proverb, *Vox populi vox Dei*. Upon examination, the first two words of this sentence turn out to have been highly ambiguous. And though their meaning shifted as the centuries rolled along, the words themselves remained as they were. This is what has happened to famous works of art as well, both literary and pictorial. They remain great masterpieces, but the reason why they are praised varies from age to age. One need only think of the fortunes of the *Aeneid*, *Hamlet*, *Don Quixote* in the history of literature, and of the *Mona Lisa*, Bruegel's *Fall of Icarus*, Piero della Francesca's *Resurrection* in the history of painting.

Not only has the denotation of the *vox populi* changed, but its connotation has changed also. Whereas the *populus* in literature was for many centuries the butt of jokes, to be used for comic relief in serious drama, it became an object of pity and later of aesthetic charm. Popular opinion was in Roman times to be despised, if considered at all; it began to be sought only after the French Revolution. As all that was left of primitive man, the peasant became the prototype of "natural" man and hence his standards of right and wrong and even of beauty and ugliness were to be accepted by everyone. But the People as a collective body of individuals included more than the peasantry; it also came to number among its members small artisans, the poor, the exploited, those who are called today "the underprivileged." The peasant in Bruegel, the urban lowlife in Caravaggio, turned into saints and martyrs. And when one came to the nineteenth century, Courbet and Millet painted both types, not in an idyllic fashion but with plain realism. There is even reason to believe that the ballet dancers of Degas were not intended to be fairylike creatures of the opera but hard-working girls, angular rather than graceful, and no more ethereal than his laundresses and absinthe drinkers. Thus where the Voice of the People in ancient times meant the voice of the Elders or the Prince Electors or sometimes the Barons, it came to mean the voice of the laboring man, whether rural or urban. The "Folk" became a solid body of human beings in which was vested the right to speak for all, whether in matters of value or of fact.

To do complete justice to this story would require such broad knowledge of religious, political, economic, and aesthetic history that probably no one man could succeed in covering the entire ground. Whether such a polymath exists or not, I am not the man. Consequently, I have attempted merely to write a group of historical sketches, indicating the high points in the narrative and leaving the rest to someone of greater erudition. I shall be amply satisfied if I have outlined a story of interest to some future historian. Not only have I not written a full history of a cluster of ideas, I have not even proposed much in the way of explanation. In fact, I doubt that causal explanations of a scientific type—and what others are there?—are possible when one is dealing with individual occurrences and not with classes of events.

There will also be found in these essays too much documentation for some readers and too little for others. I apologize to the former by pointing out that it is wiser to cite the very words of a man than to paraphrase them. Whether one is a professional scholar or not, one is better off knowing precisely what ideas are attributed to a person quoted. To the latter I can simply say that with Montesquieu I believe that to write well is to skip the intermediate ideas. Ignoramuses are not likely to waste their time on a book like this, and nothing is gained by overloading the pages of a book with footnotes. My quotations form, as it were, a little anthology of opinions. I have simply used my own judgment in determining what to leave out. In dealing, for instance, with the *fabliaux* I have seen no reason to quote several where one will do. Similarly, I have thought that Shakespeare was a better representative of the

Elizabethan Age than Shakespeare plus a dozen other contemporary dramatists. This may seem to be a lack of thoroughness. But, like the first recorded Boaz, I have left something for the gleaners.

The bibliography lists only those books and articles which I have either quoted or referred to. Other works which I have read but not quoted are not listed. The purpose of the list is to show what editions I have used, for in some cases texts vary from edition to edition. I may add that those cited are usually those which I happen to own, not those which would be the most fashionable or the most current.

I cannot close without a word of thanks to my many friends who have patiently helped me when I asked for help: to Professor Grace Frank, Mrs. Bryson Burroughs, Drs. John Baldwin, Harold Cherniss, Morris D. Forkosch, E. H. Gombrich, Henry Rowell, and Owsei Temkin. To the National Endowment for the Humanities I owe a special debt of gratitude for giving me six months of freedom in which to work without interruption. The staff of The Johns Hopkins Library has as always spared no pains to assist me in that spirit of cooperation that has always distinguished Johns Hopkins. There are of course many others who helped me without realizing what they were doing, above all the students who have followed my courses and taught me by their questions, and to them I express my thanks as well.

G.B.

Ruxton, Maryland

VOX POPULI: ESSAYS IN THE HISTORY OF AN IDEA

THE PROVERB'S ANNALS

Few popular slogans have had the history of Vox populi vox Dei. And few have been more ambiguous. For just who composed the populus, how it expressed its divine voice and how its reputation varied are problems which have never been thoroughly explored. The one detail of the proverb's history that is certain is its genesis in Judeo-Christian beliefs. It thus cannot be one of those proverbs whose origin is lost in the very distant, the prehistoric past.

Esteem for the People is a modern phenomenon, though its origin lies well back in occidental history. The vox populi was first thought to be authoritative in the election of kings and bishops; it later became an arbiter of taste. The development of what has been called folk-art, accompanied by an almost passionate love of it, is something that only a series of volumes could adequately expound. Yet a brief synopsis of this curious history may prove to be at least a stimulus to other and younger historians. It should be of some interest to Americans for, after all, our Constitution is in legend written by the People, who are held to be sovereign, and rights are expressly reserved for them in Article IX of the Bill of Rights.[1] Our national elections are believed to be conducted on the principle of universal suffrage, though this belief is not always grounded in practice. Our mass media of communication are directed by men who hold that they should give

1. Professor Lily Ross Taylor in her Roman Voting Assemblies, chap. I, points out the similarities between the methods of electing officers in the Roman Republic and in our national conventions. That the Romans were also supposed to be sovereign as a people is recalled as late as the fourth century A.D. by Claudian in his De consulatu Stilichonis, Book III, ll. 106 ff., though by that time popular sovereignty had completely disappeared.

the People what the People want. And since the development of public opinion polls, we have found our rulers studying them, following them as guides, and thus probably modifying their future results. If the People are behind some measure, it is usually believed to be a good one; if they are against it, the measure is therefore bad. This is no doubt the most prudent belief to hold if one is a politician whose career depends upon popular support. But as in all such procedures, the beneficiaries attempt to influence those whose opinions they claim to follow. One sees the same sort of thing in families, where the children have to do what their parents tell them to do but have learned how to bribe the parents to urge them to do what they would have done without urging.

Behind all this is the shadowy notion that men have a faculty of knowing what is right and wrong without study or even reflection. Men do know what they want. And they are likely to identify the fulfillment of their desires with the good. The dispute about whether the realization of a wish makes it good or whether goodness is a standard in terms of which our wishes should be organized is one that has worried philosophers since the time of Plato, if not before. Fortunately we need not try to settle that issue in a purely historical study. But I should point out that the people who use the proverb with approval assume that in case of popular desires, desire creates goodness.[2] The People are assumed to have an infallible source of knowledge, knowledge that is self-substantiated, requiring no analysis or criticism. The proverb is in this respect related to one of the many forms of cultural primitivism, the form that maintains that nature is better than art, that instinct is better than learning, that feelings are wiser than reason, that the "heart" is sounder than the "mind."

It is obvious from the very wording of the proverb that it

2. And here I should no doubt explain that when I am speaking of people collectively, as the People, I spell the word with an initial capital. In the lower case, I refer to people distributively.

could not have been phrased, except in Hebrew, before the spread of Christianity. The term *vox populi* did occur in Latin, though naturally not identified with the *vox Dei*, in Lucan's *Pharsalia*, which was written in the middle of the first century A.D. In the first book of that poem (ll. 270–75) we find the phrase in a passage running,

> The Curia, mindful of the rebellion of the Gracchi, set aside the law and expelled the tribunes who had divided the city by their disagreements. The exiles seeking the help of their leader and the standards which were nearby, were assembled by Curio the bold, in a venal speech. He, the one-time voice of the People, dared to defend freedom and to mingle armed potentates with plebeians.[3]

The idea that people in general, the human race, might have a voice was not entirely foreign to Roman thought. Stoicism was accustomed to the idea of a *consensus gentium* if not to a *consensus Romanorum*, and it was always true and always to be followed. Moreover, in the divisions of Roman society it was traditional to express the interests of the various social classes as if each had one peculiar to itself and antagonistic to those of the other social classes. But all this simply shows that the term *vox populi* in itself would not have been obscure or strange to readers of Latin. What Romans thought of popular opinion is another matter, and I shall leave it until my second essay.

Since the proverb has obvious affiliations with Hebraic and Christian thought, one looks for hints of it in the two Testaments.

3.

Expulit ancipiti discordes urbe tribunos
Victo jure minax jactatio curis Gracchis.
Hos jam mota ducis, vicinaque signa petentes
Audax venali comitatur Curio lingua:
Vox quondam populi, libertatemque tueri
Ausus, et armatos plebi mescere potentes.

Here the *vox populi* means an individual who is the mouthpiece of the people and it carries no eulogistic charge. Lucan had no great admiration for Curio. See the poetic apostrophe to him in Book IV, ll. 799 ff. I owe this reference to my colleague, Professor Henry Rowell. *Populus*, moreover, here means *plebs*.

Assuming that we know what we mean by "the People," and confining ourselves exclusively for the time being to the New Testament, one is frustrated by the exegetical skill required to make the relevant texts consistent. For there are just as many passages that would lead one to believe that Christianity was to be the religion of the poor and oppressed if they are the People as there are others that seem to support the antithetical idea. Not only do the Three Kings (literally, *Magi*) come to adore the new-born Jesus, but also the Shepherds. The significance of the two Adorations is probably nothing more than the suggestion that both high and low, weak and powerful, join in acknowledging Him. It has sometimes been said that the Twelve Apostles were chosen from the working class and that therefore Christianity was to be a religion of the lowly. But as a matter of fact the occupations of only five of them are given in the canonical texts: four are fishermen and one a publican or tax collector. Comment has been made on the fact that God was incarnated as the son of a carpenter, but the carpenter in question was of a line of kings descending from David. In the *Magnificat*, the Lord is praised for putting down the mighty and exalting them of low degree, for filling the hungry and sending the rich away empty (Luke 1:52–53). But the first miracle was at a wedding feast and consisted of providing good wine for the guests (John 2:9). In the Beatitudes the meek are to inherit the earth, and the reviled and persecuted are called the salt of the earth. But Jesus also said that He had come not to send peace but a sword. In the Sermon on the Mount (Matthew 6:20), men are told not to lay up treasures on earth but to lay them up in Heaven, to take no thought for their food or drink, nor for their clothing. They are, in fact, to take no thought for the morrow. But later (Matthew 25:1–12) the five foolish virgins "took their lamps and took no oil with them." And when the Bridegroom came, they had to ask the five wise virgins for oil, with lamentable results. And what would one who believed in taking no thought for the morrow make of the parable of the talents? And when the multitude was "very great" and had nothing to eat (Mark 8:1), Jesus performed the miracle of the loaves and fishes and fed four thousand people, though He had previously urged His disciples to take no thought for their food and drink.

It is easy enough to harmonize these apparently discordant passages by treating them as allegories showing the power of the Incarnate Lord. But the great majority who read and heard them were not trained in exegesis and they tended to emphasize either one side of the teachings or the other. Some interpreted the main lesson of Christianity as a program of communal life, as Saint Ambrose did, help for the poor, protection for the weak, which is almost precisely what the Lollards asked for. Some, on the other hand, justified the structure of power as manifested in the ecclesiastical hierarchy. In Matthew 19:21 and 24 we read, "If thou wilt be perfect, go and sell that thou hast, and give to the poor, and thou shalt have treasure in heaven. . . . It is easier for a camel to go through the eye of a needle, than for a rich man to enter into the kingdom of God." Yet when at the Passover the woman brought ointment and poured it on Jesus' head and the disciples were indignant at the waste of money which might have been given to the poor, Jesus said, "Why trouble ye the woman? For she hath wrought a good work upon me. For ye have the poor always with you, but me ye have not always." Hence when a man of wealth endowed an abbey or spent huge sums on the decoration of a church he could always cite this example rather than the former.

At the very time of the Peasants' Revolt in England, great sums were being expended on what must have seemed like luxury to the poor, and this in the name of piety. Churchmen like Saint Ambrose might preach communism, and Saint Bernard might rail against the lavish decoration of churches, but there were others, like Suger of Saint Denis, who saw no problem there. I am not attempting to say what the "real" meaning of these New Testament verses was or to harmonize texts that seem discordant. I am simply

trying to show why pious Christians could take one set of statements by themselves and see in them the kernel of a religion that
was much more complicated than they seemed to realize. The
Church as an organization never practised asceticism, though certain of the religious orders did to an extreme degree. But neither
did she preach extravagance, though the Vatican has never been a
hermit's cell. How was an unsophisticated Christian to know
which tendency was right? When the Lollards moved in the direction of simplicity and poverty they were persecuted not only
by the state but by the Church herself.

The question of popular authority and wisdom cannot be
answered until one has decided just who are the People. They
are not everybody; that much is clear. How they were distinguished from the non-People will have to be taken up by itself,
for it involves normative as well as descriptive judgments. Before
entering upon that problem, I propose to give the recorded background of the proverb as far as I have been able to trace it.

Alcuin: The First Appearance of the Proverb

The usual dictionaries of quotations attribute the proverb
Vox populi vox Dei to Alcuin, though he himself says it was current in his time, the late eighth century. In any event, no one has
found an earlier occurrence of it. We now give in translation the
entire text in which it appears, in a letter to Charlemagne. It is
dated, according to its latest editor, Dümmler, about 798.

1. A will is of force after men are dead: otherwise it is of no strength
at all while the Testator is alive. For before death the general consensus confirmed it. And so one cannot violate at a later date what
could not be condemned at an earlier.
2. Whoever is found to be displeasing to a testator and is also
especially abusive is one unworthy to be mentioned in a will. For
example: Chanaan was made a slave because he dishonored his
father; Esau lost his place as elder because of his intemperance;
Reuben and his younger brothers were subject to rebuke by their

father. And finally, "He who shall curse his father . . ." and so on.

3. It is natural that the blessings of fathers on their sons be passed along by inheritance. They, however, fight against nature who are disobedient or contumacious toward their parents. He therefore will be a proper heir who has kept the orders previously fixed by his parents.

4. It is one thing to grant something with undue indulgence, another to have been given one's rightful due. Nor can those things be taken back from what is due which it has been agreed were obtained from real merit. Indeed a diversity of merit demands a diversity of reward.

5. He who is nobly born and has been given his inheritance legitimately, has not been found in contempt either of the Old Law or the New, nor injurious to his father, nor harmful to the people, he should be very sure of inheriting with the Lord's compassion.

6. When the head is broken, it is obvious that every member languishes, since from the strength of the head comes the soundness of the whole body. Nor can the members glory in that false health which is found not to be in the head.

7. If the truth is sought here, it is not unknown; if the reason, it is not doubtful; if the authority, it is not uncertain. For the authority stands out clearly and the reason is obvious and the truth itself cannot be hidden.

8. All such matters seem grouped in a threefold division, a division of the willing and the unwilling and those who stand in between, so that they may be linked to those from whom they may benefit. Hence the willing should be properly aided; the unwilling strongly opposed; and the doubtful either rationally convinced or circumspectly neglected. And to all must it be shown that authority cannot be corrupted nor reason conquered nor truth in any way overcome.

9. The people in accordance with divine law are to be led, not followed. And when witnesses are needed, men of position are to be preferred. Nor are those to be listened to who are accustomed to say, "The voice of the people is the voice of God." For the clamor of the crowd [vulgi] is very close to madness.

10. There is a popular proverb: from hardness something survives, from softness, on the other hand, nothing remains. Nevertheless wisdom ought to wait upon constancy and constancy upon perfect wisdom, so that constancy may be wise and wisdom constant.

11. The preaching of peace should be carried on so that no false assertions can be induced under the name of piety. For just as the

breaking of the peace is the worst of things, so it is blasphemous to negate the truth. Finally, true unity and peaceful truth do much in unison.

12. And, I maintain, things of this sort must be drilled into the simple, because ignorance of the truth can force multitudes to stray. But contrariwise, the enemy is confounded when the truth is made clear, friends are unified, and in fact all will equally lack excuses [for their errors].

These things, I beg of you, look into worthily and diligently. The greatness of your faith renders my smallness impatient on your behalf, gives me daring beyond my powers, for only he loses faith who has never had it. May He in Whose hands are kings and the laws of kingdoms multiply your crowns, watch over and protect you.[4]

4.

1. *Testamentum in mortuis confirmatur*, Apostolo protestante (Hebrews 9:17). Ideoque post obitum testatoris omnimodam firmitatem obtinuit. Quod etiam ante mortem consensus omnium confirmavit. Non itaque postea valet infringi, quod antea nullo modo potuit improbari.

2. Quicunque testatori repperitur ingratus, insuper et contumeliosus existat, ipse sibi testis est, quia testamento dignus non est, ut verbi causa Chanaan patris in exhonoratio servum constituit. Esau propter intemperantiam primogenita perdidit; Ruben junioribus fratribus contumelia paterna postposuit. Ad postremum quoque: *Qui maledixerit patri* (Exod. 21:17; Lev. 20:9) et reliqua.

3. Benedictiones patrum in filio hereditare genuinum est, contra leges autem naturae pugnant qui parentibus inoboedientiam seu contumatiam parant. Legitimus igitur heres erit, qui praefixos ordines erga parentes tenuerit.

4. Aliud est indebite clementer admitti, alius ex debito competenter asscribi. Nec possunt ex debito repeti quae prorsus indebite concessum est adipisci. Diversitas siquideum meritorum diversitates exegit praemiorum.

5. Quod optime natus et hereditatem legitime consecutus neque legis antique seu novae contemptor inventus, nec adversus patrem sautius neque contra populum vulneratus, magnam debeat hereditandi gerere Domino miserante fiduciam.

6. Fracto capite subjecta quaeque languere perspicuum est, cum de firmitate capitis totius proveniat incolomitas corporis; nec possunt ea sanitate membra subdita gloriari, quam constat in capite non haberi.

7. Hic si veritas quaeritur, non est incognita; si ratio, non est ambigua; si auctoritas, non est incerta. Quoniam et auctoritas supereminet et ratio patet et veritas abscondi non potest.

8. Tripartita distributione videntur ista omnia includi, consulentium scilicet ac nocentium et eorum, qui sic inter utrosque semper ambigui sunt, ut quos obtinere perspexerint, eis se continuo socient. Sunt ergo consulentes utiliter adjuvandi, resistentes autem viriliter obviandi; dubii vero vel rationabiliter adtrahaendi, vel circumspecte dissimulandi; cunctisque mon-

There are many problems woven into this letter, but it will not be disputed that (a) Alcuin tells us that our proverb is customarily cited by some people, that (b) he identifies the People with the uneducated mob, that (c) he has no confidence in their judgment. He clearly does not believe that the People's voice is God's voice and he says what Pope Stephen was to say seventy-five years or so later, namely that the People should be led, not followed. This is of some interest since the election of Hildebrand

strandum nec auctoritatem posse corrumpi, nec rationem vinci, nec veritatem paenitus superari.

9. Populus juxta sanctiones divinas ducendus est, non sequendus; et ad testimonium personae magis eliguntur honeste. Nec audiendi qui solent dicere: Vox populi, vox Dei, cum tumultuositas vulgi semper insaniae proxima sit.

10. Vulgare proverbium est: De duro superatur aliquid, de molli vero remanet nihil. Debet tamen et sapientis ministrare constantiam, et constantis perficere sapientiam, ut sit constantia sapiens, et sapientis constans.

11. Sic exercenda est predicatio pacis, ne sub nomine pietatis inducatur assertio falsitatis. Nam sicut pacem rumpere pessimum est, ita veritatem negare blasphemum. Multum sibi denique concinunt verax unitas et pacifica veritas.

12. Haec et eiusmodi, reor, inculcanda simplicibus; eo quod ignorantia veritatis cogat errare quam plurimos. Porro veritate manifestata contrarii confundentur, amici solidabuntur, universi vero pariter excusatione carebunt.

Ista, supplico, dignanter ac diligenter insipite. Vestrae siquidem fidelitatis immensitas parvitatem meam reddit impatientem pro vobis, facit etiam supra vires audentem. Enimvero fidem non perdit, nisi qui numquam habuit. In cuius manu sunt reges et jura regnorum, ipse coronas vestras multiplicet, tueatur, obumbret.

Text from *Epistolae Karolini Aevi*, Vol. IV, ed. E. Dümmler, no. 132. In his note on *vox populi* (p. 199), Dümmler says, "*Originem huius proverbi, nescio.*" This may be evidence that the proverb was not much earlier than the ninth century. Yet the consent of the people, *pro forma*, was, as we shall see, demanded even in the election of popes. G. G. Coulton in *Medieval Panorama* (p. 28) quotes Stephen VI, Pope from 886 to 889, saying of papal elections, "The election pertaineth to the priests, and the consent of the faithful populace must be obtained; for the people must be taught, not followed." This would seem to suggest that the consent in question was not freely given. Coulton also points out, after Esmein, that consent was shown by "clamours, by acclamations or by hooting." But such consent could obviously be given only by that part of the people present. He refers to Esmein's *L'Unanimité et la majorité*, in *Mélanges H. Fitting*, Vol. 1. On shouting as suffrage, see Lily Ross Taylor's work cited in n. 1, pp. 2 and 85–86.

in the eleventh century was based almost entirely on popular acclaim and thus created a scandal. Moreover, it is not known what
was the occasion of Alcuin's letter. It obviously concerns a will,
but it is far from clear whether Alcuin was advising the Emperor
about his, Charlemagne's, will or about carrying out the provisions
of someone else's will. The letter was presumably written, if
Dümmler is right, about two years before Charlemagne was
crowned as Emperor. According to Kleinclausz,[5] Charlemagne
named his successors in 806, but Alcuin died in 804. It is, to be
sure, possible that Charlemagne had talked the matter over with
him before 806, but it would have to have been before 800, since
Alcuin was stricken with paralysis in that year. Charlemagne's will
was made about 811,[6] which date makes it even more unlikely
that the letter concerns it. And in any event, what would the
voice of the People have had to say about this? The consent of
the People was held to be necessary, as I have said, in the ceremony
of electing a bishop and sometimes in the election of a ruler. The
matter in hand may even have been Charlemagne's distribution
of crowns to his sons from the various lands he had conquered.
But all this is speculation.

Sometimes popular consent was thought desirable when appointments to less exalted offices were made. Einhard, recording
Charles's accession to the office of *maior domo*, feels it important
to add, "which honor was not usually given by the People to any
but to those who were pre-eminent by nobility or birth or wealth"
(*qui honor non aliis a populo dari consueverat quam his qui et
claritate generis et opum amplitudine ceteris eminebant*).[7] Again,
in speaking of the accession of Charles and Carloman, he says that
the Franks "solemnly and in general convention" (*solemniter ge-
nerali conventu*) elected them and when, after the death of Carloman, the brother of Charles, Charles was chosen king, it was by

5. A. Kleinclausz, *Charlemagne*, p. 310.
6. *Ibid.*, p. 347.
7. *Vita Caroli imperatoris*, *PL*, VII, col. 28.

"the consent of all the Franks" (*consensu omnium Francorum*).[8]
Just how general or how entire this consent was cannot be discovered now, and it is probable that the phrases are both simply
ceremonious. They indicate how the tradition of popular consent
was upheld and nothing more.[9] For even when a usurper took the
throne for himself, he used the same type of formula. Thus in
the *Francorum regum capitularia* we find that the election of Boso
(October 15, 879) occurred with the "consent of God, by the
suffrage of the saints . . . with one mind and like vote and with
entire consent" (*nutu Dei, per suffragia sanctorum . . . communi
animo, parique voto, et uno consensu*);[10] but surely no one would
take such phrases any more seriously than one would take the
style of "King of France" which was attributed to England's kings
until the twentieth century. But what must be taken seriously is
the felt necessity of including them. For the inertia of custom
explains not only the continuance of a verbal tradition but also
its acquisition of sanctity.

The Election of Kings and Bishops

The consent of the People to the election of bishops has an
even older history than has been suggested so far. The *Catholic
Encyclopedia* in the article "Bishop" maintains that up to the
sixth century "the clergy and the people elected the bishop on
condition that the election should be approved by the neighboring
bishops," an account that may be considered to be the authoritative doctrine of the Church. But Hastings' *Encyclopedia of Religion and Ethics*, in the article on "Laity," traces popular election
of bishops back to Acts 6:3–5. In that passage there is an account
of a dispute between the Greeks and the Hebrews concerning the
alleged neglect of widows. Then (verse 2), the Apostles called

8. *Ibid.*, col. 29.
9. Cf. Kleinclausz, *Charlemagne*, pp. 82, 205, 221.
10. See *PL*, CXXXVIII, col. 787 ff.

"the multitude of disciples" together and said to them (verse 3), "Look ye out among you seven men of honest report, full of the Holy Ghost and wisdom, whom ye may appoint over this business." After choosing them, they "set them" before the Apostles (verse 6) and when the Apostles had prayed, "they laid their hands upon them." [11]

In the Old Testament there is authority for the popular election of civil as well as religious chiefs. The main source for the popular election of a king is obviously that of Saul. In I Samuel 8:7 we find that the people came to Samuel and asked for a king. Samuel prayed for guidance and the Lord said to him, "Hearken to the voice of the people in all that they say unto thee" (*Audi vocem populi in omnibus quae locuntur tibi*).[12] Samuel points out the miseries they will undergo if they are given a king, but (8:19) "Nevertheless the people refused to obey the voice of Samuel; and they said, Nay; but we will have a king over us" (*Noluit autem populus audire vocem Samuelis sed dixerunt: nequamquam rex enim erit super nos*). The end of the incident in the biblical account runs (8:22): "And the Lord said to Samuel, Hearken unto their voice, and make them a king" (*Dixit autem Dominus ad Samuelem: Audi vocem eorum, et constitue super eos regem*).[13]

11. This runs in the Vulgate: "Considerate ergo fratres, viros ex vobis boni testimonii septem, plenos Spiritu Sancto, et sapientia, quos constituamus super hoc opus. Hos statuerunt ante conspectum apostolorum et orantes imposuerunt eis manus." In the Didache, 15, which seems to date from the second century, the people are bidden to elect for themselves bishops and deacons and the seven are called deacons in the rubric. In the fourth century, Athanasius insisted on popular elections; see his *Apologia contra Arianum*, 6. The multitude must have been what today would be called the congregation.

12. If I quote the Vulgate, it is because it was this version of the Bible that most medieval readers knew.

13. The phrase *vox populi* also occurs in Isaiah 61:6: *Vox populi de civitate, vox de templo, vox Domini reddentis retributionem inimicis suis.* This brings the two voices together, but Saint Jerome may have mistranslated the Hebrew or the Septuagint. For in the Authorized Version the people are not men-

The Vulgate then does not identify the voice of the People with that of God, though God does order His priest to listen to it. The People, moreover, are wrong in wanting a king, so the divine purpose may have been to make them pay for their foolishness. In any event, Samuel is told by God to grant their wish and he does so. And the Books of Kings are ample verification of Samuel's prophecy of the evils that accompany monarchy. Moreover, the historical books of the Old Testament establish a theory of history that became standard in Christian circles: the theory, later to be identified with the name of Saint Augustine, that historical good and evil are determined by the People's choices. The first recorded choice of the People was a mistake, and they continued to make mistakes. But the history of the proverb shows that this was to be completely forgotten.

Returning now to the election of bishops, the consent of the People was certainly required; but whether the requirement was scrupulously met and how it was met are questions to which we have no firm answers. Formal, that is, ceremonial, acclamation seems to have sufficed. In the *Libelli de Lite*, for instance, there is a passage from Cardinal Humertus' *Adversus Simoniacos* which somewhat clarifies the matter: "Whoever is consecrated as a bishop must first, according to the decretals of the saints, be elected by the clergy, then sought for by the people, and finally consecrated by the bishops of his province in accordance with the judgment of the metropolitan." [14] The consent of the People is given, it

tioned. Instead the phrase is translated, "A voice of noise from the city." In the *Twenty-Four Books of the Holy Scriptures . . . According to the Massoretic Text*, translated by Isaac Keeser, the translation is like that of the Authorized Version, except that "tumult" takes the place of "noise."

14. "Quicumque consecratur episcopus, secundum decretales sanctorum regulas prius est a clero eligendus, deinde a plebe expetendus, tandemque a comprovincialibus episcopis cum metropolitani iudicio consecrandus"; MHG, *Libelli de Lite*, Book I, chap. 5, p. 108. If there is any question about my translating "plebe" as "people," note the sentence which follows: "Neque enim aliter certus et fundatus vel verus episcopus dici vel haberi poterit, nisi certum clerum et populus quibus praesit habuerit et a comprovincialibus suis

will be observed, after the election, not before, and it is reasonable to assume that once a man's fellow bishops had chosen him, the consent of the People would follow automatically. Yet it was sometimes held to be the best evidence of a bishop's legitimacy. Optatus, for instance, defending Caecilianus against the charge of causing the Donatist schism, points out that he was elected *suffragio totius populi* (*PL*, XI, col. 919); and in the Decretals of Burchardus of Worms, Book I, chap. 12, we read that, "no one is to be ordained bishop, unless the clergy and parishioners are assembled and are unanimous" (*Nullus est ordinandus episcopus, nisi convocatis clericis et parochianis, et in unum consentientibus*). But as early as the Council of Carthage (A.D. 254) we find it noted (*PL*, III, col. 1025) concerning the Bishops Basil and Martial who were accused of lapsing into idolatry,

> that it has been established by divine authority that with the people present before the eyes of all a priest be chosen and proved worthy and suitable by open judgment and testimony, just as in Numbers God gives this advice to Moses, "Tell Aaron etc." God orders that a priest be elected before the whole synagogue, that is, He teaches and shows that there ought to be no ordination to the priesthood save in the presence of the public conscience, so that with the people present evil deeds may be detected and merits witnessed, and that there be a just and legitimate ordination which shall have been justified by the suffrage and judgment of all.[15]

auctoritate metropolitani, ad quem vice apostolicae sedis cura ipsius provinciae pertinet consecratus fuerit." Cf. also below, the second essay, p. 49. My colleague, Dr. John Baldwin, has invited my attention to a passage in Petrus Cantor's Commentary on Ezekiel 33 (Paris, Bibl. Mazarine, 178, fol. 160v b), where the proverb appears. The gloss reads: "Quod sacerdos vel prelatus judex a populo eligendus." This would look as though popular election were not confined to bishops.

15.

"Quod et ipsum videmus de divina auctoritate descendere ut sacerdos plebe praesente sub omnium oculis deligatur et dignus atque idoneus publico judicio ac testimonio comprobetur, sicut in Numeris Dominus Moysi praecepta dicens, Apprende Aaron etc. (Num. 20:25, 26). Coram omni synagogo jubet Deus constitui sacerdotum, id est, instruit et ostendit ordinationes sacerdotales non nisi sub populi assistentis conscientiae fieri oportere, ut plebe praesente vel detegantur malorum crimina vel bonorum merita

Here, for once, we have a purpose given, the revelation, if fitting, of any crimes and misdemeanors that a candidate for the episcopal chair may have been guilty of. After this passage the text refers to Acts 6:2, which we have already quoted, to show that this applies to all ranks from bishops to deacons. Why the clergy would not have known of a candidate's evil deeds and merits without consulting the People is not discussed. By the time of Charlemagne's *Capitularis*, the phrase *per electionem cleri et populi* was a commonplace.[16]

In the election of Gregory VII, as I have suggested, it was the voice of the People rather than the voice of the clergy that assured him the papal throne.[17] In his own words he writes, after relating the news of his predecessor's death to Desiderius, Abbot of Monte Cassino, April 23, 1073, "Suddenly, while our lord the pope was being carried to his burial in the church of Our Saviour a great tumult and shouting of the people arose, and they rushed upon me like madmen, so that I might say with the prophet, 'I am come into deep waters where the floods overflow me. I am weary with my crying; my throat is dried.'" And three days later, writing to Wibert of Ravenna, he adds that the populace left him "neither time nor opportunity to speak or take counsel, and dragged me by force to the place of apostolic rule, to which I am far from being equal. . . ." Whether the crowd was acclaiming him as pope or as ruler of Rome is not clear. But then it was probably not clear to the crowd either. It is well known what a stormy career he had, once in the seat of power, and there was indeed question about the legitimacy of his election. But we have a letter from Wido, Bishop of Ferrara, on the matter which leaves no doubt

---

praedicentur, et sit ordinatio justa et legitima quae omnium suffragio et judicio fuerit examinata."

The reasoning is paralleled in the marriage ceremony in the words, "If any man can show just cause. . . ."

16. See *PL*, XCVII, col. 521; Part I, sect. 1, par. 78.

17. I take my quotations from Ephraim Emerton, *The Correspondence of Pope Gregory VII.*

that popular acclamation gave him a legal right to the Papal See and was in accordance with tradition. The letter runs:

> There are some who cast slanderous doubts on the coming into power of Hildebrand and who speak of his election as a crime. But when the case is carefully investigated, the charge seems utterly false and made shamelessly rather than prudently. For, as I have learned and authenticated from the testimony of very pious men of excellent reputation, when Alexander of blessed memory was dead but not yet buried, the clergy and the people, the whole senate in unison, by a single vote of all, by a complete consensus, by the greatest desire, violently dragged him [Hildebrand] along and tore him into a thousand pieces. He was elected by the clergy, demanded by the people, confirmed by the suffrage of all the bishops and priests. Hence we might indeed say of him what Cyprian said of Cornelius, that he was made a bishop by God, by the judgment of Christ, by the testimony of almost all the clergy—or, as I might say more truly, of absolutely all—by the vote of the people who were then present, by the congregation of aged priests and honorable men, though it had happened to no one before him, when the place of Alexander and the See of Peter fell vacant. This rule of ordaining bishops has been ratified in the canons, decided by the fathers, and approved as settled by the elders.[18]

Gregory himself merely emphasized the popular clamor and one would imagine from his letter that no regular election had taken place. It is true, as Wido puts it, that, if all occurred as he

18.

"Sunt qui Ildebrandi calumpnientur ingressum, quique eius criminentur introitum. Sed re diligenter inspecta, falsum videbitur omne, quod profertur, et quod inpudenter magis quam prudenter opponunt. Nam, ut a viris religiossissimis didici et fama ferente recognovi, beatae memoriae Alexandro defuncto necdum humato, clero et populo, omni senatu pariter collecto, uno omnium voto, pari consensu, summo desiderio violenter attractus et in mille partes discerptus a clero eligitur, a populo expetitur, episcoporum et sacerdotum omnium suffragio confirmatur. Ut enim de eo dicamus, quod de Cornelio Ciprianus asseruit, factus est episcopus de Deo, Christi eius iuditio, de clericorum pene omnium—et ut verius dicam, omnino omnium —testimonio, de plebis, quae tunc affuit, suffragio, de sacerdotum antiquorum et bonorum virorum collegio, cum nemo ante se factus esset, cum Alexandri locus et sedes Petri vacaret. Haec regula ordinandorum episcoporum a canonibus statuitur; a patribus decernitur, a veteribus praefixa probatur."

Wido Episcopus Ferrariensis *de Schismate Hildebrandi, Libelli de Lite MGH,* Book I, chap. 1, p. 534.

relates it, tradition was simply continued. But, as all readers of medieval history know, there was widespread doubt about what actually had happened. In the case of secular rulers, there was also argument about the role the *populus* was to play. The question seems to have been hotly debated from at least the eleventh century on. One of the firmest believers in popular power was Manegold of Lauterbach who insisted that the People not only had the right to elect a king but also the right to depose one. To depose is obviously different from to elect, but if the People have both powers, they are to all intents and purposes omnicompetent. The following quotation illustrates Manegold's point of view.[19]

"King" is not the name of a kind but of an office. Therefore the royal rank and power, just as it arises above all worldly powers, so he who is instituted to wield it must not be the wickedest or vilest, but one who, as he surpasses all others in situation and rank, must surpass them in wisdom, justice, and mercy. For he who must assume the care of all must shine above all others by the greater grace of his virtues, must strive to wield the power which has been handed over to him with the greatest balance of equity. For the people do not raise him over themselves that he may freely exercise tyrannical power over them, but that he may protect them from the tyranny and evil of others. But when he who is elected to restrain the wicked and defend the upright begins to nurture depravity in himself, to grind down the good, to exercise cruel tyranny upon his subjects which he ought to have rejected, is it not clear that he must deservedly fall from the rank granted to him, that the

19. *Manegoldi ad Gebehardum Liber, Libelli de Lite, MGH,* esp. sect. XXX, p. 365, ll. 5–31. The best account of his theory of sovereignty that I know is G. P. W. A. Hoch's *Manegold von Lauterbach und die Lehre von der Volksouveräntät unter Heinrich IV.* For his idea of the People's Voice, see *Libelli de Lite* as cited. The tradition of the popular election of kings uses the words "the People" in a very restricted sense. In what is now England, the Witan are said to have had the power of election; in France, Louis the Stammerer (877–79) was elected by the nobles and the bishops; in the German states, the emperor was elected by only seven electors: the three Rhenish archbishops (Mainz, Cologne, Trier), the Palatine of the Rhine, the Duke of Saxony, the Margrave of Brandenburg, and the King of Bohemia. In the Visigothic kingdom of Spain, as in Poland, the king was elected by nobles. For a brief but authoritative account of the election of kings in France, see Maurice Duverger, *Les Constitutions de la France,* pp. 11 ff.

people may be liberated from his domination and their subjection to him, since the pact for the sake of which he was constituted has already been broken by him?

Nor could anyone justly and reasonably accuse them of perfidy, since they have in no way broken faith with him first. If we may take an example from less noble matters, if anyone for an appropriate wage turns over his swine to someone to be fed and this man does not feed them but steals them, slaughters or loses them, would he not know, after retaining the promised wage for himself, that he should discharge him with reproaches from feeding his swine? If, I say, this is observed in low things, as in the case of the swineherd who does not feed his swine but loses them, so much the more rightly with just and defensible reason must he who tries not to rule over man but to lead them astray, be deprived of all power and rank which he has over men as the condition of men differs from that of swine. . . . It is one thing to reign, another to tyrannize over one's kingdom.[20]

The target of this passage is undoubtedly Henry IV, the emperor who tried to depose Gregory VII and was in turn excommunicated by the pope and did penance at Canossa. Manegold's

20.

"Quod rex non sit nomen naturae, sed vocabulum officii. Regalis ergo dignitas et potentia sicut omnes mundanas excellit potestates, sic ad eam ministrandam non flagitiosissimus quisque vel turpissimus est constituendus, sed qui sicut loco et dignitate, ita nichilóminus ceteros sapientia, iusticia súpere pietate. Necesse est ergo, qui omnium curam gérere, omnes debet gubernare, maiore gratia virtutum super ceteros debeat splendére, traditam sibi potestatem summo equitatis libramine studeat administrare. Neque enim populus ideo eum super se exaltat, ut liberam in se exercendae tyrannidis facultatem concedat, sed ut a tyrannide ceterorum et improbitate defendat. Atqui, cum ille, qui pro coercendis pravis, probis defendendis eligitur, pravitatem in se fóvere, bonus contérere, tyrannidem, quam debuit propulsare, in subiectos ceperit ipse crudelissime exercere, nonne clarum est, merito illum a concessa dignitate cadere, populum ab eius dominio et subiectione liberum existere, cum pactum, pro quo constitutus est, constet illum prius irrupisse? Nec illos quisquam poterit iuste ac rationabiliter perfidiae argúere, cum nichilóminus constet illum fidem prius deseruisse. Ut enim de rebus vilioribus exemplum trahamus, si quis alícui digna mercede porcos suos pascendos committeret ipsumque postmodo eos non pascere, sed furari, mactare et perdere cognosceret, nonne, promissa mercede etiam sibi retenta, a porcis pascendis cum contumelia illum amoveret? Si, inquam, hoc in vilibus rebus custoditur, ut nec porcarius quidem habeatur, qui porcos non pascere, sed studet disperdere, tantô dignius iusta et probabilitione omnis, qui non homines regere, sed in errorem mittere conatur, omni potentia et dignitate, quam in homines accepit, privatur, quanto conditio hominum a natura distat porcorum. . . . Aliud est regnare, aliud in regno tyrannidem exercére."

letter asserts the right of the People both to elect and to depose a king and to do this on the premise of a primordial compact. It is, moreover, significant that the assertion is made by a prelate, though whoever else could have done it in the eleventh century might be questioned. Yet Alcuin had been a prelate too, and he was far from being enthusiastic about the rights of the *populus*. But by Manegold's time the biblical tradition seems to have had greater currency, as in the famous expression *populus maior principe*.[21]

I will conclude this section with the use of the proverb in the election of a bishop. There is a story dating from the first half of the tenth century that it was used to persuade a reluctant candidate for the archbishopric of Canterbury to accept his election. The candidate was Odo. According to his biography in the *DNB* by the Rev. William Hunt, Odo, a pagan, was adopted by one of Alfred's nobles—Aethelheim or Athelm—who had him baptized. On the death of Wulfheim (942), Archbishop of Canterbury from 923, Odo was offered the post by King Eadmund. He declined on the ground that it ought to be filled by one who was a monk. This difficulty was overcome by having him given the cowl at the monastery of Fleury, whereupon he accepted the archbishopric. The story of his accession is told by William of Malmesbury in his *De gestis pontificorum Anglorum*.[22] "Since the approval of all the bishops was given to the royal will, at last the most reverent overcame the rigor of his assertion and fell in with the common opinion, recognizing that proverb: *Vox populi vox Dei*." [23]

In this case the People were the bishops and it looks as if their voice had been the *vox regis* rather than their own. But whatever the facts, the proverb was seen to be of force and appro-

21. "The People are greater than the sovereign." For references to this principle, which was far from being applied, see Otto Gierke, *Political Theories of the Middle Ages*, p. 151, n. 164.

22. *PL*, CLXXIX, col. 1451 B.

23. "Sed cum regiae voluntati episcoporum omnium assensus accederet, tandem vix reverendissimus propositi sui rigore edomito, in communem perrexit sententiam, recognitans illud proverbium: vox populi vox Dei."

priate. It was, moreover, kept in currency, for William of Malmesbury's book was written two hundred years after the event in 1125.

The Deposition of Edward II: The People as the Magnates

We now skip two centuries and come to the deposition of Edward II where the proverb was used in a political context. In the Parliament of 1327 the following charges were brought against the king, most of them unfortunately justified, none of them of immediate importance to the rank and file.

1. He was unfit to govern.
2. He had refused to listen to his wise counselors.
3. He had neglected the public business.
4. He had brought about the loss of Scotland, Gascony, and Ireland.
5. He had destroyed the Church.
6. He had badly mistreated the great laymen.
7. He had broken his coronation oath.
8. He had brought the realm to the brink of ruin.[24]

Parliament found these charges proven, and, in the words of James Mackinnon, "The Archbishop of Canterbury sanctified the transaction by a sermon on the theme, Vox populi vox Dei." [25] The archbishop in question was Walter Reynolds, and the sermon was delivered at the coronation of the new king. Why he chose this proverb for his text I have not discovered, nor have I found the sermon itself. Since I have not read Reynolds' own words, I have no way of knowing precisely how his sermon fitted his text, but judging from the account of the abdication in Murimuth, no sanctification of the act was demanded. Murimuth's account reads:

A certain number of persons (a group of bishops, earls, abbots) were sent to the king at Kenilworth, and they said to him and

24. See, among others, Sir James H. Ramsay, Genesis of Lancaster, pp. 160 ff.
25. The History of Edward III (1327–1377), p. 12.

urged him diligently to renounce his royal rank and crown, and permit his eldest son to reign in his place; otherwise they themselves would renounce their homage to him and elect another king in his stead. When he heard this, with weeping and outcries he replied that he was very pained that he should have deserved such treatment from the people of his realm, but in view of his inability to do otherwise, he said that he was pleased that his son was so acceptable to his whole people that he would succeed him and reign in his place.[26]

There are one or two details about this event that are worth emphasizing. In the group of persons who waited upon the king there were no commoners from the laity, and thus the words "*totus populus*" must be taken with a grain of salt.[27] In the second place, before the abdication the Londoners rebelled, but apparently in favor of the king, not against him. In the third place, the charges were drawn up by Bishop Stratford, not by a lay commoner; and as for the People, a political theorist could possibly

26.

"Certus numerus personarum mitterentur ad regem apud Kenilworth, et sibi dicerent et eum requiverent diligenter quod renunciaret dignitati regiae et coronae, et quod permitteret filium suum primogenitum regnare pro eo; alioquin ipsi redderent sibi homagia sua et alium eligerent sibi regem. Quibus auditis, ipse cum fletu et ejulatu respondit quod ipse multum doluit de eo quod sic demeruit erga populum sui regni; sed ex eo quo aliter esse non potuit, dixit quod placuit sibi quod filius suus fuit toti populo sic acceptus quod ipse sibi succederet, regnaturus pro eo."

Adam Murimuth, *Continuatio Chronicarum, sub* A.D. 1327, ed. Edward Maunde Thompson, p. 51.

27. But accounts differ. In Walsingham's *Historia Anglicana,* ed. H. T. Riley (Vol. I, p. 186), the deputation included, "tres milites ac etiam de Londoniis et aliis civitatibus et magnis villis, et praecipue de Portubus, de qualibet certus numerus personarum," etc. In the proclamation of Edward III on mounting the throne, we read that the crown was given him by his father "spontanea voluntate" and brought about "communi consilio et assensu Praelatorum, et Comitum, et Baronum, et aliorum magnatum, necnon communitatum, totius regni" (1187). The discrepancy can probably be explained by noting that Murimuth dates from the first half of the fourteenth century and was a contemporary of the events he was chronicling, whereas Malmesbury died in the fifteenth century and knew his history only at second hand. What interests me is his desire to add representatives of the Commons and the cities to his list.

maintain that they were present in the person of their parliamentary representatives. Yet in what sense of the word could a parliament of that day be called popular? In spite of all this, it is notable that the action against the king had to be presented as an act of the People as a whole, and that Reynolds emphasized this in choosing the text for his sermon.

John Gower: The People as Abused

Internal conditions during the reign of Edward III were stormy, and in 1381 Wat Tyler's rebellion broke out when Richard III, then fourteen years old, was king. Gower, who had great sympathy with the peasants, used the proverb in his *Mirour de l'Omme*, and we begin now to see how it is largely converted to the popular cause. The passage in which we are interested runs,

> Ly sage ce nous vait disant,
> Selonc que peuple vait parlant
> L'estat de l'omne s'appara:
> Escript ausi j'en truis lisant,
> Au vois commune est acordant
> La vois de dieu; et pour cela
> Catun son fils amonesta,
> Q'il ne soy mesmes loera
> Ne blamera; car sache tant
> Ou bons ou mals quelqu'il serra
> Le fait au fin se moustrera;
> N'est qui le puet celer avant.[28]

It was not much after the appearance of this poem that *Piers Plowman* was written; and from another quarter appeared John Wyclif (ca. 1320–84). Wyclif turned out to be an innovator in both theology (see his *Trilogos*) and politics. He was a supporter of "popular consent." In fact, one of the errors for which his teach-

28. See *The Complete Works of John Gower*, ed. G. C. Macaulay. The passage quoted is from lines 12721 ff., pp. 147–48. For a historical account of the rebellion, see Walsingham's *Chronicon Angliae*, Rolls Series, 1874, and, of course, Froissart.

ing was condemned in 1418 by Martin V in the two bulls *Inter cunctas* and *In eminentis* is the following: "The people can by their own decision correct delinquent masters." [29] This was no worse than many an ecclesiastic had preached—witness our passage from Manegold, which could be supplemented by other passages from Marsilio of Padua—but when combined with Wyclif's views on the real presence, on poverty, and on the "Two Swords," it was anathema. Consequently, he came to be associated in the minds of readers with the rebels. But the proverb was apparently frequently heard at the time, for another of Chaucer's contemporaries, Hoccleve (1365–ca. 1450), wrote in his *Regement of Princes* (1411–12),

> Thus, my good lord, wynneth your peoples voice,
> for peoples vois is goddes voys, men seyne.[30]

Who the men in question were and on what occasions they said it is not told, but the very fact that it is not told shows that the words could be referred to as current. It must have been a well-known slogan. Books called *De regimene principum* were far from rare and they all contained the usual commonplaces. That this was one such is of some interest. Actually, Hoccleve himself was a bit sceptical of the divine origin of popular opinion. In stanzas 422 and following he tells the story of a king who made strict but wise laws. The people would not obey them. To induce obedience the king announced that they had been decreed by Apollo, to whose shrine he then went for consultation. He managed to persuade his subjects to obey the laws in his absence, but he died in Greece. His orders were that his body be thrown into the sea lest, if he were taken home for burial, the people would think that his death freed them from their oath of obedience. He thus prolonged his

---

29. "Populares possunt ad suum arbitrium dominos deliquentes corrigere." Most conveniently to be found in H. Denzinger, *Enchiridion symbolorum*, no. 527.

30. *The Regement of Princes*, ed. F. J. Furnivall, Vol. 72, stanza 413, p. 104.

absence indefinitely, and the laws continued in force. Hoccleve saw in law a basis for royal security. As he says in stanza 397,

> . . . lawe is bothe lokke and key
> Of suerte; whil law is kept in londe,
> A prince in his estate may sikir stonde.

None of this supports the doctrine of popular supremacy. In fact, our previous quotation from Hoccleve could be interpreted simply as advice of a Machiavellian sort: to win the support of the people, let them believe that their voice is the voice of God.

Commynes: The People as the King's Subjects

It is not only in England that one finds the proverb used. The *Mémoires* of Philippe de Commynes dates from the last quarter of the fifteenth century.[31] In the third book, fourth chapter, of this work, Commynes tells of the defeat of Alfonso of Aragon by the French in 1495 and of his flight from Naples back to Spain. The defeat apparently was easily carried out and Commynes here quotes Pope Alexander VI as saying,

> Les Francoys y sont alles avecques des esperons de boys et de la craye en la main des fourriers pour marcher leurs logis, sans aultre payne.

This ignominious defeat, says the chronicler, is divine punishment and sets an example to all other kings and princes.

> Par quoy conclud ce propos, disant, après l'avoir ouy dire a plusieurs bons hommes de religion et de saincte vie et à maintes aultre sorte de gens (qui est la voix de Dieu que la voix du peuple), que Nostre Seigneur les vouloit pugnir visiblement, et que chascun le congneut et par eulx donner exemple à tous roys et princes de bien vivre et selon ses commendemens. . . .

Such an attitude may be merely an attempt to bolster one's ideas with common sense, and, as we have seen, no philosophic premises are invoked to justify the proverb, nor are inferences drawn from it.

---

31. I use the edition of Joseph Calmette, Vol. 3.

George Gascoigne: The People as the Populace

Commyne's attitude is different from that of the Renaissance writers. As we approach that period the wind changes. In a man like Gascoigne one expects and gets no general ideas, and he is sceptical about the truth of the proverb. That he feels the need of introducing it is historically interesting, however, for if it were not being repeated generally, there would be no point here in mentioning it. In his *Dulce bellum inexpertis* included in his *Posies* (1572), after stanzas of introduction dealing with what poets, painters, and astronomers have to say about war, he comes down to the common people:

> Well then, let see what sayeth the common voice,
> These olde sayde sawes, of warre what can they say?
> Who list to harken to their whispring noise,
> May heare them talke and tattle day by day,
> That Princes pryde is cause of warre alway:
> Plentie brings pryde, pryde plea, plea pine, pine peace,
> Peace plentie, and so (say they) they never cease.
>
> And though it have bene thought as true as steele,
> Which people prate, and preach above the rest,
> Yet could I never any reason feel,
> To think Vox *populi vox Dei est,*
> As for my skill, I compt him but a beast,
> Which trusteth truth to dwell in common speeche,
> Where ever Lourden will become a leech.[32]

These verses were written during the reign of Elizabeth I and at the height of her popularity. With a sovereign as brilliant and as "personal" as Elizabeth it was natural that a swashbuckling poet should not assume the stance of a Hoccleve. The period was one in which autocrats were in the ascendancy and for the next two centuries the proverb was to be treated lightly. In Pierre de Sainct-Julien, for instance, we find it quoted, but hardly gospel.

32. *Complete Works of George Gascoigne,* ed. John W. Cunliffe, Vol. I, *The Posies,* p. 142.

Pierre de Sainct-Julien: The People as the Poor

Le Roy qui aura annobly, et affranchi tel richereau de tout subside, ne veut pourtant que les quottes qu'il souloit payer soient raiees des rooles, comme l'equité le requerroit: ains le Prince veut tousiours avoir ses sommes entieres, et ses receptes plustost fortes que foibles, sans se soucier qui les paye. Par ce moyen il est force que le reste des pauvres habitants, desquels le richerau a acquis quasi tous les heritages, supportent ce que le n'agueres Roupturier, et devenu Noble, vouloit payer. Cela advenant, et tenu pour maxime le proverb vulgaire,

> Qui est aymé de Populus,
> Il est aymé de Dominus.

Aussi qu'il est dit: que la voix du peuple est la voix de Dieu: ie laisse à iuger a ceyx qui le sçavent, les belles benedictions, que le peuple donne à l'invention et aux executeurs.[33]

These words were published in the year of Henry III's murder, and though his successor was designated by him as his heir, it was almost ten years before he would abjure his Protestantism and consolidate his power. That Sainct-Julien should introduce the notion of the people's voice into his account of paradoxical situations is not surprising. Not only was the king an adventurer and opportunist in the eyes of many, but the land was full of *nouveaux-riches* whose former taxes were now being paid by the People. And since the People's voice is God's voice, all is as it should be. On the other hand, Sainct-Julien did write a pamphlet to prove that the kingship of France was elective and not hereditary, and in his *Mélanges* he had insisted that even legitimate succession had to be confirmed by the decision of the Twelve Peers and approved by the Three Estates.[34] This is one of the few opinions of those who speak of "the People" that takes the term literally. For the Twelve Peers plus the Three Estates includes everyone but the women, the children, and the king himself.

33. *Meslanges historiques et Recueils de Diverses matieres pour la plupart Paradoxales, et neantmoins vrayes*, p. 636.
34. *Ibid.*, p. 12. Cf. Léonie Raffin, *Saint-Julien de Balleure*, pp. 90–91. I owe this reference to my friend Professor Tom Tashiro.

Francis Bacon: The People as the Multitude

The proverb was also used in the political underground during this period, for in 1620 Naunton wrote to Buckingham that he was trying to find the author of a political pamphlet called *Vox Populi, or News from Spain.* This seems to have been an attack on the foreign policies of both England and the United Provinces.[35] Bacon himself had no very high opinion of the common people. In his essay on "Seditions and Troubles," he says, "Common people are of slow motion if they be not excited by the greater sort; and the greater sort are of small strength except the multitude be apt and ready to move of themselves." In short, the two classes are interdependent. Yet in his "Expostulations to the Lord Chief Justice Coke," he writes,

> Supposing this to be the time of your affliction, that which I have propounded to myself is, by taking this seasonable advantage, like a true friend, though far unworthy to be counted so, to shew you your true shape in a glass; and that not in a false one to flatter you, nor yet in one made by the reflection of your own words and actions; from whose light proceeds the voice of the people, which is not unfitly called the voice of God.[36]

Is Bacon maintaining here that the Lord Chief Justice is the intermediary between the People and God and that therefore what he announces is *ipso facto* both the voice of the people and that of God? It would be more prudent not to adventure into mind-reading here, nor to try to reconcile what he says about the People in his essay on "Seditions" with what he wrote to Lord Coke. His theory of the Four Idols would suffice to show that he had no confidence in innate wisdom of any kind. The whole purpose of the *Novum Organum* was to correct the common errors of mankind.

35. See Spedding's *Life and Letters of Bacon,* Vol. VII of the Spedding-Ellis-Heath edition of the *Works,* p. 153.
36. See *The Works of Francis Bacon,* new ed., by Basil Montague, Esq. Vol. VII, p. 297.

Montaigne: The Passionate Multitude

Much the same might be said of Montaigne. Montaigne's scepticism was more extensive than Bacon's, and if he had any systematic ideology it was the kind of nominalism that stopped at the confrontation of individual people and events. To put experience into words is bound to land the nominalist in paradox, for words, when descriptive, are by their very nature logical reals. The paradox was ignored by Montaigne, if he was aware of it, and he seldom hesitated to generalize when it served his purpose. Thus in his essay on the discipline of the will, in which he follows his usual practice of referring his observations to himself, he is willing to generalize about the facility of demagoguery.

> I have seen wonders in my day in the indiscreet and prodigious facility of people, suffering their hopes and beliefs, to be led and governed as it has pleased and best fitted their leaders: above a hundred discontents, one in the neck of another: and beyond their fantasies and dreams. I wonder no more at those, whom the apish toys of *Apollonius* and *Mahomet* have seduced and blinded: Their sense and understanding is wholly smothered in their passion. Their discretion has no other choice but what pleases them and furthers their cause. Which I had especially observed in the beginning of our distempered factions and factious troubles. The other which is grown since, by imitation surmounts the same. Whereby I observe, that it is an inseparable quality of popular errors.[37]

The instances to which he is referring in this passage are the Protestant revolt and the *Ligue*. He condemns both as stifling reason in passion. But such movements succeed because the People are willing to be manipulated by their leaders. This is said as a simple observation, and nowhere have I found in Montaigne the sort of bitter and sarcastic description of the multitude which his disciple, Pierre Charron, published. Charron's *La Sagesse* was first printed in 1601, only six years after the first edition of the *Essays*. In it he castigates the common people with an acerbity that even Alcuin left unexpressed.

37. *Essays*, III, 10. Florio's translation, spelling modernized.

The populace is but a wild beast. Whatsoever it thinks is but vanity, what it says is false and erroneous, what it reproves is good, what it admires is bad, what it praises is dishonorable, what it does and undertakes is but folly, *non tam bene cum rebus humanis geritur, ut meliora pluribus placeant: argumentum pessime turba est.* The mob is the mother of ignorance, injustice, inconstancy, idolizing vanity, which to wish to please is impossible. Its motto is *Vox populi vox Dei,* but it would be better to say, *Vox populi vox stultorum.* But the beginning of wisdom is to keep clear of them and not to let oneself be carried off by popular opinions.[38]

If a source is needed for this passage, it will probably be found in Montaigne's essay on *Fame.* Here the essayist is specifically referring to popular judgments of human accomplishments, of great men and their characters.

We are often driven to empanel and select a jury of twelve men out of a whole country to determine of an acre of land. And the judgment of our inclinations and actions (the weightiest and hardest matter that is) we refer it to the idle breath of the vain voice of the commone sort and base rascality, which is the mother of ignorance, of injustice, and inconstancy. Is it reason to make the life of a wise man depend on the judgment of fools? . . . "Is there anything more foolish than to think that all together they are oughts, whom every single one you would set at noughts?" Whosoever aims to please them has never done. It is a But that has neither form nor holdfast. . . . "Nothing is so incomprehensible to be just weighed as the minds of the multitude." Demetrius said merrily of the common people's voice, that he made no more reckoning of that which issued from out his mouth above, than of that which came

38.
"Le vulgaire est une beste sauvage, tout ce qu'il pense n'est que vanité, tout ce qu'il dit est faux et erroné, ce qu'il reprouve est bon, ce qu'il approuve est mauvais, ce qu'il loue est infame, ce qu'il fait et entreprend n'est que folie, *non tam bene cum rebus humanis geritur, ut meliora pluribus placeant: argumentum pessima turba est,* la turbe populaire est mère d'ignorance, injustice, inconstance, idolatre de vanité, à laquelle vouloir plaire ce n'est iamais fait: c'est son mot, *vox populi, vox Dei,* mais il faut dire *vox populi, vox stultorum.* Or le commencement de sagesse est se garder net, et ne se laisser emporter aux opinions populaire."

De la Sagesse, "dernière édition" (Paris, 1630), Book I, chap. 52, p. 13. The English in the body of my text is my own translation. The Latin quotation might be translated, "Human affairs are not so well arranged that the better pleases the greater number; the very evil mob is the proof."

from a homely place below, and says moreover, "Thus I esteem it, if of itself it be not dishonest, yet can it not but be dishonest, when it is applauded by the many." No art, no mildness of spirit might direct our steps to follow so straggling and disordered a guide. In this breathy confusion of brutes, and frothy chaos of reports and of vulgar opinions, which still push us on, no good course can be established. Let us not propose so fleeing and so wavering an end unto ourselves. Let us constantly follow reason. And let the vulgar approbation follow us that way, if it please. And as it depends all on fortune, we have no law to hope for it, rather by any other way than by that.[39]

Clearly Charron did little more than transmit his master's opinion in more violent language. Montaigne does not repeat the whole proverb that concerns us, but his reference to the *voix du peuple* in the scatological terms of Demetrius shows that he had the phrase in mind. But by this time humanistic learning had changed the ideas of scholars about the wisdom of the multitude. When one remembers that cardinals in Italy looked down on printed books and insisted on having their reading matter in manuscript, that one of the apologies for emblems was their unintelligibility to the crowd, that the parables in the New Testament were discussed as dealing with matters too sacred for the masses to learn, one can see that there would be little sympathy with ordinary opinion.[40] But as we approach the seventeenth and eighteenth

39. Florio's translation, spelling modernized, Book II, Essay 16. The quotations are from Aelian, *Variae Historiae*, II, chap. 1; Cicero's *Tusculans*, V, 36; and Cicero's *De finibus*, II, 15. I saw no good reason to include the Latin since translations of the quotations were in the text.

40. See my introduction to *The Hieroglyphics of Horapollo* (Bollingen Series XXIII) for information on the value of arcane knowledge. For a possible source of Montaigne's opinion of *la tourbe*, and a source which is fairly typical of the Humanists, see Guicciardini's *Ricordi*, no. 140: *Chi disse un populo, disse veramente un animale pazzo, pieno di mille errori, di mille confusione, sensa diletto, sensa stabiltà* ("To speak of a people is to speak in truth of a foolish beast, full of a thousand errors, of a thousand confusions, without pleasures or firmness.") The *Ricordi* is now available in English as *Maxims and Reflections of a Renaissance Statesman*, trans. Mario Domandi. Cf., in that edition, series B, no. 5, p. 100; no. 123, p. 125; and no. 156, p. 134. See also my second essay below.

centuries we find that popular claims for recognition in both political and religious areas are being met with hostility from the literati, though, as everyone knows, the hostility was futile.

Sir Thomas Browne: The Multitude Again

A generation after the publication of the first edition of *La Sagesse*, Sir Thomas Browne expressed in suaver language an opinion of the People similar to Charron's. His *Pseudodoxia Epidemica* came out in 1646, six years after Parliament was dissolved, four years after the outbreak of Civil War, one year after the beheading of Laud, and three years before that of Charles I. It is as a whole a catalogue of "vulgar errors," and hence demonstrates to those willing to be convinced that the voice of the People sometimes tells lies. After listing various errors of the mob, Browne writes,

> It much accuseth the impatience of Peter, who could not endure the staves of the multitude, and is the greatest example of lenity in our Saviour, when he desired of God forgiveness unto those, who having one day brought him into the City in triumph, did presently after, act all dishonour upon him, and nothing could be heard but Crucifige, in their Courts. Certainly he that considereth these things in God's peculiar people, will easily discern how little truth is in the waies of the Multitude; and though sometimes they are flattered with that Aphorism, will hardly believe, the voice of the people to be the voice of God.[41]

La Fontaine: The Vulgus

La Fontaine was as dubious of the validity of the people's opinion as his contemporary in England was. In his fable on Democritus and the people of Abdera (Book VIII, 26) he admitted his prejudice—easily done in view of the social climate of the Court and the Academy.

41. *The Works of Sir Thomas Browne*, ed. Geoffrey Keynes, Vol. II, Book I, chap. 3, p. 29.

> Que j'ai toujours hai les penseurs du vulgaire?
> Qu'il me semble profane, injuste et téméraire,
> Mettant de faux milieux entre la chose et lui,
> Et mesurant par soi ce qu'il voit en autrui?

> Le maître d'Epicure en fit l'apprentissage.
> Son pays le crut fou: petits esprits? mais quoi?
> Aucun n'est prophète chez soi.

La Fontaine has the Abderites send for Hippocrates to cure Democritus of his supposed insanity. But the philosopher is immersed in his books. His examiners begin to reason about metaphysics and then,

> Ils tombèrent sur la morale
> Il n'est pas besoin que j'étale
> Tout ce que l'un et l'autre dit.
> Le récit précédent suffit
> Pour montrer que le peuple est juge récusable.
> En quel sens est donc véritable
> Ce que j'ai lu dans certain lieu
> Que sa voix est la voix de Dieu?

This scepticism is in keeping with the prevalent mode of satire during the seventeenth and eighteenth centuries, satire infused with a bitterness that had seldom been felt since the days of Juvenal. It was directed not toward one social class but toward types of human beings, as in Molière or La Bruyère, or toward humanity in general, as in Swift. The pretentiousness of certain men, their avarice, false ambition, brutality, mendacity, in short their weakness of virtue and strength of vice, these became the targets of the social critic, as they had always been. To quote passages from all the satirists would be impossible and enough has been said to sketch lightly the history of the proverb.

La Bruyère: The People as Underdog

The work of a moralist like La Bruyère was to emphasize types of people rather than humanity itself, whereas La Rochefoucault did the very opposite. In fact, La Bruyère was willing to admit that he spent his life in observing men and his mind in untangling their vices and silliness. Speaking of himself in the third person, he says,

S'il donne quelque cour a ses pensées, c'est moins par une vanité d'auteur, que pour mettre une vérité qu'il a trouvée dans tout le jour nécessaire pour faire l'impression qui doit servir à son dessein.[42]

His work was supposed to be that of scientific observation, but instead of first setting up classes of character, as Theophrastus did, he examined individuals and used them as materials for classification. It is therefore possible to identify each of the men he is criticizing, though he gives them a Greek or Latin name. To see the human race as a collection of individuals, none of whom is completely like any other, was something that may be said, without more exaggeration than is customary, to have begun with Montaigne, when he announced that he was writing a self-portrait. Strictly speaking, this ought to have led a man to say nothing about the People as possessing a voice common to them all and like the voice of anyone in particular. But La Bruyère did not go that far. On the contrary, one finds him generalizing about men and women, about courtiers, about wits and men of wealth, but his usual tendency is the drive toward individuality. There is a good deal in La Bruyère about the influence of property on character, and there is the well-known contrast between the fate of a rich man and that of a poor man.[43] But why there is this gap between great wealth and extreme poverty he never seeks.

By the end of the eighteenth century the medieval principle *populus maior principe* had been pretty well justified in action. In

42. Essay on "Ouvrages de l'Esprit" in *Les Caractères ou Moeurs de ce Siècle*, chap. 1, "Les Caractères de la Bruyère," p. 21.

43. Essay on the "Biens de Fortune," conclusion. One of the most striking of such passages occurs in "Les Grands," pp. 256–57, where he compares "les deux conditions des hommes les plus opposées," the rich and the poor whom he calls here "*le peuple.*" He ends this discussion by saying that if he had to choose between being "*un grand*" or "*un homme du peuple,*" "*je ne balance pas, je veux être peuple.*"

both the United States and France the People had seemed to win out, and when one looks backward one wonders why this was not evident to the Bonapartes, the Metternichs, the Wellingtons, and their successors in authority. There were dissident voices well into the twentieth century, and there will probably always be some who cannot reconcile themselves to facts. In the United States, Alexander Hamilton's famous speech in the Federal Convention on June 18, 1787, is often cited as a case in point. "The voice of the People," he is reported to have proclaimed, "has been said to be the voice of God; and, however generally this maxim has been quoted and believed, it is not true to fact. The people are turbulent and changing; they seldom judge or determine right." [44] But on the whole few of the writers have ever attempted to justify the innate wisdom of the People. During the nineteenth century, however, one man at least made a suggestion which is allied to the doctrines of the *consensus gentium*, the *lumen naturale*, and the Scottish common-sense philosophy. This man was Archbishop Trench.

Archbishop Trench: Consensus Gentium

The voice of the People, says the Archbishop, is not "every outcry." On the contrary, "the proverb rests on the assumption that the foundations of man's being are laid in the truth; from which it will follow, that no conviction which is really a conviction of the universal humanity, but rests on a true ground; no faith,

44. See *The Records of the Federal Convention*, ed. Max Farrand, Vol. I, p. 299. It is worth noting that this is preceded by the words, "All communities divide themselves into the few and the many. The first are the rich and well born, the other the mass of the people." As far as human nature in general was concerned, the Constitution embodied a definite conception of what it was believed to be. See A. O. Lovejoy, *Reflections on Human Nature*, Lecture II, "The Theory of Human Nature in the American Constitution and the Method of Counterpoise," pp. 37–66.

which is indeed the faith of all mankind, but has a reality corresponding to it; for, as Jeremy Taylor has said, 'It is not a vain noise, when many nations join their voices in the attestation or detestation of an action'; and Hooker, 'The general and perpetual voice of men is as the sentence of God Himself. For that which all men have at all times learned, nature herself must needs have taught; and God being the author of nature, her voice is but his instrument.' " [45] Unfortunately the Archbishop had not heard the voice of the Opposition and his notion of universality seems to have been limited to the universe of his associates. By means of terming all who disagree about those opinions which he calls universal by the invidious name of exceptions or "not truly human," he proves his point. Thus such ideas as taboos against incest, and the existence of a "First Cause, Creator and Upholder of all things," are indeed universal. But in the opening lecture of his book he quotes a quatrain from James Rowell (ca. 1594–1666) which turns all proverbs into the voice of God. The verses run,

> The people's voice the voice of God we call;
> And what are proverbs but the people's voice?
> Coined first, and current made by common choice?
> Then sure they must have weight and truth withal.

This is perhaps as good a conclusion to the chronicles of our proverb as any. We have done no more than brush in lightly the fortunes of a maxim over the centuries. Its origin is unknown; but its use to justify political and ecclesiastical policies make it appear to be a bit of very ancient wisdom. There are some strange features of its use, of which one is the failure of anyone to raise the question of just who the People were whose voice was that of God. For no one that I have come across has applied it to all human beings regardless of age, sex, wealth, lineage. The next

45. Richard Chenevix Trench, *Proverbs and Their Lessons*. The first edition of this book, a series of lectures "delivered to young men's societies," is dated 1857.

essay will try to clarify the problem of who the People were and what their reputation was.[46]

46. Since writing this collection of essays I have come upon an article called "Vox Populi Vox Dei," by S. A. Gallacher, in *Philological Quarterly*, Vol. XXIV (January, 1945). This article traces the origin of the proverb, as far as possible, and includes some references which I have not used. It should be read both as an excellent supplement to my essay and for its own intrinsic interest. I owe the reference to my colleague, Dr. John Baldwin.

II

WHO ARE THE PEOPLE?

The quotations cited in the first essay are evidence that no one has been quite sure what he was referring to when he spoke of the People. They also show that some men thought well of the proverb and others ill, which would be true of any idea. But it is also obvious that writers conceived of society as divided into at least two groups, one of which was the People and the other variously named. The distinction might be fundamentally that between the governed and the governors. But this in turn would be based on the sort of government of which one approved; or— and this is not improbable—the sort of government of which one approved would depend on what one thought of those who were to be governed. In an absolute monarchy the People might be everyone except the monarch, and if one approved of absolute monarchy it would be because one had no very high opinion of the governed. Here the theme of the fickle mob, or the uneducated masses, or the lower classes, or something similar enters the picture. In a limited or constitutional monarchy the People would be a smaller group but still large enough to include everyone but the king and those individuals capable of limiting his power, the barons under Edward II, the Congress of the United States in relation to the Executive and the Supreme Court. At the other extreme one might have a government like that of the Athenian polis or the New England township, as those communities are described in the textbooks, and here almost everyone would be "The People" and would be thought of as at least intelligent enough to vote. Hence the distinction ought not to arise in such a context. But the structure of no society is merely political, and if Athens had its *hoi polloi,* the New England towns had their people who lived on the wrong side of the tracks.[1]

Surely there is no need to insist that economic distinctions also play a major part in differentiating members of all communities but the simplest. No proof is needed that in all historical societies there has been a distinction between the rich and the poor, though this may not have been true in primitive communistic societies. The poor then become the People and the rich the anti-People. In many places the poor had no say in political decisions, for even when there was a semblance of democracy, voting was based on a property qualification. Tenney Frank has shown how this worked out in Republican Rome.

[In the Servian army] the wealthiest men, who could afford to provide both armor and horses, were chosen for the cavalry. Of these there were chosen eighty centuries (8000) of men who were wealthy enough to provide heavy armor for service in the first line. They were called men of the first class. The second, third, and fourth classes provided twenty centuries each, the fifth class thirty, and from among the numerous poor who had no property only five centuries were taken. . . . [This organization] introduced the principle of classifying the citizen-body according to wealth, a classification later used by the founders of the republic in creating their primary assembly for voting and law-making purposes. That assembly, based upon wealth, then gradually displaced the old-time assembly of brotherhoods. The conservative character of the republican government is in large measure due to this early adoption of the timocratic principle.[2]

There have been communities where all voting was limited to the propertied class and others where voting for certain offices was so limited. The poll tax has sometimes been justified on the ground that a man who could not afford to pay the usually small

1. For the survival and increase of social distinctions in an old New England community, see W. Lloyd Warner and Paul S. Lunt, *The Social Life of a Modern Community,* where the stratification of classes is laid out in detail.

2. Tenney Frank, *A History of Rome,* p. 29. The brotherhoods of which he speaks were the ancient *curiae.*

sum imposed was not fit to vote. Whatever the argument, the connection between wealth and political power, or potential power, has been intimate. No one to speak of has ever wanted to be poor, the exceptions being saintly characters like Francis of Assisi, or the Greek Cynics who thought that property was a burden, or austere souls like Thoreau, who thought that money was the root of all evil. But in opposition to them there have been also some men who maintained that economic prosperity was a reward of virtue, the virtues of hard work, self-discipline, self-denial, all rolled up in one. In the last half-century this has been attributed to the rise of Protestantism, but intellectually it could be traced back to the Parable of the Talents. It is the philosophy of Poor Richard, and it cannot be denied, should anyone care to deny it, that the accumulation of capital has been considered an ideal by most Americans and, I suspect, by a good many Europeans and Asiatics as well. For capital gives one power accompanied by prestige, and most of us are sensitive to the charms of both.

There have always been more poor people than rich, surely a *vérité de la Palice*. And there have always been more powerless people than powerful. Power can in fact be most effectively exercised if concentrated in a few hands. As Odysseus said, "The rule of many is not a good thing; let there be one king, one ruler to whom Zeus has given the sceptre." We may be as democratic in ideal as we wish, but we always have to grant the claims of efficiency in time of crisis. As the Romans appointed a dictator when in great danger, so the Americans concentrate power in the hands of the President during a war. The legend first told, I believe, by Livy and put into verse by Shakespeare in *Coriolanus*, of the belly and the other organs, is an example of how government by the Many was conceived. There seems indeed to have been an unpleasant connotation associated with the very words, "the Many," "*multitudo*," "the Crowd," all of which are antitheses not merely to the Few, but also to the Better Sort, the Elite, the

Upper Classes, the people who are what would now be called by the sociologists, "the In-Group." To men who spoke in such words the People were simply the Majority.

Finally, there has been a conception of the People that had mystical overtones and was especially influential in and after the eighteenth century. As we shall see in the fourth essay, an idea of something called "The Folk," usually in German, "Das Volk," became popular. The Folk were the aboriginal men from whom either all of us or a nation or a society or a race descended. The Folk contained the residual primitive soul of the group in question. Just as the individual who can claim descent from the paladins of Charlemagne or the Norman conquerors of England has greater prestige than one who knows only the names of his grandparents, so the Folk, having existed in spirit if not in flesh since the beginning, has seemed to be nobler than the individuals who composed it. Purity of race in societies of mixed blood became an asset, just as pure blood in dogs or cows is an asset. And though the Volksseele might and often did manifest itself in the poor and even in the ignorant, it never lost its claim to nobility. If the word "noble," as seems likely, is derived from the Greek, meaning "to know," either the noble himself or his ancestors were knowledgeable or known, and people may feel that it is better to have ancestors who are known than ancestors who are unknown. In view of the indisputable fact that human beings cannot be spontaneously generated, we must all have the same ancestors, for there are not enough for each man to have his own. But ancestor worship has never depended on anything other than just knowing the names of those whom one is worshiping. Hence, if there is such a thing as a German Seele inherent in the German Volk, its traits when known are to be reverenced. But in all modern societies in the Occident blood is mixed. In France alone there is ancient Greek and Phoenician blood, Latin blood, Celtic, Frankish, and German blood, to say nothing of the vestiges of the

English who fought for a hundred years in that country and cannot be expected to have practiced continence while there. I am not writing a treatise in demography and need give no further examples, but the knowledge that a people is of mixed descent does influence its self-appraisal. If it is true that the Helots of Sparta were descendants of a primitive conquered people, as the lower castes in India are said to be, or perhaps the Saxons in Norman England, there would be an analogy to the prestige of the *Volksseele* in historical fact. The Spartan soul would not be found in a helot nor an Aryan soul in a Dravidian nor an American soul in an Italian or Jewish immigrant. The case of the Saxons is different, for their language prevailed over Norman-French, and it was not very long before the upper classes in England became English, whereas on the Continent it was the conqueror's language that prevailed. Perhaps the collective soul inhabits the dominant language. In the United States, though the number of citizens of non-seventeenth-century forebears is much greater than the number of those who trace their lineage back to the men of the *Mayflower*, the *Ark and Dove*, or the *God Speed*, yet the latter are the People in the sense of being in their own opinion *The Americans*. It has not been unusual for a man whose ancestry is not Anglo-Saxon to be asked what sort of surname he bears. He is thus made aware by the less tactful or the more patriotic that he is not of the representative group, though he may nevertheless be of the majority. He is one of the People in the political sense; he can be of them in the economic sense; but he is not of them in the social sense.

The distinction between the People and the anti-People appeared early in Roman history in the famous *SPQR*. Whatever the origin of the emblem—for an emblem is what these initials became—there can be no question that sharp distinction was made in it between the *Populus* and the Senate or Elders. The Senate was originally composed, according to legend, of one hundred men who were followers of Romulus and chosen by him, the Ramnes. These men were in theory counselors, but became in practice a legislative and indeed governing body. The inclusion of the People in the emblem does not prove that they had any governmental functions whatsoever in the earliest days of the Republic. But by 494 the plebeians rebelled and it was at that time that two officers were elected by the Plebeian Council (*concilium Plebis*), which did not cease making trouble until imperial times. Finally in 287, two centuries after First Secession, the *Lex Hortensia* was passed which gave equal rights before the law to plebeians and patricians. But the social, as distinguished from the political, status of the *plebs* remained low. In time, the consuls were chosen from the plebeians as well as from the patricians, but it never became customary. It is worth noting that in Livy's words (Book II, xxxii) which are presumably justified, the tribunes were chosen as a help *adversus consules* and no patrician could be given the office. Just what evils had been committed by the patricians has to be investigated incident by incident, but one can use one's imagination, which is aided by the contempt that not only patricians but others poured upon men who rose from the *plebs*. A man like Cicero's brother Quintus is represented in *De legibus* as having called the Tribunate *pestifera* "born in sedition and making for sedition." His objection is that "it stole all honors from the Fathers, made all low things equal to the high, stirred up trouble and confusion." [3] Cicero's weak reply is that the tribunes kept the *plebs* in check and put an end to the rebellion. Quintus, it is to be observed, does not agree and even objects to the secret ballot. But Cicero points out that the secret ballot safeguards the people's liberty. And, he adds, the ballots before they are cast, should be first shown to "our best and most eminent citizens" in order to obtain their advice. "Do you not see, that if corruption

3. Book III, ix, 20. "Patribus omnem honorem eripuit, omnia infima summis paria fecit, turbavit, miscuit."

should be silent, that they would ask when voting for the opinion of the aristocrats? Thus our law grants the appearance of freedom, retains the authority of the aristocrats, and eliminates the causes of strife." [4] The law in question was not one already in existence. It was one imagined by Cicero himself. No comment is needed about the equivocation.

The Tribunate actually did succeed in widening the gap between the *plebs* and the patriciate. It was as if in the United States the Negro population had been legally organized with two or more officials elected by them to see that their civil rights were respected. They would obviously be a group of second-class citizens not only in practice, as they are now, but also in law. So the plebeians were organized, and the fact that they were plebeians rather than patricians was constantly rubbed into them, though the tendency towards absolutism, which came to a head in Augustus, put all Romans on the same footing as far as their freedom went. To return to the emblem *SPQR*, *senator* was the name of an office; *populus* was not. The former were the governors, the latter the governed, whatever may have been intended by the phrase. An analogous distinction is made in the Constitution of the United States, which names "the people of the United States" as the ordainer and establisher of the document, and, after describing the legislative, executive, and judicial powers, speaks of the "rights of the people" in Amendments IV, IX, and X, as if their authors knew that the People were different from their government. The distinction is clearly one made by common sense. Yet in spite of the fact that women were as much among the governed as men are, an amendment was required to give them the right to vote. This then introduced a new differentia into the definition of The People—the suffrage.

4. *Ibid.*, Book III, xvii, 39. "Non vides, si quando ambitus sileat, quaeri in suffragiis quid optimi viri sentiant? Quam ob rem lege nostra libertatis species datur, auctoritas bonorum retinetur, contentionis causa tollitur."

Populus in Latin

Now all this may seem like pedantic quibbling. But the question of who belonged to the *populus* was not always clear to the Romans themselves. Cicero, for instance, is firm in maintaining that the term is not equivalent to "all men." In *De republica* he says, "The Commonwealth is the people's wealth; but the people are not every assemblage of men associated in any way whatsoever, but an assemblage of many men associated by common acceptance of the law and the sharing of a useful service." [5] Evidently men might be living in the same locality and yet not belong to the People if they did not accept the same laws and co-operate in the same service, probably military. The definition obviously allows for the existence of a minority group within a population, a group with its own laws and services. The cohesive matter within a People turns out to be morality. On the other hand, in his oration *Pro L. Murena*, we find Cicero making a further distinction between the *populus* and the *plebs*, in his phrase, "so that this matter might work out to the advantage of the people and the plebeians of Rome." [6] Similarly Livy, speaking of the Tribunate, says, "This office is not of the people but of the plebeians." [7] And in the next century Martial (VIII, 15) makes a threefold distinction of the people, the knights, and the senate (*Dat populus, dat gratus eques, dat tura senatus*). Even a Roman, if asked to identify the voice of the People, would have been puzzled.

The puzzle continued to tease some men as late as the second century A.D. For in Aulus Gellius (Book X, xx, 5 ff.), where the definitions of *rogatio, lex, plebisscitum,* and *privilegium* are re-

5. Book I, xxv, 39. "Res publica res populi: populus autem non omnis hominum coetus quoque modo congregatus, sed coetus multitudinis juris consensu et utilitatis communione sociatus." The pun which opens this quotation is inevitable. *Res* is one of the most multivalent words in Latin.
6. "Ut ea res populo plebique Romanae bene eveniret."
7. Book II, 56. "Non enim populi, sed plebis eum magistratum esse."

quested, the authority of Ateius Capito is cited. By this time one might imagine such distinctions to be obsolete, but for reasons of conversation, if for none more practical, they apparently continued to be interesting. "Capito," he says, "in the same definition sharply distinguished the *plebs* from the *populus*, since in the *populus* are contained all the parts of the state and all its ranks, whereas that part should be called the *plebs* in which the patrician families of citizens are not included. A plebiscite therefore according to Capito is a law which the plebeians, not the people, approve." [8] This, I need not point out, is significantly different from Cicero's definition.

The Roman appraisal of the *plebs*, we see, was similar to that entertained by the Greeks of *hoi polloi*. And we find passages in Latin authors deploring the taste and judgments of the Many, as we do in our own times. Livy, for instance (Book XXXI, 34), is firm in saying that *nil tam inaestimabile est quam animi multitudinis* ("nothing is so valueless as the minds of the multitude"). Cicero is in full agreement. In his *De finibus* (Book II, xv, 49) he criticizes Epicurus in his usual manner for maintaining that the right (*honestum*) is pleasure. This opinion, he says, might be held by the Multitude, but as for himself,

I think that this is usually shameful, and, if occasionally it be not shameful, then it is not shameful because that which is right and proper in itself has been praised by the Multitude. We do not believe that something is said to be right because it is praised by the Many, but because it would be such that even if men were ignorant of it or if they said nothing about it, it would still be of a praiseworthy and beautiful kind. [9]

8. " 'Plebem' autem Capito in eadem definitione seorsum a populo divisit, quoniam in populo civitatis omnesque eius ordines contineantur, 'plebes' vero ea dicitur, in quo gentes civium patriciae non insunt. 'Plebisscitum' igitur est secundum Capitonem lex, quam plebs, non populus accipit."

9. "Ego autem hoc etiam turpe esse saepe iudico et, si quando turpe non sit, tum esse non turpe cum id a multitudine laudetur quod sit ipsum per se rectum atque laudabile; tamen non ob eam causam illud dici esse honestum quia laudetur a multis, sed quia tale sit ut, vel si ignorarent id homines vel si obmutuissent, qua tamen pulchritudine esset specieque laudabile."

And in the *Tusculans* (Book V, xxxvi, 103–4), he returns to the theme, saying that popular approval is not to be sought:

> It must be understood that popular glory is not to be sought for its own sake nor is obscurity to be feared. . . . For what is more stupid than to think that those whom you despise individually as mechanics and barbarians are something [estimable] as a group? [10]

And Cicero continues with the observation that the *honores populi* are to be rejected even when unsought. The voice of the People as the voice of the majority is clearly not the voice of any god in the opinion of the Romans I have cited. But there must have been many other Romans who disagreed; otherwise their criticism would have had no target.[11]

Claudian

One might expect that as time went on the meanings of the terms that interest us would have become fixed. But if we may take Claudian as a good example of fourth and early fifth century

---

10. "Intellegendum est igitur nec gloriam popularem ipsam per sese expetendam nec ignobilitatem extimescendam . . . quidquid stultius quam, quos singulos sicut operarios barbarosque contemnas, eos aliquid putare esse universos?" Cicero refers in this passage to a fragment of Heraclitus on the stupidity of the Ephesians, who exiled Hermadorus. Fragment 114 (Bywater). But Heraclitus was a famous misanthrope and his remains are peppered with anti-popular comments. Roman contempt for the *mobile vulgus* is perhaps too well known to require much in the way of documentation. Everyone knows Horace's *Odes* III, 1 and 2, the latter with its *nec . . . ponit secures arbitrio populares aurae.*

11. One is tempted to continue this discussion, but the temptation must be resisted, for to yield would be to overload these pages with quotations. As social history moved on more ranks were added to those existing in the ancient world. In the fifth century A.D. we find Sidonius Apollinaris listing as the various ranks, the *plebs*, the *curia*, the army, and the college. Gibbon, from whom I take this quotation, adds, "This language is ancient and constitutional; and we may observe that the *clergy* were not yet considered as a distinct order of the state." *Decline and Fall*, chap. 36 (Everyman ed., Vol. iii, p. 422, n. 2).

Latin, we shall see that he was no more certain of what *populus* denoted than his predecessors had been. Though the poet was limited in his choice of words by the exigencies of meter, yet his indifferent use of *populus*, *plebs*, and *vulgus* suggests, if it does not prove, that the finer shades of meaning had been lost. He uses *vulgus* in *In Rufinum* (Book II, l. 399) to mean simply the public in the amphitheatre; in the same poem (l. 427) he uses *plebs* for the people who came to acclaim the death of Rufinus; in *In Eutropium* (Book I, l. 210) he speaks of selling *populos* for profit, and in Book II he writes of men whose origin is *humili de plebe* (l. 342), as if the *plebs* had several strata; in his panegyric on the fourth consulate of Honorius (l. 298) it is the *populus* which is obedient to a magistrate who obeys his own laws; and in *De consulatu Stilichonis* (Book III, l. 183) it is again the *populus* which is not ungrateful to its benefactor; in his panegyric on the sixth consulate of Honorius, the Senate and the People become *cum plebe patres* (l. 332); and in the same poem later on (l. 611) the imperial genius rules the *populus* again. One cannot, to be sure, know whether the diversities of meaning were intended or whether a fourth century reader would be sensitive to them. But in several of the passages cited sense would be hardly changed—though meter would be—if one word were substituted for another.

Saint Augustine and Isidore of Seville

Augustine, whose special interest in history is known to everyone, felt it necessary to give his own definition of People. He had no great admiration for the human race as it had developed after the Fall. In the *City of God* (Book XIX, 23–41) he defines *populus* in essentially moral, not political, terms. The People are a group of persons bound together by a love of justice. In the second book of the same work (chap. 21) he uses the definition which we have quoted from Cicero. But since he had already made his fundamental distinction between the City of Man, founded by

Cain, and the City of God, founded by Abel (Book XV, 1), it was obvious that the City of Man was based on fratricide. Hence, when he spoke of the *populus* he was thinking of those who belonged to the City of God, for there was little hope that the City of Man would ever improve. The citizens of the City of God are, to be sure, governed by the *vox divina*, which is God's Wisdom (*Sapientia*) speaking through seers and prophets (Book V, 19). But he never, as far as I have been able to discover, says anything of the *vox populi*. In view of his low opinion of human constitutions it was hardly to be expected that he would have found much good to say about any human pronouncement. The history of the City of Man is an almost uninterrupted series of sins followed by disaster.

Augustine also flatly declares that when men are not bound together by "the love by which man loves God as God should be loved, and one's neighbor as oneself . . . there is neither that society of men bound together by a common acceptance of law and a community of interests . . . [nor] a people [*populus*]. . . . Hence there is no state [*respublica*] for where there is no *res populi*, there is no *populus*" (Book XIX, 23). The echo of Cicero is sharp, and the notion that a People had to be constituted on the basis of religious beliefs, with consequent moral agreements, was carried into the accepted dogmas of the Middle Ages. The inference was that Society as a unity was not to be taken for granted; it had to be achieved. And later, when the quarrel about the Two Swords arose, the ground for it was prepared by the idea of the two Cities which had always existed side by side and in discord. If the City of Man was founded by Cain, no one who believed this could possibly think that its citizens were anything better than the members of the *vulgus*. It would be a simple matter for such a person to conclude that Caesar's heir was Cain's heir and the pope the heir of Abel. But other men existed too and they were not to draw that conclusion. The thirteenth century, for instance, was no more ready to grant that the emperor was subordinate to the pope than Dante was.

One of the most influential sources of definitions in the Middle Ages is the *Etymologies* of Isidore of Seville. He is firm in distinguishing the People, who are "associated in agreement about the law and in peaceful communion," from the *Plebs*, who are the mob. "The people," he says, "make up the whole state [*civitas*], the mob [*vulgus*] is the *Plebs*." And since there are always fewer elders than juniors, the *Plebs* are always the majority.[12] Whether Isidore in using the word *civitas* was differentiating the population into those individuals who were associated by their acceptance of law and peaceful communion from those who were not so associated, I cannot pretend to say. He clearly uses the words "the People" for the total population which includes the Patricians, that is, the Elders. How he distinguishes the *vulgus*, except by their numbers, from the rest of the population is obscure, unless he means that everyone except the Patricians is part of the *vulgus*. He would not in any event have accepted our proverb as true, if he was consistent, for he could not have believed that the voice of the total population was divine.

We have referred in passing to the dispute about the relation between temporal and spiritual power. At times the dispute turned upon the question of the origin of the powers under con-

12. Since I may have been too free in expanding Isidore's sense, I shall quote the Latin: "Populus enim humanae multitudinis iuris consensu et concordi communione sociatus. Populus autem eo distat a plebibus, quod populus universi cives sunt, connumeratis senioribus civitatis. Plebs autem reliquum vulgus sine senioribus. 6. Populus ergo tota civitas est, vulgus vero plebs est. Plebs autem dicta a pluralitate. Maior est enim numerus minorum, quam seniorum . . . Vulgus est passim inhabitans multitudo, quasi quisque quo vult." *Etymologiae*, Book IX, iv, 5–6. The most sensible definition of *plebs* and *populus* is that given by Lily Ross Taylor (*Roman Voting Assemblies*, pp. 60 ff) : "The voters in the tribes under the presidency of a tribune were known as *plebs*. . . . Under the presidency of a consul or praetor the voters were the *populus*."

sideration. No one doubted that the Holy See had a beginning in time; its history could be traced backward to Saint Peter, from him to the High Priests of Israel, to the first High Priest, Aaron, and possibly even to Abraham or Melchizedek. This glorious history was hard to rival. But, as we have already pointed out, kingship was instituted by God Himself in the divine command to Samuel. On the other hand, when God said, "*Audi vocem populi,*" He did not specify the constitution of the *populus*. In II Kings (II Samuel) 5:1–5, a pact (*foedus*) is established between the Elders (*senioribus*) of Israel and David. The Elders were not the whole people of Israel, it is obvious. Hence this passage could be cited as scriptural evidence for the popular origin of monarchy, for the Elders, though only a part of the population, could be identified with the *populus* if one meant by that word what Cicero and Saint Augustine meant by it. The social compact, then, was not made by the total population, and I doubt that anyone who believed in it ever thought it was so made. Gierke points out[13] how the notion of a social compact is connected with the limitations of the *plenitudo potestatis* of both pope and emperor. That absolute power could be limited, an apparent paradox, could be demonstrated both dialectically and empirically. Dialectically all power could be shown to come from God and even His Vicar on earth was subject to His will. But experience, too, showed that neither pope nor emperor had ever been omnicompetent. Even the famous bull *Unam Sanctam* had to recognize that the two areas of dominion were different. Such arguments arose fairly late in the Middle Ages, though Charlemagne too had some doubts about his rights to the imperial crown. Between the sixth and the tenth centuries, however, the conditions for debate were hardly favorable. Action took the place of argument. Moreover, such events as the sack of Rome by the Goths and the establishment of Gothic power in Italy were effective barriers to anyone who wanted to maintain either the superiority of the traditional

13. *Political Theories of the Middle Ages,* p. 37.

secular or religious power or the origin of either. It was not until the eleventh century that a Gregory VII could vigorously assert the supremacy of papal authority and its source in popular acclaim. The vigor of his words was not and could not be paralleled by that of his deeds; yet they could keep his ideas in circulation and alive and, after all, for our purposes that is sufficient. If there had not been some strong belief in popular sovereignty it would not have been possible for a man like Rienzi to revivify and realize for a short time the idea of a popular state. Whether the Romans who shouted "*Popolo, popolo!*" as a cry of victory had much of an idea what they were shouting, I doubt, but the force of a slogan is not to be measured by its meaning. It should also be noted that in Rienzi's case his plan was carried out through the co-operation of a pope.

On the level of common sense the matter boils down to the fundamental distinction between those who are governed and those who do the governing. As Aristotle pointed out clearly, constitutions can be differentiated on the basis of how many individuals belong to each group. But whether one is living in a monarchy, an oligarchy, or a democracy, people form the group which is being governed.[14] These men and women are identified in ordinary speech as the People. In fact, until recent times there have always been three groups of people in all states, not two, for slaves have never been part of the *populus*. Nor is it true that the Church put an end to slavery, as has been claimed.[15] In the

14. Though as the number of functionaries grows, the number of the governors grows. And if one thinks of the power of lobbyists, the secret government, it becomes even more difficult to find anyone who does not have some share in government. Hence the People, like the King, has two bodies, one of which is active and the other acted upon.

15. See G. G. Coulton, *Medieval Panorama*, p. 322. "Narbonne," he says, "had a slave-market at a regular tariff: two slaves there cost as much as a mule, two mules as much as a horse. Two prelates in England, Lanfranc of Canterbury and Wulfsten of Worcester, share the credit of having put a stop to the selling of native slaves to the Irish. But in Southern France and Italy the slave-trade continued all through the Middle Ages, and the milder servi-

United States, where slavery is no longer an issue, there are still three classes of citizen: those who govern, those who are governed, and those who disfranchise themselves through negligence, poverty, or fear. In the 1960 presidential election only 63.5 per cent of persons presumably eligible to vote voted; in 1964, only 62 per cent. But the percentage varied from region to region: in Alabama only 36 per cent voted in 1964, in Mississippi only 32.9, whereas in Idaho 75.8 per cent voted, and in Massachusetts 71.3. It seems absurd to talk about popular government when voting is restricted either voluntarily or by compulsion to 35 per cent of those ostensibly eligible to vote.

No such doubts troubled the medieval writers so far as political problems were concerned. In Gierke's words:

> An ancient and generally entertained opinion regarded the Will of the People as the Source of Temporal Power. A friendly meeting took place between this traditional opinion and that Patristic Doctrine of the State of Nature which the Church was propagating. That doctrine taught that at one time under the Law of God and the Law of Nature community of goods, liberty and equality prevailed among mankind. It followed that Lordship made its first appearance as a consequence of the Fall of Man. It followed also that the authority of Rulers was grounded on human ordinance.[16]

How "generally accepted" this opinion was may be disputed, but that it had abundant support need not be argued. The *lex naturae* was accepted long before its supposed implications for political philosophy were drawn out of it. It was often used in primitivistic debates in Antiquity and was part and parcel of popular opinion, if only in the identification of the Golden Age or the *Saturnia regna*

---

tude of villenage was justified on moral and economic grounds by orthodox medieval philosophers; Wyclif alone has been marked as an exception to this general rule. No Pope or Church Council fulminated against slavery; the Archbishop of Narbonne, in 1149, left his Saracen slaves by will to the Bishop of Beziers; and in 1251, another Archbishop of Narbonne complained that the viscount had withheld from him his rightful profit on two slave-markets, to the amount of 2500 sols, or about £15,000 in modern purchasing power."

16. *Political Theories of the Middle Ages*, p. 38.

with life in the Garden of Eden. But the state of nature as a concept was not confined to political conditions. It was sometimes supposed to be technological, sometimes juristic, sometimes ethical, and sometimes even dietetic and marital.[17] It was, as far as the extant evidence goes, always defined as lacking something that was thought of as undesirable and yet characteristic of modern society: an established constitution, various artifices, marital conventions, luxury, and so on. If the mythographer was primitivistic, he would praise the state of nature; if anti-primitivistic, he would use it to measure our progress.

Since no one really knew what primitive man was like or what life in the Garden of Eden was like, the imagination was given a free rein. The arguments both pro and con had to be dialectical, if argument was used. Such items of modern society as were unfortunate must have come into being through some fault of primitive man, for whatever the goddess Nature produced must have been good and, if one were a Christian, one had the Bible as proof that "God saw everything that he had made, and, behold, it was very good." In the second place, it was understood that qualitative changes are always from a given condition toward its polar opposite. Hence the state of nature must have been diametrically opposed to the state of things-as-they-are. Thus if a critic of his society attributed its ills to luxury, to the prevalence of the arts and sciences, to codified laws, he saw in the state of nature the complete absence of these things. And since the state of nature in Christian times would have to be the state of pre-lapsarian man, it could be described with a little imagination in accordance with the first two chapters of Genesis. Though there are certain discrepancies between these texts, nevertheless both expressed the decrees of God.[18]

17. See A. O. Lovejoy and G. Boas, *Primitivism . . . in Antiquity*, pp. 14 ff.

18. I have discussed this in *Essays on Primitivism and Related Ideas in the Middle Ages.* See especially the essays on "The Original Condition of Man."

According to scripture, the establishment of monarchy was on the whole an evil. The People's Voice may be said to have made a great mistake when it requested a king. The basic error, as given in I Samuel 8 is that the People had rejected God as their ruler: "They have not rejected thee, but they have rejected me, that I should not reign over them." So in Judges 21:25, the last verse runs, "In those days there was no king in Israel: every man did that which was right in his own eyes." This would seem to imply in connection with I Samuel 8 that the election of a king was an abdication of personal autonomy, which in turn was identical with theocracy. There is, however, little if any recollection that the people of Israel erred in electing a king. One might have thought that the Thirteen Colonies, at least those in the North, might not have forgotten the warning, but in the early days of the Revolution some thought it possible to be free and also under the Crown. Perhaps the experience of the citizens of Massachusetts was enough to disillusion men with theocracy. In any event, faith in the popular will increased rather than diminished. And when errors were suspected it was usual, and still is, to look for some palliation of them, some excuse, such as lack of correct information, pressure from influential economic groups, bad leadership, as if to show that had the People been free to choose they would have chosen wisely. Yet the one authority for the first popular decision points out how wrong the People were even then. Recorded history could easily corroborate the conclusion that the People can be as wrong as a king or senate.

It goes without saying that in actual practice the ideological arguments were rarely used. When one referred to the *vox populi* as an appellate court one simply said that all the conditions of modern society that were regrettable were the result of the Fall. They were the result of one man's primordial sin. Since before that unhappy event man's will was free, it would not have been possible to predict what choice it would make. According to Saint Augustine, we were doomed now to choose the worse, even if, like

Ovid's Medea, we saw and approved of the better. Adam, moreover, was mankind as an integral whole: when he fell, we all fell.
And though Saint Ambrose might call our collective sin a *felix
culpa* in that it entailed the Incarnation and Redemption, neither
would have been necessary if we had not yielded to temptation.
This in all its ramifications might have been expected to weaken
any idea that the People, that is, anyone living after the Fall, could
speak with the voice of God when not directly quoting His
words.[19] If, on the other hand, there are any traces of free will
left in us, we might make an effort to remodel society in the likeness of Eden.

Natural Man

It was hence reasonable for later Utopians to imagine or
actually to found new Earthly Paradises, in which, unfortunately,
Adam's story was usually repeated. The regeneration of prelapsarian man sometimes seemed feasible even without the creation
of new states in the wilderness. To men persuaded of this possibility, the problem was first to define "natural man" according to
a technique mentioned above, that is, by stripping off man as he is
now the characteristics that seem evil. But one had also to assume
that natural man was living within each of us, as if in a prison
waiting for his release—a metaphor which opened Rousseau's
Social Contract. Release would come when he—or some liberator
—would destroy the unnatural man who was his jailer. To illustrate this I shall quote but one passage, for the story is well enough
known not to require a series of examples. I have chosen an appeal to Nature in the twelfth-century work of Alain of Lille as he
preached against riches.

19. Cf. Alexander Pope, *Epistles and Satires of Horace Imitated*, Epist. I,
to Augustus, ll. 89–90: "The people's voice is very odd. It is and it is not,
the voice of God."

Listen to what Nature has to say against you: Man, I have borne you without honors, without honors may you depart; without riches have I given you birth, may you come back to me without riches; without worldly glory have you come, may you leave without it. Man, do you ask to make yours that which does not belong to you? Surely those things are not yours which were not born with you. Those things cannot be yours, they cannot belong to you for long, or be yours forever. Consider that word of the philosopher, "It is a goodly possession, joyful poverty." But there is not poverty if it is joyful. For he who finds poverty befitting to him is a rich man. Not he who has too little, but he who thirsts for more is poor. If you live in accordance with Nature, never will you be poor. If you follow common opinion, never will you be rich. Nature desires but a trifle, opinion an immensity. Natural needs are limited, those born of false opinion have no end.[20]

According to Alain it seems to be possible for an individual to reform by his own means, by self-discipline, through an act of will. But as the state or the community was divided into the People and the Nobles, the Powerful, the Senate, the Court, the Magnates, so the individual was internally divided between the natural man made in the image and likeness of God and the unnatural man made in the image and likeness of Mammon. Alain, deriving from cynicism or, more accurately, from Roman stoicism, is basically attached to the ideal of self-sufficiency, autarky.

Others correlated naturalness with other traits. In Diogenes

20. "Audi quid contra te dicat Natura! O homo, sine honoribus te genui, sine honoribus redeas; sine divitiis te peperi, sine divitiis ad me venias; sine mundana gloria intrasti, sine illa exeas. O homo, quaeris facere tua quae sunt aliena? certe a te aliena sunt, quae tecum nata non sunt; tua esse nequeunt, tecum diu vel semper esse non possunt. Considera illud philosophi: "Honesta res est, laeta paupertas." Illa vero non est paupertas si laeta est. Cui cum paupertate bene convenit, dives est; non qui parum habet, sed qui plus cupit, pauper est. Si ad naturam vivas, nunquam pauper eris; si ad opinionem, nunquam dives. Exiguum natura desiderat, opinio immensum. Naturalia desideria sunt finita, ex falsa opinione, nascentia ubi desinant non habent." *Summa de arte praedicatoria*, chap. VI; in *PL*, CCX, col. 123. The tradition of Greek cynicism with its program of living in accordance with Nature rather than in accordance with opinion, *physis* vs. *nomos*, or in this case *doxa*, was probably transmitted through Seneca.

the natural was to be found in the animal; in the early Stoics it was in the reason when liberated from the passions. Fundamentally one was seeking freedom from something supposed to enchain the soul, whether it was the love of possessions, the *amor habendi*, or the love of knowledge, the *amor sciendi*. Behind the program may have been the counsel, "Sell all and follow me," where the person and teaching of Christ becomes an analogue of the Law of Nature or of the Truth that liberates (John 8:32). When the People were thought of as a paradigm of the good life, the life of freedom, it was the ruler who was to be resisted. And paradoxically enough, though our Fall came from disobedience to our Heavenly King, we were told to be disobedient to our earthly king. The anti-intellectualist was to urge men to listen to their emotions, their common sense, their instincts, their hearts, and to divorce old barren reason from their beds. The dictum *populus maior principe* was applied at first only to political mythography, but before a few centuries had passed it would be modified in phraseology and applied to philosophy, religion, and art.

Pity for the People

Meanwhile a sentiment of pity for the People was being generated. Pity was aroused by the poverty of the masses, and their poverty was apparently a kind of cement that would solidify certain common interests which their fellows of higher rank did not share. The solidarity of the People comes out clearly in such proverbs as this: "A roaring lion and a hungry bear is an impious prince to his poor people" (*Leo rugiens et ursus esuriens est princeps impius super populum pauperem*). But it is not only a prince who is criticized. For we come upon another proverb which says, "The ruination of a people is evil priests" (*Ruina populi sacerdotes mali*). It is only fair to add that it also seems that a bad superior may be appointed by God as a punishment: "Because of the people's sins the Lord has set a hypocrite over them" (*Propter peccata populi regnare facit Dominus hypocritam*).[21]

When an idea becomes proverbial one can conclude that the sentiments contained in it have gained wide acceptance. The ideas contained in these commonplaces are of no significance to us except as evidence that some individuals believed it possible for the People as a group to be harshly treated. This belief—by no means self-evident—that a group of individuals can suffer as a whole, collectively, that a class of persons may be selected because it has a certain solidarity, was inherent in such concepts as that of the *plebs patriciatus*, which would have been impossible in classical Latin, but which as *plebs tua Israel* was as early as the fifth century. No one seems to have asked himself just what was involved in a collection's becoming a unity. Such problems did not arise until the nineteenth century, when the supposed implications of collectivities were drawn out by men like Hegel and his school. It is also true that familiarity with the idea of collective guilt and atonement may have made acceptance of collective injustice less questionable than it would have been if unfamiliar.

Another truism should be ventured and that is that we have only recorded opinion to go on. Of all the opinions that may have been recorded before the invention of printing, only a small fraction are now available. That fraction cannot be said to represent more than the thoughts of a literary elite. We have no way of knowing how widespread any opinion may have been in a semi-literate society. The best we can do is to guess that when an idea agreed with what a man thought to be to his own interest, it would be espoused by him. But even that is dubious. To have asked a tenth- or even a fifteenth-century Frenchman whether he believed in the principle *populus maior principe* would have been to elicit a vacant stare of incomprehension. We have, moreover, seen too frequently in the last two hundred years people fighting

21. Chosen from Othlo (eleventh century), *Libellus proverbiorum*, ed. G. C. Korfmacher (Chicago, 1936), pp. 40, 72, 58, respectively.

for causes which they neither understood nor were equipped to understand. How then equate their actions with their beliefs? It was the philosophers who wrote about the *consensus gentium*, inherited guilt, vicarious atonement, and the sovereignty of the emperor or pope.

Just as there were people who identified the consensus with the truth, so there were others who identified it with nonsense. It has been emphasized that no one seemed very sure who the People were. Yet until one knew who they were one could not tell whether one admired their ideas or not. The *populus-plebs* might be despised, whereas the *populus-pauper* might be eulogized. The *populus principans* could be esteemed as the voice of God, whereas the *populus subditus* might be ordered to remain silent and obey. In Christian circles it was apparently no more trouble to believe that the People as a whole could sin, or be sinned against, than it was to believe that they could be, in fact had been, redeemed. But if such beliefs presented no obstacles, in spite of their logical intricacies and paradoxes, then it would be easy to attribute to the People as a whole a host of other properties. Indeed, ever since Hesiod had described his various "races," golden, silver, heroic, bronze, and iron, since Hellenes and barbarians had been differentiated, it had become a pastime of writers to compose generalized accounts of various peoples whom they might either laud or look down upon.

National Traits

It has always been easy to say that there are exceptions to every rule, and even before statistical investigations were known, deviants from the norm could be brushed aside. This practice has continued to our own times and bids fair not to die out. One can still characterize nations, social classes, economic groups, as sober, brave, chaste, friendly, hostile, drunken, lubricious, or thieving, to choose only a few of the more familiar adjectives. Usually the application of such epithets is a literary, not a scientific, device. There was a time when John Bull, Uncle Sam, and Marianne were used by caricaturists as the Dottore, Arlechino, and Pantaleone were used in the *commedia dell'arte*, to symbolize nations, cities, or groups within nations. Such stereotypes have seldom been used by ethnologists or social psychologists, though Hitler employed them in propaganda with tragic results, and the practice is not unlike that used by Marxists who lump together all the bourgeoisie and all the capitalists and give their members collective traits. I imagine that the segregationists in the United States actually believe that there exists a Negro soul or mind or collective unconscious which is transmitted by generation even into people who have more white blood than black.

It is probably true that when a group of human beings lives in relative isolation its traditions will solidify and may become characteristic of it alone. We see this in speech, costume, art, religion, and social etiquette. But that it is to be laid to the public expression of a group-soul is doubtful, for none is needed to explain it.

Ages

The legend of the Ages, according to which all human beings living between certain dates would have the same general character, intellectual and moral, gave support to the idea that individuals behaved as they did as a function of their "times." Indeed, as we shall see in a later essay, some of the German philosophers maintained that the times themselves had a spirit or character, not the statistical mode of measured ways of behaving, but rather as an over-individual something which determined the behavior of the individuals. The Voice of the People now turned into the Voice of the Age, Period, or Time.[22] And that voice was of such a nature

22. The following from James Thomson, author of the *City of Dreadful Night*, is the most extreme version of the influence of a "time" or "age" on

that it utilized individuals as its mouthpiece. In short, a man acted as he did because the Age made him do so. Thus individuals could be said to express their times, reflect their times, speak for their times, and apparently their times were cut off from them as a cause is cut off from its effects. The question of what would happen to a time or age if its human components were removed from it seems not to have puzzled writers who believed in ages. Hence when expressions like "the Mediaeval Mind," "the Renaissance Man," "the Victorian mentality," were used one might have expected some discussion of how one knew who embodied these fictions. But aside from Hegel's—and Emerson's—universal man, little was done in this field of inquiry. And such phrases as "the childhood of the race," "America comes of age," "the search for national identity," fused into one basic metaphor, that humanity as a whole has a mind or soul or spirit or character, and the logically independent metaphor that it has a history that parallels that of an individual.

In Saint Augustine's story of the ages, one of the earliest Christian versions and certainly the most influential, this parallelism was detailed.[23] The seven days of Creation symbolized, he thought, the seven ages of man. The first age, from Adam to

the people living in it. It is from "The Poems of William Blake" of 1865. (First printed in the National Reformer in 1866. Reprinted in The Speedy Extinction of Evil and Misery, p. 216.)

"[Like the mountain peaks which are first illuminated by the rising sun] so the Spirit of the Ages, the Zeitgeist, is developed universally and independently by its own mysterious laws through mankind; and the eminent men from whom it radiates the expression of what we call a new aspect (the continuous imperceptible increments of change having accumulated to an amount of change which we can clearly perceive, and which our gross standards are fine enough to measure), the illustrious prototypes of an age, really cast but a faint reflex upon those beneath them; and while pre-eminently interesting in biography, are of small account in history except as prominent indices of growth and progress and decay, as early effects not efficient causes. They help us to read clearly the advance of time; but this advance they do not cause any more than the gnomon of a sundial causes the procession of the hours which it indicates. . . ."

23. De Genesi contra Manicheos, I, 23 (PL, XXXIV, cols. 190 ff). Cf. Boas, Primitivism . . . in the Middle Ages, pp. 177 ff.

Noah, is the age of infancy; the second, from Noah to Abraham, that of childhood; the third, from Abraham to David, that of adolescence; the fourth, from David to the Babylonian captivity, that of youth, "the certain adornment of all ages"; the fifth, from the Captivity to the Advent, that of maturity (*presbytes*); the sixth, the present, is that of senescence, when "a man is born who now lives spiritually"; and the seventh will be that of the cosmic Sabbath "which has no evening." This outline of history was repeated throughout the Middle Ages from the time of Eugippius to that of Hugh of Saint Victor. But none of these accounts perceived the problem of collective minds, and all, for that matter, tacitly admitted differences among the individuals belonging to any single age. Consequently, the same question arises of who represents or speaks for his age and how he is selected. Were such a question answered, then the People could be said to be metaphorically present in their representative. Whether his voice could be identified with the voice of God is more dubious. The one man who might be said to speak with God's voice is the pope and even he only within the limitations which were defined in 1870.

Diversity within an age was not formally recognized until the time of Auguste Comte. His predecessors, Vico and Herder, were more given to emphasizing the homogeneity of ages. The men of Vico's heroic age not only thought alike but framed laws, wrote poetry, and worshiped their gods in a uniform manner. But Comte saw that in his metaphysical and positivistic ages there would be survivals from earlier periods. Since his basic metaphor was the mental life of an individual, he could grant that just as some adults behave like children and others like adolescents, so in the positivistic period there would be theologically and metaphysically oriented individuals. For him the People would be those men most in tune with the prevailing and characteristic key, or else their antitheses, the hangovers from the past. Since he admitted this possible diversity, he put a small group of scientific experts in charge of society. Like Comte, I suspect, the Marxist of today would grant that even under the dictatorship of the proletariat there would be vestigial traces of primitive communism and capitalism, though such traces would tend to disappear. But the proletariat as a class becomes the People and whatever is achieved in a communistic state is presumably planned for the satisfaction of their interests.

Le Peuple

The attempt to identify the People in France was especially strong after the downfall of Charles X. Before the Restoration and during the Revolution the People were apparently the sans-culottes. As Hannah Arendt puts it:

> The words le peuple are the key words for every understanding of the French Revolution, and their connotations were determined by those who were exposed to the spectacle of their sufferings, which they themselves did not share. For the first time, the word covered more than those who did not participate in government, not the citizens but the low people. The very definition of the word was born out of compassion and the term became the equivalent for misfortunate and unhappiness—le peuple, les malheureux m'applaudissent, as Robespierre was wont to say; le peuple toujours malheureux, as even Sieyès, one of the least sentimental and most sober figures of the Revolution, would put it.

In a note later in her book, Dr. Arendt adds, "Le peuple was identical with menu or petit peuple," and it consisted of "small businessmen, grocers, artisans, workers, employees, salesmen, servants, day laborers, lumpenproletarien, but also of poor artists, play actors, penniless writers." [24]

The one man who was clear about his identification of the People was Michelet. In a short book entitled Le Peuple, pub-

24. From Hannah Arendt, On Revolution, p. 69 and p. 293, n. 18. The second quotation is translated by her from Walter Markov, Ueber des Ende der Pariser Sansculottenbewegung, in Beitrage zum neuen Geschichtbild (Berlin, 1956).

lished in 1846, two years before the final ousting of monarchy, he flatly maintained that *le peuple* was the peasantry.[25] To Michelet the outstanding virtue of the peasant is his wedding to the land (p. 33), and that marriage is a tie which springs from a deeply seated love between men and the earth. He is distinguished from other men by a *don de travailler, de combattre, au besoin, sans manger, de vivre d'espérance, de gaîté courageuse* (p. 35). But this is not all: he is also a child and therefore a genius, relying more on instinct than on reason. To Michelet reason is anathema. It is perverse and has dissociated men from one another. The greatest need of humanity is fellowship cemented by love (p. 141). It is the absence of the critical faculty that distinguishes the peasant. He has been corrupted, it is true, by the *bourgeois* who live, of course, in cities, but when he can be found in his rural state he will be seen to be motivated by friendliness (*l'amitié*), which in Michelet seems to be the equivalent of Christian charity, and which has no need of reflective thought. "Instinctive thinking," he says, "is close to action, is almost action; it is almost at once an idea and an act" (p. 148). Where now is one to find this man of instinctive action? Only in the outstanding popular leader, the man of genius: "in him is placed the great soul. We are all astonished to see the inert masses vibrate in tune with the least word he says, to hear the roar of the Ocean be silent at the sound of this voice, the waves of the people swell about his feet. . . . Why then be astonished? This voice is that of the people; dumb in itself, it speaks in this man, and God speaks with him. Here is where one can truly say, Vox *populi, vox Dei*." [26] The meta-

25. I use the edition brought out in Paris in 1946 by Lucien Refort, which is an exact reprint of the original with notes and commentary. All quotations are from this edition.

26. The French of these sentences runs: (1) "la pensée instinctive touche à l'acte, est presque l'acte; elle est presque en même temps une idée et une action." (2) En lui [le génie] réside la grande âme. Tout le monde s'étonne de voir les masses inertes, vibrer au moindre mot qu'il dit, les bruits de l'Océan se taire devant cette voix, le vague populaire trainer à ses pieds. . . . Pourquoi

physics of this last test is again that of Hegel, the metaphysics of a collective soul in an "eternal" man. But if there is anything rational in this soul, it is the reason of Hegel's concrete universal. Michelet pointed out in this little book that the French were frightened of what they called Communism and Terrorism (p. 113). But, as he also pointed out, the Terror was not made by the peasants (the People), but by the bourgeois and nobles, "minds cultivated, subtle, bizarre, sophists and scholastics." As for communism, he laughed it out of court on the ground that every Frenchman was a proprietor and would not give up his property as long as he could hold on to it. How long this would be under communism as it exists in reality rather than in books, he did not foresee. But Michelet was more of an orator than a critical historian. As Lucien Refort says, Michelet's "ideas emerge from his love or his antipathy much more than from the modalities of reasoning." That goes far to explain both the popularity and the lack of precision in his work.

The Constitutional Convention ·

We have, I hope, seen that this lack of precision is not peculiar to Michelet. Consider for a moment the opening of the preamble to the Constitution of the United States: "We the People. . . ." The authors of that document were neither representative of the colonial population nor did they mirror its ideas. There were plenty of loyalists in that population, including Franklin's son William. Moreover, the final draft of the Constitution was the result of a compromise, and one colony, Rhode Island, was absent, and deliberately, at all of the debates. The compromise was a happy one; but it was a compromise nevertheless. The heart of its

---

donc s'en etonner? Cette voix, c'est celle du peuple; muet en elle même, elle parle en cet homme, et Dieu avec lui. C'est là vraiment qu'on peut dire, 'Vox populi, vox Dei.' " This might be contrasted with the opinion of Heinrich Heine, Michelet's contemporary, in his *Geständnisse*, in *Werke und Briefe*, Vol. 7, pp. 121–22.

philosophy, the separation of powers, was a point on which some of the most stalwart revolutionists were divided. The lack of consensus on most points had always characterized the colonies. It took from 1777 to 1781 for the Articles of Confederation to be ratified by the thirteen states and from 1787 to 1790 for the Constitution to be accepted by them all, though it went into effect in 1789. The conflict of interests in the Continental Congress was manifest in the earliest days of its deliberations, some delegates insisting on remaining loyal to the King, others declaring for independence; some wanting to open all the ports to all shipping, others to supervise what was later to become international commerce; some wanting financial and military aid from foreign nations, others shrinking from so "treasonous" a gesture. But what else was to be expected when delegates from twelve different colonies, of various social and economic institutions, of different national origins, met together to deliberate? The formation of our Constitution, not to mention its ratification, illustrates the power of disagreement and debate in producing a final consensus, as it also illustrates resignation to what one is convinced is inevitable. Franklin's famous saying, "We must all hang together, gentlemen, or we shall all hang separately," assuming it to be authentic, dates from 1776, but it may well contain the nuclear thought that was decisive. Yet his words were scarcely a program. Hamilton's well-known opinion of the voice of the People, expressed in 1787, is evidence enough that he shared some of the traditional estimates of "the Multitude" usually held by aristocrats. He certainly did not think of himself as one of the Multitude. John Adams, who did not sit as a delegate to the Convention, showed plainly enough that he realized the difficulty of defining the word "the People." "It is certain, in theory," he wrote to James Sullivan, "that the only moral foundation of government is the consent of the people. . . . To what extent shall we carry this principle? Shall we say that every individual of the community, old and young, male and female, as well as rich and poor, must consent, expressly to every act of legislation?" [27] His decision was that of Harrington, that "power follows property." The People then became the owners of property. And presumably the Voice of the People was the voice of the propertied class. They alone had something at stake when legislation was being debated.

This was in fact the opinion of several of the most influential delegates. Elbridge Gerry (Massachusetts) argued that "the Cincinnati would in fact elect the chief magistrate in every instance, if the election be referred to the people." "The most dangerous influence," said John Dickinson (Delaware), "of those multitudes without property and without principle with which our country, like all others, will soon abound." Most of the state constitutions required their voters to own property, in sums ranging from twenty pounds in New York to sixty pounds in Massachusetts, though Pennsylvania, Delaware and New Hampshire had already come out for free elections. Hamilton, in the speech just referred to, flatly said, "All communities divide themselves into the few and the many. The first are the rich and well born, the other the mass of the people. . . . Can a democratic Assembly, who annually revolve in the mass of the people, be supposed to pursue the public good?" Catherine Drinker Bowen, from whose *Miracle at Philadelphia* I take these quotations, says, speaking of Madison, "Present day readers may be a trifle dashed to find the Father of our Constitution urging, in effect, that the American rich put up barriers against the American poor, who with power in their hands could be dangerous." The fact is that the delegates were afraid of popular uprisings like Shay's Rebellion. To them, to quote Mrs. Bowen's admirable study again, "Democracy signified anarchy; *demos* was not the people but the mob." [28]

27. Quoted from Page Smith, *John Adams*, Vol. I, pp. 258–59.
28. *Miracle at Philadelphia*, p. 45. It becomes clearer and clearer as one studies the journals of Madison, that the leading delegates with the exception of Franklin, looked back to Rome not only for their vocabulary but for many of their main ideas. Hamilton was far from being alone in his distrust of the poor.

It has taken over a century for our concept of the People to change in any significant manner. Phrases like "the consent of the people" or even "the consent of the governed" have never been taken literally. One can see in reading the political history of the United States how the denotation of "the People" has spread, property requirements, religious affiliations, sex, color, national origin, being gradually removed. And even when restrictions on the franchise have been annulled by law, the inhabitants of certain regions have not always been agreeable to accepting and obeying the law. The Fourteenth Amendment has been fortified by recent legislation and is still defied, not only by the people of various southern states but even by the governors and legislators of at least two of them. The executives in question have been acting as they do with full support from the white majority as tested in elections. And yet Lincoln's words which close his Gettysburg Address will be repeated in schools and political harangues as if sacred: "Government of the people, by the people, for the people. . . ." [29] Daniel Webster in 1830 had already spoken of the "people's government, made for the people, made by the people, and answerable to the people," and he apparently saw no problem involved in telling his fellow senators whom he was referring to.[30] As so

29. William Rappard in his lecture "Les Etats-Unis et l'Europe," printed in *Le Nouveau Monde et l'Europe* (p. 43), quoted an anticipation of Lincoln's words. In 1830 Judge Schinz had said, "Alle Regierung der Schweiz mussen es erkennen, dass sie bloss aus dem Volk, durch das Volk, und fur das Volk da sind." But the phrase had already been used by the *Comité du Salut public* in 1793. Posters for the first play given under governmental auspices in Paris, August 6 of that year, bore the words, "De par et pour le Peuple." See the first edition of Romain Rolland's *Le Théâtre du Peuple*, p. 77, n. 1.

30. In his Second Speech on Foot's Resolution, January 26, 1830. See *The Works of Daniel Webster*, Vol. III, p. 321. Since writing this book I have received a full discussion of one concept of the People which should be mentioned. It is "Who are the 'People' in the Preamble to the Constitution," by Morris D. Forkosch, *Case Western Reserve Law Review*, Vol. 19, no. 3 (April, 1968). It is definitive.

often in the history of ideas, one finds that the emotional effect of a term is a function of its obscurity and sometimes proportionate to it. In succeeding essays we shall see some examples of this. In a context like this, charm counts for more than clarity.

III

THE PEOPLE IN LITERATURE

To identify the voice of the People with that of God is to attribute to them a superiority that no individual, except possibly the Pope, has ever claimed to possess. No one, to the best of my knowledge, has ever said that any man other than a prophet could be God's spokesman on earth. There have, to be sure, been mystics who have seen God face to face and have heard His voice; but their voices under day to day conditions were not held to be divinely inspired. According to our proverb it was the collective voice of the People that was divine, not the voice of any individual. But men who were sceptical of this notion could argue that the collective voice was simply a multiplication of individual voices and that the latter could be as ignorant as their history or inherent character made them. How could a hundred fools be collectively wise? This was the question of men like Cicero. On the other hand, there was in European literature the tradition of the Wise Fool.[1] The Wise Fool is best known to modern readers in the person of King Lear's Fool, who has the prerogative of telling the truth, however unpleasant, to his master. Moreover, he knows the truth. Sometimes the Wise Fool appears as the village simpleton, or, as in some of Grimm's fairy tales, the third son, shrewder and more astute than his two older brothers, and even, in *Puss-in-Boots*, as an animal. He appears in Andersen's story of "The Emperor's Clothes" in the character of the little child who is innocent of flattery, as if maturity were an obstruction to wisdom. In the long

---

1. Best described by Enid Welsford in her *The Fool. His Social and Literary History* (London, 1935), esp. chapter 4. As an example of the Wise Fool even in popular literature, see the ballad of "King John and the Abbot of Canterbury," in Percy's *Reliques*, 2d ser., Book III, no. 6.

run this reduces to the doctrine that something called Nature is better than Art, that instinct is better than reason, that for certain kinds of knowledge "book learning" is a waste of time. Antiintellectualism is nothing new. It is simply one form of cultural primitivism. For reasons that are no longer discoverable men seem to have thought that in primitive times the human race was able to steer its way among obstacles by some sort of unlearned congenital knowledge, which could be found only in those individuals who had not been tainted with instruction. Such individuals were identified during the course of history with the peasant or artisan, the madman, the seer, the child, and in the early nineteenth century with the woman, whose intuition was surer than man's intellect. They were never members of the ruling class.

My first two essays have shown that there has been a basic ambiguity in the phrase, "The People." At the risk of needless repetition, let me say that at times it meant a group within the state which held a certain political position—a group that elected its rulers and gave consent to the form of government under which it lived or proposed to live. At other times it meant a group selected from a religious context which acclaimed bishops on their election. And in yet other times it meant a social group of very low prestige—peasants, artisans, the poor, usually the uneducated.[2] When we speak of government by popular consent we are using the term in the first sense and are not committing ourselves to any appraisal of the good taste or manners or religious insight of the People. But when we speak of "popular novels" or of "vulgarity," we do so in a tone of disparagement. We seem to assume that social status is independent of political status. We seldom fuse the two and, at least in the United States, it has often been admitted in private conversation if not in print that the taste, manners, and literary background of our political potentates are not such as would be approved by the arbiters of the elegancies.

2. And sometimes, as when a case in court is termed "The People vs. So and So," it seems to denote almost everyone.

The self-made man is highly regarded in terms of ecological success. But those who feel that they have the right to appraise the
conduct of others will give him a low mark in social etiquette.
This naturally will be called snobbishness, and in a democratic
society snobbishness is condemned. But this requires qualification.

There is a historical link between the political and social
senses of the term, "the People." (The religious sense has not
been used for years.) If the People are the *plebs* or the *vulgus* or
the *multitudo* (*hoi polloi*), they will almost by definition be those
men who have (a) no inherited property, (b) no individual political
power or influence, (c) no experience of the arts or pastimes of the
leisure class, and (d) none of the prestige that comes from wearing
the proper clothes, speaking with the approved accent, knowing
the right people, and so on *ad nauseam*. They are, as contemporary sociologists might say, the Out-group. Indeed, the very fact
that there are so many of them lowers them in the eyes of the
socially élite. We all grow up in the belief that "all things excellent are as difficult as they are rare," and by a simple conversion
of Spinoza's statement we infer that the rarer things are the more
excellent. The tastes and manners of the Many make them undesirable associates. In books they may be said to have the noblest
qualities as a mass, but in real life the social class that fixes the
standards of approbation rarely substitutes courage, endurance,
initiative, or plain hard work for good manners. And by good
manners is meant the manners that may be in style at the time
the appraisal is made. This is important, for sometimes through
la nostalgie de la boue the manners and language that one generation considers to be those of the gutter turn into those of the
drawing room. The characteristics of the *vulgus* have usually been
dispraised, but sometimes the manners of the upper classes are
taken over by the lower, and then those gestures which were
thought of as the height of elegance become first quaint, and then
amusing, and then downright vulgar. While this progress is going
on, the reverse may be accompanying it, and those forms of be-

havior which were condemned in the time of one's grandparents become smart. The change is revealed even in the evolution of adjectives of praise: witness the word "genteel."

The People are not always the poor, but the poor are usually an important part of the People. Unfortunately, Western Europe had good reasons for not admiring them, assuming that reasons were needed. The court of last resort was always the Bible and, though both Testaments preached charity, brotherly love, alms, kindness, and the equality of all men in the sight of God, there were texts aplenty to justify the hard of heart. Biblical exegesis seldom paid much attention to contexts, except in self-defense. Thus we find that "the poor shall never cease out of the land" (Deut. 15:11); "the Lord maketh poor, and maketh rich" (I Sam. 2:7); "the poor is hated even of his own neighbor: but the rich hath many friends" (Prov. 14:20); and finally, "Ye have the poor always with you; but me ye have not always" (Matt. 26:11). The one safe conclusion that can be drawn from the Bible concerning the poor is that they will always exist and that the only remedy for their condition is alms. Their poverty does not confer nobility upon them; it does not make their judgment or taste better than that of their benefactors. The curious thing is that no seer or prophet envisioned any remedy other than alms for the condition which all deplored. In Christian times, as everyone knows, voluntary poverty became a form of penance. Nor was there much comfort to be found in the New Testament for the rich. But the triumph of Christianity caused all qualms about riches to vanish, and not only the worldly but the Church itself gained wealth and sought wealth. The Church could hardly have become a worldwide organization without it. It was more pleasant to be rich, and, at least until that ultimate moment before the Gates of Paradise, the poor continued to be looked down upon. And as the People had a multitude of poor members who might at any time break loose and try to overthrow the rich, they were always a threat to the peace of mind of the dominant stratum of society. It was essential that a man's uneasiness be pacified, if he were the type to sympathize with his fellow men. And the easiest form of inner pacification was to see that what one deplored was inescapable. Although it is out of chronological order, it may not be irrelevant to cite here John Winthrop's *Model of Christianity*, in which God is made responsible for this condition. "God Almighty," he says, "in His most holy and wise providence hath so disposed of the condition of mankind as in all times some must be rich, some poor; some high and eminent in power and dignity, some mean and in subjection." [3] The reason for this disposition is simple enough: it is in conformity with the rest of Creation in which variety and difference are the rule. Lest this diversity cause the universe to fall apart, one kind must depend on another and all things be interdependent. Therefore each class of men will have its own virtues: in "the great ones" there will be manifested love, mercy, gentleness, and temperance; in "the poor and inferior sort," faith, patience, and obedience. These words were written *en route* to Massachusetts Bay aboard the *Arabella*, and their author may not have had the leisure to think out the implications of his words. But it was not unusual to find an apology for poverty in the opportunity it bestowed on the rich to give alms. Alms giving was a virtue, and if there were no poor there would be no one to whom to extend one's brotherly love. And obedience was also a virtue, as is amply shown in Genesis. Hence, if there were no "great ones," there would be no one to whom to be obedient.

I have found no Puritan who went so far as the Ancients in ridiculing the poor. The Many in Greece and the *mobile vulgus* in Rome were targets of both ridicule and contempt,[4] and it would be sheer pedantry to document this generalization, for it is common knowledge.

3. I quote it as printed in Perry Miller's *The American Puritans*, p. 79.
4. Later, in Martial's time, there must have been a desire to appear poor, perhaps because ostentation was either in bad taste or because of fear of despoliation. See his famous epigram *Pauper videri Cinna vult; at est pauper* (VIII, 19).

In pre-Conquest England social status was accompanied by inequality even before the law. The punishment meted for a crime was in harmony with the social hierarchy, the killing of a serf by a nobleman being less severely punished than the killing of a nobleman by one of his peers. In the eleventh century, Wulfstan (d. 1023) delivered a famous sermon "To the English" in which he deplored the unfair treatment of the lower orders. Many persons, he said, are reduced to poverty and humiliated, "and poor men are sorely tricked and cruelly betrayed, and [though] convicted of no crime are sold into the power of strangers far from this earth [of theirs], and for a trifling theft [by their parents] children still in the cradle are by harsh law enslaved far and wide throughout this folk; and freemen's rights are taken away and thralldom is tightened and alms-right is curtailed, and—what is quickest to tell—the law of God is hated and scorned." [5]

This sort of thing is well known to historians. But what does not seem to be realized is its concomitance with the whole notion of *dignitates* inherent not only in the feudal system but in the cosmos as a whole. That the universe was a hierarchy was an idea of Plotinus, foreshadowed by Philo Judaeus but not developed by him. In Plotinus the hierarchy had three characteristics: it was logical, running from the most general and abstract down to the least general and most concrete; it was ontological, running from the most real, the *ens realissimum*, down to the least real; it was axiological, running from the best down to the worst.[6] On each level were beings of the same degree of generality, reality, and

5. As quoted in Margaret Schlauch, *English Medieval Literature and Its Social Foundations*, p. 93.

6. Plotinus' pupil Porphyry, in his *Introduction to the Categories of Aristotle*, may even have thought that individuals were the last stage of the hierarchy, for his famous Tree had *Being* at the apex and the *infima species* at the base. But it is probably obvious that individuals cannot be produced from, e.g., *humanity*, the concept, by logical means alone, unless one has previously assumed that all potentialities must be realized. This is the principle called the Principle of Plenitude by A. O. Lovejoy.

worth. By the fifth century this was developed by Pseudo-Diony-sius into the celestial hierarchy, in which the nine angelic choirs were expounded. But there was also an ecclesiastical hierarchy with the Pope at the top and the catechumens at the base. And on paper, if not in fact, when the feudal system was operating, one had the sovereign at the top and the various ranks of nobility under him running, let us say, from the royal dukes down to the serfs. In Anglo-Saxon England this seems to have been simpler. There were only four ranks: the nobles (*eorlas*), the free peasants (*ceorlas*), the freedmen (*laetas*), and the slaves (*theowas*).[7] The word "hierarchy" itself appears for the first time in Pseudo-Dionysius, and it is surmised that it was taken over from the organization of the Egyptian priesthood. The most familiar instance of any hierarchy at present would be in the armed services, where rank corresponds to the amount of power which a given officer, commissioned or non-commissioned, may have. The organization of a large corporation might be a close parallel, and there is a similar type of constitution in the Roman Catholic Church. By equating power with worth (*dignitas*), it would be an easy step to equating privilege with worth and rank and power. There is no need to point out that this is precisely what one finds in the Army and Navy. Thus one can rationalize one's feeling that the lower ranks are inherently less worthy than the upper.

Power can be of various kinds. It may amount to nothing more than social prestige which makes power effective. It may be economic or socioeconomic. But whatever it is, there is always either an overt or a concealed center of power. Once the system is fused into one's way of thinking, one needs no conscious effort to equate rank with value. The human beings at the top of the hierarchy are by that fact alone better than those farther down. And those at the bottom of the pyramid are *ipso facto* ugly, or bad,

7. M. Schlauch, *English Medieval Literature*, p. 6.

or stupid, or ridiculous. There is no sense to this if by sense one means a rational ground.

On the other hand, custom can itself make sense. There is no rational sense in the traditional submission of wives to husbands. There is to be sure the Pauline commandment: "Wives, submit yourselves unto your husbands, as unto the Lord. For the husband is the head of the wife, even as Christ is the head of the Church: and he is the savior of the body. Therefore as the church is subject unto Christ, so let the wives be to their husbands in every thing" (Eph. 5:22–24).[8] There is some sense in obeying the commands of the Apostle as emanating from God. But here "sense" is equivalent to "authority," and the man who accepts authoritative dicta does not demand reasons, causes, explanations. The wife who is self-assertive is not only a bad wife but a comic figure; and so is the private soldier who takes on the airs of a commander, or the layman who acts like a bishop. In fact, in ecclesiastic circles relief was sought from the rigidity of the system as in the Saturnalia, for example, when the hierarchy was inverted and a boy acted as bishop and a lord waited on his servants. In the nineteenth century such a reversal was taken seriously, and the pity that had been felt in earlier times became esteem for those who suffered simply because of their low rank. Figaro's well-known diatribe foreshadows this change in public opinion: "Because you are a great lord, you think yourself a great genius! . . . nobility, fortune, rank, position . . . it all makes for pride! But what have you done to have such benefits? You took the trouble to be born, nothing more." [9]

8. This has died out in the United States, but as late as Anthony Trollope's time it was taken for granted. For that matter, it was only recently that the word "obey" was dropped from the bride's marriage vows.

9. "Parce que vous êtes un grand Seigneur, vous vous croyez un grand Génie . . . noblesse, fortune, rang, des places; tout cela rend si fier! qu'avez-vous fait pour tant de biens? vous vous êtes donné la peine de naître, rien de plus." (Act V, scene 3.)

Aristophanes

The most I can do in an essay of this size is to take a few literary examples to illustrate how men of letters felt about the People. To begin with, no one would hesitate to qualify Aristophanes as a representative of Athenian opinion. He was, to be sure, a reactionary not only in politics but also in questions of behavior. He could swallow neither Euripides nor Socrates and his lampoons of both are famous. If he survived in spite of Christian prudishness, it must be because his insights into the human race or his way of expressing them, or both, seemed agreeable to his readers, though as far as ancient literature is concerned, survival is hardly a mark of excellence. Ovid's *Ars amatoria*, Strato's *Musa puerilis*, and at least half of Martial's epigrams could well be exchanged for the lost works of Sappho, Livy, Aeschylus, or Sophocles. At any rate Aristophanes did survive in part, whatever the reason, and in one of his plays (*The Knights*) Demos appears as one of the characters. The People are the victim, and in the end of the play are transformed into the Victor by something of a miracle. Two of the main characters, Cleon the Demagogue and the Sausage Seller, are of the lower classes, "unbroken by the rules of art, untamed by education," in the words of J. Hookham Frere's translation. And the brawling and cursing in which they engage is in part a caricature of democratic argument which could easily be transferred to our own times. Even the manner of public oratory is mocked as in essence the speech of carpenters and smiths. In fact, the speeches of Cleon and the Sausage Seller are full of metaphors taken from their trades, that of the tanner and the pork butcher. And when the two of them begin to court Demos, their suits are based on promises to ruin the state by wasting its money on corruptive measures. They anticipate Plato's picture of the artisan class as an incorporation of the appetitive faculties of the soul. But perhaps the most telling example of Aristophanes' opinion of the people is the passage which in Rogers' translation runs:

> Chorus: Proud, O Demus, thy sway.
> Thee, as Tyrant and King,
> All men fear and obey,
> Yet, O yet, 'tis a thing
> Easy, to lead thee astray.
> Empty fawning and praise
> Blessed thou art to receive;
> All each orator says
> Sure at once to believe;
> Wit thou hast, but 'tis roaming;
> N'er we find it its home in.

> Demos: Wit there's none in your hair.
> What, you think me a fool!
> What, you know not I wear,
> Wear my motley by rule!
> Well all day do I fare,
> Nursed and cockered by all;
> Pleased to fatten and train
> One prime thief in my stall.
> When full gorged with his gain,
> Up that instant I snatch him,
> Strike one blow and dispatch him.[10]

Since *The Knights* ends with Demos restored to youth and vigor, through the good offices of the Sausage Seller, and with Cleon punished, the comedy cannot be said to be only an attack on popular government. It is, rather, an attack on a specific demagogue. On the other hand, the rejuvenescence of the People is simply a return to the good old days of our fathers, preached on almost every occasion by the poet. The Demos of the first part of the play is the People of contemporary Athens, flattered by a demagogue and a sausage seller, a victim of every sort of political corruption. The Demos of the last scene is quite different. For the Demos of our fathers was incorruptible, and sausage sellers

10. *The Knights*, trans. Benjamin Bickley Rogers (Loeb Classical Library), Vol. 3, p. 233, ll. 1111–30.

and tanners were kept in their place. The question of how a group of aristocrats could become so weak and so susceptible to the bribes of the vulgar is, needless to say, not broached.

It is easy to forget, when talking about Athenian democracy, that the Demos was far from being the total male population of Athens. The term did not cover the slaves, some of whom were well-educated prisoners of war, nor the resident aliens, the *Metoikoi*, nor, of course, the women. In Herodotus (I, 196) it was a term contrasted with the "fortunate," the commoners as contrasted with the Gentry. In Thucydides (V, 4) it distinguished the Plebeians from the Men-in-Power (*hoi Dynatoi*). Thus, after the fifth century it could be used with a pejorative connotation. In fact, as early as Solon, we find the distinction made between the "mass of the people" and "those who [are] rich in power, who in [wealth] are glorious and great," as if such a division were inevitable.[11] But there is a possibility that Aristotle's dispraise of manual work led him to base the distinction on economic status. For we find him objecting to granting citizenship to artisans as men who cannot "practice virtue."[12] Since virtue, as defined in the *Nicomachean Ethics*, depends on one's having leisure, the dogma appears understandable. There are plenty of sentences and anecdotes in Greek literature which assert the courage, the ingenuity, the candor of the poor, just as there are others which assert that the rich have antithetical traits. But it is not to be expected that a man of the common people will have the qualities of the nobleman. That would be, if nothing more, a contradiction in terms. Perhaps the best evidence of this is Odysseus' different treatment of men "of noble birth or high rank" and "men of the Demos" in the *Iliad*

11. Quoted in Aristotle, *Athenian Constitutions* (chap. 12), trans. Frederic G. Kenyon, in the Oxford Aristotle.

12. *Politics*, 1278 a: "In ancient times," he says, ". . . the artisan class were slaves or foreigners and therefore a majority of them are so now." And a bit later he adds, "No man can practice virtue who is living the life of a mechanic or laborer." (Trans. Jowett, revised.)

(II, 188–206). To the latter he uses harsh names and threats, to the former friendly persuasion, a custom not unusual even in modern armies.

Plautus

One naturally turns to the plays of Plautus as examples of Roman comedy. But Plautus, unlike Aristophanes, is not a social critic. He has two stock comic figures, the Pimp and the Slave, both insolent. His humor is largely confined to verbal repartee and insult. Even the Miles Gloriosus, though the remote progenitor of Falstaff, is only a buffoon. That the comic characters come from the *Plebs*, when not slaves, is true, but that their comic traits are identified with their plebeian origin is not true. Plautus had a certain sympathy—or perhaps I should say "uncertain"—for some members of the *Plebs*. The chorus of fishermen in *Rudens* illustrates this.

> The poor in every way live miserably
> Especially if they have no trade and have never learned any skill.
> Whatever they happen to have at home must suffice for them.
> Now we, you can see how rich we are from our costume.
> These hooks and these rods, they are our trade and our living.
> Daily from the city to the sea we trudge for fodder.
> That is our [sport] our gymnastics and our wrestling.
> Sea urchins, limpets, oysters, sea-mussels, shell-fish, mussels, ribbed
>   scallops, are our catch.
> And then we go on to fishing with hook and stone.
> Our food we get from the sea; if nothing turns up
> And if we catch no fish, well, covered with salt washed clean,
> Home we go secretly, to bed without supper.[13]

13.

> Omnibus modis qui pauperes sunt homines miseri vivont,
> praesertim quibus nec quaestus est, nec artem didicere artem ullam:
> necessitate quidquid est domi id sat est habendum.
> nos iam de ornatu propemodum ut locupletes simus scitis:
> hisce hami atque haec harundines sunt nobis quaestu et cultu.
> Cotidie ex urbe ad mare huc prodimus pabulatum:
> pro exercitu gymnastico et palaestrico hos habemus;

This speech is not a protest. That it was a funny speech one hardly dares assert, for to a modern reader it seems pathetic. But then *The Taming of the Shrew* is said to be funny, and not merely to Elizabethan ears. Shylock, too, may have been a comic character—as was Herod in the mystery plays.

The association of buffoonery with the lower classes, insofar as they are laborers and peasants, has been fairly consistent up to modern times. This clearly does not imply that the upper classes were uniformly praised. One would merely have to read Juvenal to be disabused of that idea. But in aesthetic matters the taste of the *vulgus* was held to be inherently lower than that of the aristocracy. Ben Jonson, translating Horace, has him say, "The Roman gentry, men of birth and mean,/Will take offence at this," that is, "of ever-wanton verse, bawdy speeches and unclean." Jonson must have suspected that the Roman gentry, like the English, were just as wanton, bawdy, and unclean in their speech as the "men street-born." But it was the custom to overlook this and to attribute purity of taste to the gentry and impurity to the multitude, just as Shakespeare usually gives prose to the comic figures and blank verse to the serious. But this goes back at least to Scaliger. In Scaliger's opinion comedy uses characters from low city life or the country, whereas tragedy uses kings and princes. There seemed to be something intrinsically funny in both the appearance and

---

echinos, lopadas, ostreas, balanos captamus, conchas,
marinam urticam, musculos, plagusias striatas;
post id piscatum hamatilem et saxatilem adgredimur.
cibum captamus e mari: si eventus non evenit
neque quicquam captumst piscium, salsi lautique pure
domum redimus clanculum, dormimus incenati.

II, 290 ff., ed. C. E. Harrington. It is worth noting that the lot of the fisherman is almost always described as hard and melancholy, even in the piscatory eclogues. Cf. the *Letters* of Alciphron, probably third century A.D. Dr. Henry Marion Hall in his *Idylls of Fishermen* (p. 2) tries to explain this on mythological and historical grounds. See below, p. 149, for how the life of the shepherd became a happy motif in Christian literature, though four of the Apostles were fishermen and none of those named in the Gospels are called shepherds.

speech of boors, clowns, yokels, pedlars, grave-diggers, servants, private soldiers. They were just not to be taken seriously.[14]

In fact, the very adjective "vulgar" as a term of dispraise is good enough evidence that whatever emanates from the *Plebs* is in bad taste. Vulgar humor and vulgar speech, like popular opinion and popular songs, are all on the same aesthetic level—though the same humor, meanings, opinions, and songs when translated into the vocabulary of the upper classes will be acceptable. There is an analogy to this in the substitution of Greek and Latin derivatives for words of Anglo-Saxon origin where the latter are vulgar both in the sense of being low in the social scale and in the sense of being indecent. Warner and Lunt, to whose work I have already referred, have found that the speech of the upper-upper class sometimes coincides with that of the lower-lower class. But what amounts to affectation in the upper-upper comes naturally to the lower-lower. One may affect the manners and speech of a class one looks down on and never feel the need to endow it with one's own political and social privileges. The southern aristocrat suckled by a Negro "Mammy" rarely felt it his duty to grant her the vote. The black blood of America's mulattoes counts for more than their white blood. Yet even if one discounts racial prejudice, there exists also social prejudice, expressed in taboos regarding good and bad addresses, appropriate families into which one may marry, approved schools and colleges, and even Christian sects.[15] This need not be tied to any economic factor at all. The upper social stratum may contain a large number of people with only moderate incomes, and the richest families in a community may be sneered at because of the newness of their wealth, the source of it, or the social stratum into which they were born. Any excuse will serve to justify one person's contempt for another. The adjective "vulgar," with all its ambiguities, will prove omnicompetent.

14. Roman opinion should be supplemented by Trimalchio's account of his rise from rags to riches in the *Satyricon*, chapters 75 and 76. It is a typical satire of the *nouveau riche*.

15. Cf. G. William Dumhof, *Who Rules America?*, chapter 1.

The Mysteries

Social status is not always the measure of esteem when one comes to the English mystery and morality plays. Whereas in the Chester Pageant of *The Deluge* Noah's wife is the typical village scold, in the Coventry Nativity Play it is King Herod who is ridiculed. When seeing the former, surely one was supposed to be amused to hear Noah's wife say to her husband who was trying to induce her to enter the ark,

> Yea, sir, set up your sail
> And row forth with evil heale,
> For without any fail,
> I will not out of this town.
>   But I have gossibs every one,
> One foot further I will not go;
> They shall not drown, by St. John!
> If I may save their life.
>   They loved me full well, by Christ!
> But thou will let them in thy chest,
> Else row forth, Noah, whether thou list,
> And get thee a new wife.[16]

Yet Noah's wife, for some reason now lost, is usually represented as a scold in such plays. In the Towneley *Deluge* she delays the departure, scolds Noah for his self-centeredness, hits at him— blows that he returns—and when she enters the ark, cannot find anything good to say about it.

> I fa[i]th I can not fynd,
> Which is before, which is behynd,
> Bot shall we here be pynd,
>   Noe, as haue thou blis?

Whereupon she leaves the ark and has to be almost beaten into returning aboard.[17] This, I assume, was funny. And similarly the

16. Text from *Everyman and Other Interludes* (Everyman ed.), p. 34.

17. See John Matthews Manly, *Specimens of the Pre-Shaksperean Drama*, Vol. 1, pp. 21 ff. It is only fair to the memory of Noah's wife to say that in *Noah and Lamech* she behaves very well.

Shearmen and Tailors who put on the Nativity Play must have grinned when Herod, swearing by Mahound, spoke of himself as "he thatt made bothe hevin and hell," "the cawse of this lyght and thunder." [18]

Who wrote the plays is not always known, but the original authors must have been literate—though no doubt the actors also inserted improvisations. The identity of the authors would be of use in determining their probable prejudices. If they were abbots or nobles they might have made their shepherds and artisans crude and farcical. On the other hand, the fact that the plays were given for town rather than gown to some degree explains the simplicity of their subject matter. And to that consideration must be adjoined the historical fact that the end of the fourteenth century was the period of peasants' and workers' rebellions. Of this more below.[19]

Chaucer

That the People are inherently crude in their tastes comes out vividly in *The Canterbury Tales*, which, it should not be forgotten, were written in the same period as *Piers Plowman*. The stories are by and large in conformity with the character of their narrators, though presumably Chaucer wanted his readers to think that all the pilgrims enjoyed all the tales. The tales of the Miller and the Reeve are, one imagines, the kind of story that Chaucer thought millers and reeves would be likely to tell. But whereas he has his fun with Miller and Reeve, with Merchant and Man of Law, with the Wife of Bath and the Doctor, he treats the poor Plowman, the Clerk, the Shipman, and the Parson with respect.

18. *Ibid.*, p. 137.
19. This should be supplemented by a reading of the Second Shepherd's Play (Towneley) and the opening of *Johan Johan Tyb and Syr Johan*, with its 110 lines on how Johan Johan is going to beat his wife. Or, to take a later example, see Act 3, scene 3, of *Gammer Gurton's Needle*.

Hence there would seem to be no relation between professional or economic status, and decency or indecency. As a matter of fact, he writes an apology for the Miller's tale in the prologue, and adds,

> And therefor, who-so list it nat y-here,
> Turne over the leaf, and chese another tale.

And in the Shipman's prologue, after the Man of Law has dilated on patience, kindness, and charity, and the Priest has rebuked the Host for his swearing, Chaucer has the Host say, "I smelle a loler in the wind," as today in the United States one would smell a communist. There is no concluding any social philosophy in Chaucer.

So much is probably obvious. There is no simplifying a great poet like Chaucer. He satirizes even himself, as in the prologue to *Sir Thopas* and the Host's interruption of that tiresome ballad. Chaucer was able to understand every human character and to give each full empathy. He did not take himself so seriously as scholars have taken him. The one character about whom he is really bitter is the Pardoner. It would be prudent, if overcautious, to say merely that he was more interested in individuals than in classes of men. That he accepted rank and its privileges is indubitable; but that he held any theories about their origin or development is very questionable. The closest approach to a generalization about manners and social class is in the tale of the Wife of Bath (ll. 1146–59), strange though that may seem:

> Heer may ye see wel how that genterye
> Is nat annexed to possessioun
> Sith folk ne doon the fyr, lo! in his kinde.
> A lordes sone do shame and vileinye;
> And he that wol han prys of his gentrye
> For he was boren of a gentil hous,
> And hadde hise eldres noble and vertyous,
> And nil himselven do no gentil dedis,
> Ne folwe his gentil auncestre that deed is,
> Ne nis nat gentil, be he duk or erl;
> For vileyns sinful dedes make a cherl . . .
> Thy gentillesse cometh fro god allone;
> Than comth our verray gentillesse of grace,
> It was no-thing biquethe us with our place.

But this was a commonplace even in the fourteenth century. Another commonplace is found in the Clerk's tale, in the author's interpolation beginning (lines 995–1001).

> O stormy peple! unsad and ever untrewe!
> Ay undiscreet and chaunging as a vane,
> Delyting ever in rumbel that is newe,
> For lyk the mone ay wexe ye and wane;
> Ay ful of clapping, dere y-nogh a jane;
> Your doom is fals, your constance yvel preveth,
> A ful greet fool is he that on yow leveth.

It is usually wrong to attribute to an author the opinions expressed by one of his fictional characters, but this particular passage is given to the author himself by the editors and presumably he is speaking in it *in propria persona*.

Anonymous Authors

There is a large assortment of poems and prose passages which could be chosen to indicate opinion about the People in the Middle Ages. But only an anthology would do them justice. One very curious attack is printed by Thomas Wright in his *Anecdota Literaria*. It is entitled *Des vilains*.[20]

> Or escoutez un autre conte.
> A toz les vilains doint Dex honte
> Qui je hui matin se leverent;
> Et si di-je pechié, qu'il erent
> Les terres qui portent le blé:
> Ne en iver, ne en esté
> Ne finent-il de traveillier,
> Chascuns jor, por ce gaaigner
> Don clerc juvent, et autre gent.
> Lo pain et lo vin en semant,
> Tot lo gaaignent li vilain,
> Et tot l'avon-nos par lor main,
> Il sofrent lo froit et lo chaut,
> Por gaaignier; mais moi ne chaut,

20. London, 1844. Pp. 53–54. The source is MS Berne, no. 354, fol. 57, vo.

Dex male honte li envoit.
Or ne sofrent ne chaut ne froit
Por nos, mais il font por argent,
Il nos selent moult chierement
Tote la rien que il nos vandent;
Totjerz à nos enginer tandent,
Moult sont felon, si con moi sanble.
Se il voient.iij.clers ensanble,
O .iiij. en une compeignie,
Don n'i a vilain qui ne die,
"Esgardez de ces clers bolastres;
Par ma foi, il est plus clerjastres
Que berbiz ne que autres bestes."
Max feus lors broisse les testes
As vilains qui ce vont disant!
Plaust à Deu lo roi puissant,
Que je fusse roi des vilains,
Je feisse plus de mil ainz
Et autretant de laz feisse:
Dont je par les cos les preisse:
A mal port fussent arivé!
Jà vilains ne fust tant osé,
Que il un mot osast parler,
Ne mais por del pain demander,
O por sa pastrenostre dire.
Moult aussent en moi mal sire,
Et totjors m'apelassent maistre;
Mais por ce que rois ne puis estre,
Vos en lairai atant lo conte.
Dex lor doint à toz male honte,
Si voirement, con je voldroie,
Dame-Dex ma proière en oie.[21]

21. Professor Grace Frank has been kind enough to provide me with the
following translation of these verses:

Now listen to another tale.
May God give ill fortune to all the peasants
Who arise this morning;
And even though I speak sinfully, may they keep wandering over
The lands that bear the grain:
Neither in winter nor in summer
May they cease working,
Each day in order to obtain
That which clerks and others enjoy.
In sowing bread and wine
Peasants gain everything

Campanella

The number of verses written in contempt of the peasant is probably no greater than the number of satires against women, of which some are ferocious, or those against the clergy. The four-teenth century was given to satire, and it would require a large volume to include even a fair sample of it. But there is a poem

----

> And everything we have from their hands.
> They suffer cold and heat
> To gain [those things], but I do not care.
> God gives them this ill fortune.
> They do not suffer heat or cold
> For us, but for money.
> They ladle out to us very dearly
> Everything that they sell us;
> They always tend to cheat us,
> Very wicked they are, it seems to me.
> If they see three clerks together
> Or four in a group
> There is no peasant who does not say,
> "See those deceitful clerks;
> By my faith there are more bad clerks
> Than sheep or other animals."
> May evil fire brush the heads
> Of the peasants who go saying these things.
> Would to God, the powerful King,
> That I were king of the peasants.
> I would make more than a thousand fish-hooks
> And just as many snares
> By which I might take them by their cods.
> They would have arrived at a sorry port.
> Never would a peasant be so bold
> As to dare to speak a word, not even
> To beg for bread
> Or say his paternoster.
> He would have a harsh lord in me
> And would always call me master.
> But since I cannot be king
> I'll now leave off telling this tale.
> May God give them all ill fortune
> As truly as I should wish
> That the Lord hear my prayer.

This should be contrasted with another poem printed by Wright in the same volume (p. 64), entitled *Des putains et des Lecheoirs*, in which God is said to have established three orders of men: clerks to whom He gave alms and tithes; knights (*chevaliers*) to whom He gave lands; and peasants to whom He gave plowing.

dating from two centuries later which deserves a special place in an essay such as this, for it emphasizes a new aspect of the social question. It is written by Campanella.

Il popolo è una bestia varia e grossa
ch'ignora le sue forze; e però stassi
a pesi e botte di legni e di sassi,
guidato da un fanciul che non ha possa,
ch'egli portria disfar con una scossa:
me lo teme e lo serve a tutti spassi.
Né sa quanto à temuto, ché i bombassi
fanno un incanto, che i sensi gli ingrossa.

Cosa stupenda! e s'appicca e imprigiona
con le man proprie, e si dá morte e guerre
per un carlin di quanti egli al re dona.
Tutto à suo quanto sta fra cielo e terra
ma nol conosce; e se qualche persona
di ciò avise, é l'uccida ed atterra.[22]

Here we happen to know that the author was involved in an uprising in Naples, spent twenty years in prison, and presumably was speaking with deep feeling. His sonnet does more than repeat platitudes. It is the one poem I have found in this field which expresses the irony of popular stupidity combined with power. It anticipates the lament that has been heard in the nineteenth century and occasionally in the twentieth, that the People do not realize how easily they could liberate themselves. And to add to

22. John Addington Symonds in his *Sonnets of Michael Angelo Buonarrotti and Tommaso Campanella* (p. 143) translated this sonnet as follows:

The People is a beast of muddy brain,
That knows not its own force, and therefore stands
Loaded with wood and stone; the powerless hands
Of a mere child guide it with bit and rein:
One kick would be enough to break the chain;
But the beast fears, and what the child demands,
It does; nor its own terror understands,
Confused and stupefied by bugbears vain,
Most wonderful! With its own hand it ties
And gags itself—gives itself death and war
For pence doled out by kings from its own store.
Its own are all things between earth and heaven;
But this it knows not; and if one arise
To tell the truth, it kills him unforgiven.

the irony, they would kill the man who would tell them. Campanella told them, and should one wish to know the fate he suffered, one has only to read the sonnets he wrote in prison.

Spenser

Campanella's sonnet, as I say, refers to the People as unrealized political power. But in France and in England this power had been realized and had made itself felt in rebellions that terrified the propertied class. One finds echoes of the revolts in strange places. Echoes of Lollardry, for example, recur even in *The Faerie Queene*, as we have heard them in Chaucer. In the Second Canto of Book V we find the People personified as the Mighty Gyant, satirizing the whole movement of class rebellion as a process of leveling which is against the decrees of God and Nature.

> He sayd that he would all the earth uptake
> And all the sea, divided each from either:
> So would he of the fire one ballaunce make,
> And one of th'ayre, without or wind or wether;
> Then would he ballaunce heaven and hell together,
> And all that did within them all containe,
> Of all whose weight he would not misse a fether:
> And looke what surplus did of each remaine,
> He would to his owne part restore the same againe:
>
> For-why, he sayd, they all unequall were,
> And had encroched uppon others share;
> Like as the sea (whiche plaine he shewed there)
> Had worne the earth; so did the fire the aire;
> So all the rest did others parts empaire,
> And so were realmes and nations run awry.[23]

Obviously the remedy is to reduce all things "unto equality."

> Therefore the vulgar did about him flocke,
> And cluster thicke unto his leasings vaine,
> Like foolish flies about an hony-crocke;
> In hope by him great benefits to gaine.

23. See W. Gordon Zeeveld, "Social Equalitarianism in a Tudor Crisis," *Journal of the History of Ideas*, Vol. 8, no. 1 (1946), pp. 35–55.

But Artegall, the Man of Justice, sets the Gyant and his disciples right. Based on the doctrine of cosmic balance, his doctrine is one of stability: "All change is perillous, and all chaunce unsound." But this has little effect upon the Gyant, who replies:

> Therefore I will throwe downe these mountaines hie,
> And make them levell with the lowly plaine;
> These towring rocks, which reach unto the skie,
> I will thrust downe into the deepest maine,
> And as they were, them equalize againe.
> Tyrants, that make men subject to their law,
> I will suppresse, that they no more may raine;
> And Lordlings curbe that commons over-aw,
> And all the wealth of rich men to the poore will draw.

But Artegall retorts with the familiar answer: all is in the hands of God whose ways are beyond our understanding.

> What ever thing is done by him is donne,
> Ne any may his mighty will withstand;
> Ne any may his soveraine power shonne,
> Ne loose that he hath bound with stedfast band.
> In vaine therefore doest thou now take in hand
> To call to count, or weigh his workes anew,
> Whose counsels depth thou canst not understand;
> Sith of things subject to thy daily vew
> Though doest not know the causes, nor their courses dew.

The result is that Artegall's companion, iron Talus, pushes the Gyant off his eminence and "down the rock him throwing, in the sea him drowned." This arouses the people who "rose in armes, and all in battell order stood." But they, like the Gyant, are exterminated by Talus, since Artegall had qualms "his noble hands t'imbrew in the base blood of such a rascall crew." Lest one think this to be of only dramatic relevance, reference should be made also to Spenser's *A View of the Present State of Ireland*, in which the remedy for Ireland's troubles is not very different.

Spenser also seems to have had a feeling that social rank endowed people with special qualities which were congenital. In one place he goes to a ridiculous extreme in maintaining that skill in equitation is innate in men of noble blood:

In brave poursuit of honorable deed,
There is I know not [what] great difference
Betweene the vulgar and the noble seed,
Which unto things of valorous pretence
Seemes to be borne by native influence;
As feates of armes, and love to entertaine:
But chiefly skill to ride seemes a science
Proper to gentle blood: some other faine
To menage steeds, as did this vaunter, but in vaine.[24]

He even goes so far as to be able to spot in a foundling—a wild man, living in the woods and unable to speak any recognizable language—his noble forebears.

O what an easie thing is to descry
The gentle bloud, how ever it be wrapt
In sad misfortunes foule deformity
And wretched sorrowes, which have often hapt!
For howsoever it may grow mis-shapt,
Like this wyld man being undisciplynd,
That to all vertue it may seeme unapt,
Yet will it shew some sparkes of gentle mynd,
And at the last breaks forth in his owne proper kynd.[25]

The rebels of whom Spenser is thinking are probably those who took part in the rising of 1549 in the reign of Edward VI. These men of Exeter and Norfolk were presumably fighting the increasing enclosures. Their leader was the famous Robert Ket, a tanner. The charge of communism raised by Spenser was as common then as it is today in the United States, for one of the few

24. Book 2, canto 4, stanza 1. "This vaunter" is Braggadocchio.
25. Book 6, canto 5, stanza 1. In stanza 2 we find that this wild man has been "rudely borne and bred/Ne never saw faire guize, ne learned good," but nevertheless showed "some token of his gentle bloud," in his treatment of Serena. We are told that "when time shall be to tell," we shall find out who the wild man really was. But The Faerie Queene comes to an end before we are told. In the case of another foundling, Pastorelle, a birthmark serves as identification; she too had the bearing of a woman of noble birth though brought up by those marvelous shepherds in whom Spenser had a special interest.

universal traits of historical mankind seems to be the fear of losing property.[26]

Shakespeare

It is inevitable in an essay like this one to say a word about Shakespeare. *Coriolanus* is the tragedy of a man beaten down by the people whom he had tried to help. Shakespeare shared with Chaucer the ability to put himself inside his characters, so that their speeches become precisely what one would have expected them to say. In the case of Coriolanus he had some help from Plutarch. He follows the tradition of introducing artisans and the lower classes for comic relief, but he does not confine his satire to them.

One might think that the choice of Gaius Marcius for a hero was evidence of anti-popular sentiment on Shakespeare's part. But that the *plebs* are fickle was nothing new in literature, and that Marcius was notoriously opposed to their demands is clear from history. Indeed, Shakespeare makes good use of this information to open the play. The one significant particular in which Shakespeare and Plutarch differ is in Plutarch's justification of the resentment of the *plebs* against the patricians: they had lost their property, were destitute and hungry, and had been reduced to servitude. Plutarch also maintains that the Senate did nothing to alleviate their suffering and, when some of the more moderate senators favored helping them, that Marcius sternly opposed them. He says that even those who admired Marcius for his courage and austerity were disgusted by his haughtiness and imperious temper. None of this appears in Shakespeare. The angry citizens who open the tragedy mince no words and make their accusations without dramatic motivation. Marcius is called "chief enemy to the people"; he is to be killed at once; he is "very dog to the common-

26. See G. M. Trevelyan's *England in the Age of Wycliffe* on this charge during the rebellion of 1381.

alty"; and the good that he has done was done "to please his mother and to be partly proud." Dramatically the whole of the plot is contained, as in a germ, in this opening passage. The dénouement is occasioned by his mother's intercession; his pride blocks every attempt to reconcile him to the people. He mocks at popular approval:

> Bid them wash their faces and keep their teeth clean . . .
> 'Twas never my desire yet to trouble the poor with begging . . .
> Better it is to die, better to starve,
> Than crave the hire which first we do deserve.

And so it goes. Yet Shakespeare realizes that a mob without a leader is impotent and shows us the citizens swaying first toward Coriolanus and then, under the suggestions of Sicinius and Brutus, abandoning him. It is the technique of mob rule, which he uses also in *Julius Caesar*, the technique of flattery skillfully blended with suggestion. But anyone likely to read these pages will have recalled the lines I have in mind (Act II, scene 3) and can be spared their repetition. The one conclusion that seems reasonable is that *Coriolanus* is the tragedy of pride, *superbia*, and that it is only accidentally the expression of its author's social views. The most one can say is that the voice of the people echoes the voice of the demogogue.

We have mentioned Mark Antony's oration and it may be useful to compare the attitude of the people toward Coriolanus with their attitude toward Caesar. In the opening of *Julius Caesar* the Tribunes, Flavius and Marullus, drive the Carpenter and the Cobbler, along with their fellows, from the streets, where they have assembled to celebrate Caesar's triumph. In words resembling those of Coriolanus, they are called blocks, stones, "worse than senseless things." And they "vanish tongue-tied in their guiltiness." Their guilt is ingratitude to Pompey. And in Casca's account of Antony's offering the crown to Caesar we find that "the rabblement hooted, and clapped their hands; and threw up their sweaty night-caps, and uttered such a deal of stinking breath because

Caesar refus'd the crown, that it had, almost, chok'd Caesar." But the uncomplimentary description goes on in the dialogue between Casca and Cassius (Act I, scene 3), where the Romans are sheep to Caesar's wolf, hinds to his lion. So in the funeral scenes, the people swing from Brutus to Antony at the touch of oratory. And probably the most frightful scene in Shakespeare is that in which the mob attacks Cinna, the poet, a scene which is irrelevant to the tragedy of either Brutus or Caesar but shows how fiercely and irrationally the People will behave when aroused (Act III, scene 3). The one dramatic purpose of this scene would seem to be a demonstration of mob violence stimulated by oratory, and hence a denunciation of policy determined by popular acclamation.

Some consideration should perhaps be given to the *Second Part of Henry VI*, of which Jack Cade's revolt is an incident. But though Cade's forces are described as "a ragged multitude of hinds and peasants, rude and merciless," calling "all scholars, lawyers, courtiers, gentlemen" "false caterpillars" (Act IV, scene 4), it is only by inference that one can uncover a definitely hostile judgment of the People as a whole. For there is an equally severe judgment of all the villains in all the plays, be they commoner or noble. Cade's rebellion may have been justified by the condition of the peasants and maybe Shakespeare should have tried to justify it in his play. It took place one hundred and fifty years before *Henry VI* was written, and it is treated almost as a farcical interlude, with Cade's insistence on being addressed as Lord Mortimer, ordering the burning of London Bridge and the Tower, and the destruction of all records—"my mouth shall be the parliament of England" (Act IV, scene 7)—and his decreeing the common ownership of all things. Shakespeare follows history in having Buckingham and Lord Clifford offer pardon to all who will forsake Cade and return home. And he follows tradition in having Cade himself berate his troops for their vacillation. Again, as in *Julius Caesar* and *Coriolanus*, we find the populace swinging over, to their leader for a time, only to switch once more after a speech from Clifford. The *topos* of the fickle crowd has to be carried out. Small wonder that Cade leaves the scene crying, "Was ever feather so lightly blown to and fro as this multitude?" But before jumping to any conclusions about Shakespeare's contempt for the People, it would be best to recall Richard II's dethronement (*Richard II*, Act IV, scene 1) and the king's comments on courtiers.[27] The fairest conclusion on Shakespeare's views of society and popular control of its destiny is that he shows no sympathy either with the mob or with demagogues, regardless of status. He occasionally shows some sympathy for individuals of the lower classes but on the whole has no interest in them as serious dramatic material. Nor did his contemporary dramatists.

Shakespeare was living in a time when England was free from Rome, when a queen of unquestioned popularity was on the throne, and when the realm as a whole was quiet. It remained, moreover, internally peaceful until the time of the Puritan Rebellion. But this was not typical of English history; revolt and anarchy, despotism and invasion, had punctuated it from the earliest recorded times. It has been said that in the beginning the king was elected by the free choice of the People, an opinion based in all probability on Tacitus's *Germania*.[28] Regardless of the vagueness of the word "people," one can envision the history of England as the growth of popular freedom and the decline of royal power. There was progress and retrogression in this history. Revolts against vested authority with accompanying disorder amounting to something close to anarchy occurred in the eighth century, in the middle of the tenth, in the early thirteenth under Richard I, as well as under John and later under Henry III. Simon Montford

27. See also Act 5, scene 2: York's account of Bolingbroke's reception by the London crowds. For an interesting but superficial attack on Shakespeare's social views, see Upton Sinclair's *Mammonart*, chapters 35 and 36.

28. See J. R. Green, *History of the English People*, Vol. 1, p. 35. This work, though no longer in style, was based on original sources and should be revived.

and the Communes kept the middle part of the century in turmoil, though for a good cause, and in the fourteenth century came the Peasants' Revolt. One can see in this constant warfare of king against king, king against baronage, populace against feudal superior, something symptomatic of an atmosphere of discontent and the determination to appease it. Two kings were dethroned and subsequently murdered; one was forced by his barons to limit his sovereignty. The Lollards, John Ball and Wat Tyler, Jack Cade, Langland, Wyclif, these are names which show the way the winds of doctrine were beginning to blow.

The history of the French peasantry differs from that of the English only in that we have earlier records of their rebellions. Beginning with the revolt of Mariccus and his 8000 peasants (Tacitus, *Historiae*, II, 61), a revolt put down by Vitellius, the story continues with the bands known as the Bagaudae about 284. Then, skipping the centuries of which we have but the most meager information, we come to the *Parlements des paysans Normands*, roughly A.D. 1000; the *Capuchonnés* of Durand the carpenter in 1182; the *Pastoureaux*, headed by Jacob, the Master of Hungary, in the thirteenth century; the second *Pastorale* of 1320; the *Jacquerie* and the *Tuchins* in the fourteenth century; and the *Ecorcheurs* in the fifteenth, with increasing misery among the peasants. The waves of discontent mounted; they culminated in the *Commune de Romans*, with Jean Serve *le Pommier* as its chief, in the *Croquants* towards the end of the sixteenth century, and in the rebellion of the *Nu-Pieds* of 1639. None of these revolts was lasting, none was successful. It was not until 1789 that the Third Estate *supported* by the nobility was able to bring about a successful revolution and finally rid France of the Old Regime.[29] (An analogous account could be written of Rome.)

Meanwhile Englishmen were being slaughtered and towns devastated not only in foreign adventures but at home. The lower-

29. The detailed story, fully documented, of peasant revolts in France is given in Gérard Walter's *Histoire des paysans de France*.

class Englishman of the fourteenth century suffered from unusual poverty. To this poverty were added the revolt of Kent, the Statute of Laborers of 1351, the Black Death, the uprising of men like Owen Glendower, which ran into the first years of the fifteenth century, and the War of the Roses from 1453 to 1497. Then in the sixteenth century came the resistance of Parliament in 1523 to Wolsey's demands for money for the king, the Reformation, the execution of Anne Boleyn, and the religious troubles under Edward VI and Mary Tudor. Surely no contemporary of Shakespeare wanted any more treasons, stratagems, and spoils; what he wanted was peace and order. There was no peace, however, and England had to undergo another series of wars, both international and civil, and whatever merriement there was in Merrie England came by the way. Yet there was manifested throughout those centuries a determination to secure freedom from arbitrary authority, whether vested in king, noble, or prelate.[30]

Prose Fiction

Meanwhile prose fiction was undergoing a development which was to culminate in the modern novel. The miseries of the poor had been expressed eloquently by Langland, but it was not until the appearance of *Lazarillo de Tormes* (1554) that realistic description of their lives was written down as something for the literate to read.[31] The picaresque novel, whether Spanish or French (*Gil Blas*) or English (*Colonel Jack*), was presumably read as comic literature, but nevertheless the tricks played by the heroes, the insight which their stories gave into low life, the poverty and

30. Most of this is well known; but for the somber side of the reign of Edward III, one of the longest reigns in English history, see Traill's *Social England*, Vol. 2, pp. 11 ff.

31. Though there were farces on the theme of the blindman and his boy, *Le Garçon et l'Aveugle*. See Grace Frank, *The Medieval French Drama*, pp. 221 ff.

suffering of their characters, the courage and skill with which these were borne, must have elicited some sympathy from their readers. Certainly it would be difficult for a modern reader to go through *Lazarillo* and simply laugh. Laughter there is aplenty in such books, but there is as much serious criticism of life as in *Don Quixote* or *Gargantua* or, for that matter, in the comedies of Molière. The criticism comes clearly and tellingly through the humor. One has only to compare *Gil Blas*, for instance, with the *Satyricon* to see this. When Petronius wishes to condemn orientalism, to take but one example, he condemns it in so many words, stepping out of character to do so. But when Le Sage wishes to condemn Gongorism, he invents an episode in which one of his characters becomes involved. In short, the social criticism is intricately woven into the narrative.

It is a curiosity of literary history that social satire is often expressed through the mouth of an exotic—a Persian, an American Indian, a Chinese—as if a certain distance were necessary if one were to look objectively at one's society. But the same end is achieved by selecting a character from a social stratum which is not in favor—a workman, a parasite, a vagabond, a prostitute, an adventurer. Whether an author is aware of this or not, he writes as if a Gil Blas, a Roxana, a Figaro, had the distance that was needed. These people are out of society; they are foreigners to all intents and purposes. If they manifest shrewdness of insight, it comes not from applying the standards of their class to the behavior of a superior class but by utilizing generally accepted standards of behavior which are not believed to have any relevance to social status or national origin. Like the Wise Fool, the Innocent Child, the Simpleton of the fairy tales, *l'Ingénu*, they are able to penetrate the shams and pretenses of society. From the realistic point of view, it is surely fanciful to say that an artisan, a prostitute, a private soldier, has more valid knowledge of society than a doctor, a priest, or a general officer in the army. To be exploited or unfortunate confers no special intelligence on a man. In fact, if it did, the aesthetic shock of the picaresque novel would fall flat. Just as we are pleased that the youngest of the Three Little Pigs turns out to be the most intelligent, so we are pleased when a crude peasant kills a dragon and wins a king's daughter. If this were an everyday event, we should be bored to death hearing about it. Yet the Cinderella theme continues to divert the public, and even so sophisticated a writer as Bernard Shaw made effective use of it.

The picaresque novel and the accounts of low life, as in Restif de la Bretonne, prepared the public mind in the seventeenth and eighteenth centuries for taking the lower classes seriously. But before that could happen one had to pass through the dreary stage of heroizing the middle classes. Once that was done, then stories of the nobility, of the court, of the rich, became as tiresome as romances of chivalry became in the eyes of Cervantes. To read a novel by Ouida is to laugh or to be bored. Yet there is a real possibility that her incidents, if not her psychology, were plausible. After all, very rich people have existed and have lived lives that sound as fabulous to us who read them as do the happenings in the *Arabian Nights*. Again, it is unlikely that the real Giton, if there was one, would have thought the *Satyricon* of much interest. And one has yet to find a decayed southern aristocrat who looked upon Faulkner with much appreciation. Novels, like plays, give what seems to be information about society to their readers. This possibility of going beyond life as one knows it must be admitted to be a powerful element of interest in reading fiction. I do not say that "escapism" or information is the main interest in a novel. Like every work of art, a novel is a complex of many interests. But still, one that simply tells you what you already know is a dull book indeed. I suspect that the emphasis which is put upon eroticism in contemporary fiction captures the interest of the general public for the simple reason that in their daily lives they have suppressed their interest in it. To see it come out in the open is a refreshing experience, like that of seeing "dirty words" written on a wall. So sympathy for the oppressed in fiction is a good substitute for helping them.

English Lyric Poetry

I have examined a large anthology of English poems[32] to see how the People appeared in them. This anthology contains some of the work of three hundred and fifteen poets and has about one thousand poems. Most of the poetry would be called lyrical, having to do with the feelings of the poet about various subjects. Of the poems examined, only fourteen have anything to do with the fate of the underdog. In chronological order one might begin with Johnson's *London*, where a few lines of sympathy for the poor are found:

> Has Heaven reserved, in pity to the poor,
> No pathless waste, or undiscovered shore?
> No secret island in the boundless main?
> No peaceful desert yet unclaimed by Spain?
> Quick let us rise, the happy seats explore,
> And bear oppression's insolence no more.
> This mournful truth is everywhere confessed,
> Slow rises worth by poverty depressed.

A vaguely similar sympathy is expressed by Goldsmith in *The Deserted Village*:

> Ill fares the land, to hastening ills a prey,
> Where wealth accumulates, and men decay:
> Princes and lords may flourish, or may fade;
> A breath can make them, as a breath has made;
> But a bold peasantry, their country's pride,
> When once destroyed, can never be supplied.

There follows a lament for the spread of towns which has made it impossible for the poet to retire to "humble bowers and die at home." But this is purely personal and says nothing about the

32. *Great Poems of the English Language, an Anthology of Verse in English from Chaucer to the Moderns*, compiled by Wallace Alvin Briggs.

character of the peasantry except in the most general terms. It is simply sentimental nostalgia for the country, and a critic would be foolish to attempt to drag anything more out of it. Blake, however, in his little poem *London* is more forceful in his condemnation of the town, in which he hears

> How the chimney-sweeper's cry
> Every blackening church appals,

or,

> How the youthful harlot's curse
> Blasts the new-born infant's tear,
> And blasts with plagues the marriage-hearse.

It was not until the nineteenth century was well underway that a poet struck a more violent note. Shelley's *Song to the Men of England*, like Hood's *Song of the Shirt*, was a bitter exclamation of disgust and a call to action. It is, I imagine, unique in its intensity and must be about the first poem in English to address itself to the working class and urge rebellion. Hood's poem is tempered with pity for the woman and says nothing about the social system which made her employment necessary. Burns's *Cotter's Saturday Night*, Browning's *Why I am a Liberal*, in both of which one might expect something to the point, are equally empty as far as our theme is concerned. Edwin Markham's *The Man with the Hoe*, based on Millet's painting of the same title, is at best a statement of the horror that one painting excited in one man and a plea that the wrong done to God's image be righted.

> O masters, lords and rulers in all lands,
> Is this the handiwork you give to God,
> This monstrous thing distorted and soul-quencht?
> How will you ever straighten up this shape;
> Touch it again with immortality;
> Give back the upward looking and the light;
> Rebuild in it the music and the dream;
> Make right the immemorial infamies,
> Perfidious wrongs, irremediable woes?

A reply was written to Markham by John Vance Cheney (1842–1922) in which the poet calmed him by pointing out the inevitable variety of kinds in the world: The Man with the Hoe fills his place in the universal scheme of things just as everyone else does: "Need was, need is, and need will ever be/For him and such as he . . ." This might comfort the man who feels sorry for the peasant but it is questionable how the peasant himself would receive it. One similarly questions Masefield who in *A Consecration* may reject ". . . the Be-medalled Commander, beloved of the throne,/Riding cock-horse to parade when the bugles are blown," in favor of ". . . the ranker, the tramp of the road,/The slave with the sack on his shoulders pricked on with the goad," the man with too weighty a burden, too weary a load, the sailor, the stoker, the chantyman. But again, though one is interested to read of Masefield's preference for such men, one cannot suppress the question of what he thinks should be done about their problem. Hence one is grateful for Louis Untermeyer's *Caliban in the Coal Mines*, where the poet is at least capable of identifying himself with the miners and does not simply look at them and weep. But is it intimated that the unfortunate are sanctified by suffering, that being exploited confers upon one rights that the exploiters do not have? In spite of Shelley's defense of poetry, poets may indeed be the trumpets that sing unto battle, but they are hardly the legislators of the world. And those who have tried their hand at legislation, like Lamartine, were hardly great successes. In fact, after a close survey of hundreds of English poems, I should conclude that poets are more interested in their own feelings about women, landscapes, the four seasons, wine, death, their sins, and their relationship to God, than they are in the lot of their fellowmen. A more self-centered collection of writings could scarcely be found. The paradox of lyricism lies in its being put down on paper and printed: why should a man who is totally uninterested in the feelings of his fellows think they should be interested in his?

The Novel

By the middle of the eighteenth century the bourgeoisie began to be effective politically, at least in England, and had begun also to make its way into literature. *Pamela* in England,[33] *Le Fils naturel* in France, *Miss Sara Sampson* in Germany, had as those who were not their main characters members of the upper class. These books are weathervanes indicating a shift in the wind. Maybe the exploited, maybe the working class, were not so comic as had been imagined. By the end of the first third of the nineteenth century, novels began to depict what one historian calls "the really acute phases of labor and poverty." [34] Such novels include Disraeli's *Sybil*, Mrs. Gaskell's *Mary Barton* and *North and South*, Charlotte Brontë's *Shirley*, Kingsley's *Alton Locke*, and perhaps Dickens' *Hard Times*. George Eliot's *Adam Bede* is in a class by itself, not only because its hero is a rural workman, and thus not of the proletariat, but also because the causes that move the plot are psychological, not economic. Its author had no social doctrine to preach. Though all of these books utilize the old machinery of plot, love interest, coincidence, happy endings, nevertheless they all depict sympathetically the life of the poor, even when their authors become oversentimental. *Mary Barton* shows Mrs. Gaskell's intimate knowledge of the ideas, as well as the living conditions, of the factory worker. Whether Engel's *The Condition of the Working Class in England* (1844) had any influence upon English novelists I do not know, but the novelists present a similar picture in fictional form. In any event, as Mario Praz has said in *The Hero in Eclipse* (pp. 349–50), Adam Bede is presented as "the model of a hard-working intelligent man who accepts life as it is and has a deep respect

33. *Pamela*, though it seemed absurd to Fielding, was taken seriously enough to be turned into an opera, *La Buona Figliuola*, by Piccinni, with a libretto by Goldoni.

34. Frances Therese Russell, *Satire in the Victorian Novel*, p. 198.

for the social organism," and Felix Holt is a "man of the people who is a paragon of loyalty to his own social class, an incarnation of the dignity of labor." That such figures could become the protagonists of novels certainly indicates a profound change in one's appraisal of both the rural and the urban working class. After reading a certain number of such novels one begins to share the feelings of Anthony Trollope when he says in *The Warden* (1855): "Divine peeresses are no longer interesting, though possessed of every virtue; but a pattern peasant or an immaculate manufacturing hero may talk as much twaddle as one of Mrs. Ratcliffe's heroines and still be listened to." Trollope was hardly the man to identify misfortune with virtue and, though the "realistic" novel had its day in England, both Dickens and Thackeray continued to hold the public's attention. People were just getting tired of the Underdog as Hero.

It was not until 1865, and in France, that a novel appeared with a heroine from the lower classes, whose character was not prettified or romanticized. I refer to the Goncourts' *Germinie Lacerteux*.

Yet the Goncourt brothers felt the need to justify their novel by saying in a preface to the second edition:

Living in the nineteenth century, in a time of universal suffrage, of democracy, of liberalism, we have wondered whether those who are called "the lower classes" did not have a right to a novel; whether this society beneath a society, the people, should remain under the pressure of a literary interdict and the contempt of authors who up to now have kept silent regarding the heart and soul which such people might have. We have wondered if there existed still for the writer, and for the reader too, in these years of equality in which we live, unworthy classes, misfortunes too low, dramas too foul mouthed, catastrophes too ignobly terrible. We became curious to find out whether this conventional form of literature, forgotten and belonging to a society that has disappeared, Tragedy, was definitively dead; whether in a country without caste and without a legal aristocracy the miseries of the lowly and the peasants might appeal to the interest, the emotions, the pity as deeply as the miseries of the great and the rich; whether in a word the tears which are shed below stairs might bring on tears as well as those that are shed in the drawing room.

Germinie Lacerteux is the sad tale of a servant girl working for a Mlle de Varandeuil. She becomes the mistress of a worthless youth, son of a dealer in dairy products, Mme Jupillon, and under the influence of her infatuation for him, steals, drinks, wastes her savings on him, and finally dies in poverty, leaving debts which Mlle de Varandeuil feels she must pay. But though the heroine is only a servant girl, her fate is not a function of her social class at all; it is the result of passion, a passion which in other novels produces the same effect in people of the upper classes. They might not rob their employers, but would rob their parents and friends; they could also become sodden with drink, gamble away their substance, and, moreover, die in poverty. Similar comments could be made about Esther Waters, published thirty years later. Here too the heroine is a servant. She too is the victim of passion, and though she does not die in the end, she is reduced to the economic misery with which she began. Neither the social class nor the poverty of the main figures, nor their illiteracy and lack of formal education, play any role in determining the outcome of their lives. They provide the authors with local color and that is all.

Hugo

No consideration of French literature of the nineteenth century, however scanty, would be complete without some mention of Victor Hugo.

Hugo's Les Châtiments contains a strong plea for popular sovereignty, undefined. The poems which make up this volume were all written in exile and are diatribes against Napoleon III. Like all diatribes their basis is simply fierce antipathy and anger. But sometimes as in "L'Art et le peuple," Hugo forgets his anger and turns to praise, to praise in this case of art, which is "human thought which breaks all chains," which liberates peoples who are enslaved and turns a free people into a great people. Or, again, as in "Chanson"—"*Courtisans! attablés dans la splendide orgie*"—he puts himself in the place of those who are the victims of these courtiers and who live for truth, probity, honor (*la gloire*), and freedom. His ode "Au Peuple" (Book II, 2) is a cry to the People, who lie dead like Lazarus, to arise. In "A l'Obéissance passive" (Book II, 7) he recalls the triumphs of the revolutionary armies and laments their descendants who have fallen into ignominy, being used to assault the laws of their country, to kill women and children. Or, as in "Ainsi les plus abjects" (Book III, 4), he gives a brutal picture of "*Napoléon le Petit*" as a false Bonaparte, a royal "*croquant, ce maraud couronné*," whom the *vox populi* has elected, and of the People who, like terror-stricken sheep, graze between the sacristan and the game-keeper. They have been tricked into submission, but there remains in some a spark of freedom which they have the right and the duty to kindle into flame. Hugo, who wrote these lines in Jersey in 1852, may well have been thinking of himself when he wrote,

> Un français, c'est la France; un romain contient Rome,
> Et ce qui brise un peuple avorte aux pieds d'un homme.

To snatch the heart from these verses, one might say that Hugo, like Emerson, Carlyle, and before them, Hegel, was thinking that the People may be a single "representative man."

Lês Châtiments is a good example of the incorporation of abstractions into concrete works of art. Whether the poems are good poems or not is of no importance to us here: what is of importance is Hugo's use of the idea that the People, however vaguely defined, can have rights, be deprived of them, rebel to regain them. The book as a whole is an exclamation, not an argument, and must not be analyzed into an extended enthymeme. Hugo simply hated Louis Napoleon and expressed his hatred as eloquently as he could. Just what role is played by the idea of popular rights in a case of this sort is unclear. The emotional connotations of its verbal symbol probably predominate. "The People" by the middle of the nineteenth century carried with it an intense affective charge, and similarly words like "freedom," "honor," "courage," all became names for qualities which one was supposed to admire. But a philosophic analysis of the meaning of such terms would rob them of their pathos and leave them in a state of denotative nudity. The most that could be expected of them, so far as the history of ideas is concerned, would be inferences logically deduced from sentences containing them either as subjects or predicates. Logically, *Les Châtiments* is at most dogma. The reiteration of a given dogma may prove to be historically more effective than attempts to prove or disprove it. In *"Le parti du crime"* (Book VI, 11) Hugo writes,

> . . . ce gouvernement dont l'ongle est une griffe,
> Ce masque impérial, Bonaparte apocryphe,
> A coup sûr Beauharnais, peut-être Berhueil,
> Qui, pour la mettre en croix, livre, sbire cruel,
> Rome républicaine à Rome catholique,
> Cet homme, l'assassin de la chose publique,
> Ce parvenu, choisi par le destin sans yeux . . .[35]

What has he done, logically speaking, except vilify Louis Napoleon by means of epithets? The poem was stimulated by the creation of the Second Empire out of the Second Republic. At best it charges the Prince-President with breaking his word. But that is of small moment. Hugo can assume, he thinks, that his epithets will be gratefully received by a public incapable of finding them for itself. The time was at hand when the *vox populi*, as Michelet said, could be heard in the words of one man. Yet why was not Napoleon III that man?

35. In prose translation: "This government whose nails are claws, this imperial mask, fake Bonaparte, surely Beauharnais, maybe Berhueil, who to crucify republican Rome hands her over, cruel stool pigeon, to Catholic Rome, this man, assassin of the state, this upstart chosen by blind destiny."

THE PEOPLE AS POET

That the People could have a voice is connected with the idea of national or racial traits. The main difference between a *people* and *The People* would seem to be that a people is composed of all the members of a race or nation, whereas The People might name either the lower order of a given nation or the same men and women in several nations, united in their needs and aspirations regardless of national frontiers. As an example of eighteenth-century opinion on national traits, one would do well to consult that fantastic treasury known as the *Jugemens des Sçavans,* by Adrien Baillet, biographer of Descartes and *Maire de Paris.* Under the general title of "The prejudices of nations or of the country of an author," Baillet lists a large collection of traditional cultural traits. What these opinions are based on is not given; but since ethnology was an unknown science in the early eighteenth century there is no point in demanding sound evidence for any of these beliefs. Their importance to us lies in the fact that Baillet, a scholar, thought them representative of cultivated opinion. I shall list some of them.

The Orientals, we learn (p. 125), are great lovers of fiction and characterized by the poetic spirit; their theology, philosophy, politics, and ethics are "all wrapped up in fables and parables." The Jews write without solidity and possess nothing but the literature of cabalism, frivolous allegories, and gross parables. "The Holy Scriptures are entirely mystical, allegorical, enigmatic." All Egyptian thought is mysterious, disguised by hieroglyphics; the Arabs are more poetic than others have thought, though they also stand out as mathematicians. The Greeks were above all other nations in their wisdom and scientific achievement (p. 129); the

Romans excelled in the arts of government (p. 130). So it went on. These do not represent the opinion of Baillet, but are a rough sample of the opinions he had picked up in his reading. A semi-partisan of the theory of climates, he admits that "there is no air so gross, no climate so cold, no landscape so wild, no land so uncultivated, that it cannot produce minds when the trouble is taken to educate them with application and persistence" (p. 145). Hence even the Germans have been able to "surpass the Asians in humanity, the Romans in the military art and discipline, the Hebrews in religion, the Greeks in philosophy, the Egyptians in geometry, the Phoenicians in arithmetic, the Chaldeans in astrology, and all other nations in the invention and perfection of arts and manufactures" (pp. 145–46).

The differences between peoples then may be explained, as others had said before Baillet, by differences in climate. Maupertuis even went so far as to explain bodily differences in this way.[1] But as Volney was to point out later in the eighteenth century, when beliefs about the effect of climate upon habits, manners of thinking, and character had been fairly well stabilized, most countries had several climates and their people lived in them all.[2] Such considerations were overlooked, however, and the older idea that Germans, Frenchmen, Italians, and so on, each had a general character prevailed.

Now if a people is to have a voice, it must say something. And what it will have to say will express not only ideas about that

---

1. See *The Earthly Venus*, translated from *Venus Physique* by Simone Brangier Boas. But the literary tradition of racial characteristics goes back at least to Herodotus.

2. See his *Tableau du climat et du sol des Etats-Unis*, never completed, and his *Voyage en Égypte*, in *Oeuvres de C. F. Volney* (2d ed., complete; Paris, 1825), Vol. 4. In *Voyage en Égypte* he modified the general law of climates and substituted the following: "Les pays de plaine sont le siège de l'indolence et de l'esclavage; et les montagnes, la patrie de l'énergie et de la liberté." Since most countries have both hills and plains their inhabitants might be expected to vary accordingly.

world which is external to the human body, but also feelings, aspirations, resentments, and other psychical attitudes and states. To know the interests of a people is to know the orientation of its mind; and if a tradition is established among a population that science or philosophy or poetry or what you will is the most important of all interests, then the voice of the People might be expected to express opinion about those fields. If one believes that the Romans were especially gifted in government, then one ought to find problems of government discussed in their literature more frequently than other topics; and if the Germans, who in 1685, the date of the first edition of the *Jugemens*, lived in three hundred or so principalities, believed in at least two opposing religious creeds, and engaged in an unorganized economic constitution, were primarily diversified in their abilities, it may have been because their political and economic environments, rather than their climates, were diverse.

But I am not engaged in arguing for or against these opinions; I am simply noting them and their relation to our main theme. In the eighteenth century it was argued that there was such a thing as a folk-soul, which presumably determined everything of what would be called a "spiritual" nature that was done by a given folk. Once one knew what traits tradition had given to a folk, one could predict what the folk-soul (*Volksseele*) would have to say. But the matter is complicated by the allied notion that the People transcend frontiers and that what one is looking for is something pervading the human race, that is, Human Nature as it exists apart from racial or national or political or religious considerations. In the search one comes upon natural as opposed to artificial man. Where does one find natural man? One might find him by abstracting from all men their local differences and assuming that the residue is natural man. Thus some ethnologists have made a distinction, like the Greeks, between nature and custom, and by eliminating culture, nature is left. One of the most important aspects of culture is education; and the belief seems to have developed that the unschooled man is more natural than he who is educated. People have found fault with educational systems since the time of Plato at least, and this despite the obvious fact that great men have grown up under all the systems known to history. But education is clearly much broader than what one learns in schools. Most of its effectiveness comes from what one learns in all sorts of social experiences, in the streets, in shops, in church, in art museums, in play, and so on. The uneducated man would be the wild man found in a solitary den in the woods, if such a thing were possible. Wild men, children brought up by wolves, deaf mutes abandoned by their parents —these have all had their day in the court of the critics of education. None has proved satisfactorily pure, that is, free from education, for aside from all other considerations, their intelligence and other psychic traits would have had to be tested by examinations into what they could not possibly be expected to know. Such problems seldom bothered the writers who sought for natural man. The man who had not been corrupted by books or by the artificialities of the drawing room would be as natural as anyone wanted. And such men could be found in both the urban slums and the country. Though human beings have lived in cities from time immemorial, cities are usually thought of by nature lovers as an evil degenerative force sullying the purity of God's image. Thus, most men and women would have to be corrupt, not merely as a direct effect of urban life—as in the case of countrymen who have immigrated to cities—but because of the human desire to build towns and to live in them when built. Hence the cultural primitivist who seeks uncorrupted human nature will often go to the peasant or the unschooled rustic for his paradigm of what human nature ought to be, regardless of what it actually is.

There is no reason why uneducated beings should become artists or poets, and indeed the very word "art" is often opposed to "nature." But if one has reason to believe that before any systems of education existed people were engaged in painting pictures or singing songs or chanting epics, then a corollary might be that such products of unspoiled humanity would be better than comparable products which are the result of schooling. Similarly, the medical remedies of the Folk, or herbal drugs grown in one's native soil have been said to be more efficacious than chemical remedies prepared in a laboratory.[3] And again, there is the idea that handicraft is inherently better, that is, more beautiful, than machine-made artifacts; that vegetable dyes are inherently better than analine dyes; and even, in some circles, that uncooked foods are better than those prepared in a kitchen by a *cordon bleu*. When one has the temerity to ask a cultural primitivist why the natural is better than the artificial, the answer usually is not that looking and listening and tasting will prove the point, but that instinct is better than instruction, that the heart is better than the head, that what is natural is free from rules and therefore better, and so on in a metaphysical sorites.

When one comes to poetry, one finds two general theses: that the untaught poet is superior to one who follows "the rules"; that the collective mind or soul of a people will express itself in a kind of poetry that will be superior to any poems written by an individual and better for the simple reason that it has been written by the collective soul. In the first case there will usually be a search for rural poets, individuals who for some reason or other have decided to write songs or long narrative poems or other forms of verse. One thinks at once of the more famous of these men—Burns, John Clare, Stephen Duck. But along with such men there were others—like Thomas Taylor, the Water Poet—a number of whom have been discussed by Rayner Unwin in his most interesting volume *The Rural Muse* (1954). Most of these poets could be associated with the peasantry, though not all of them were

3. See, e.g., John Wesley, *Primitive Physic, or, an Easy and Natural Method of Curing Diseases*, the first edition of which appeared in 1747. My attention was drawn to this item in the history of cultural primitivism by my colleague Dr. Owsei Temkin.

actually peasants. But what does one discover when one reads the work of these inglorious, if not mute, Miltons? One finds that they have always tried to write in the manner of the educated poets, using the same meters, the same subjects, the same metaphors. An eighteenth-century instinctive poet imitates, or at least resembles, Pope; an uneducated nineteenth-century poet resembles Tennyson. In other words, there seems to be little if any originality in these obscure writers. Their aim is to approach "correct" poetry as a limit. Just as the Douanier Rousseau wanted to paint as the artists in the Louvre painted, so Duck or Robert Bloomfield wanted to write as the poets consecrated by the influential critics had written. Pope, it will be recalled, urged poets to copy Vergil, who, to his way of thinking, was Nature. Ingres suggested that Raphael would serve painters in the same way. The early rural poets in England took James Thomson as their guide. The one outstanding exception to this generalization is Robert Burns, who may have had the traditional songs of Scotland in mind, but as far as recorded literature is concerned seems to have had no master.

In 1765 Bishop Percy published his famous *Reliques*. The poems in this volume had been edited by the Bishop and were often improved, as the editor thought. The great majority of them were ballads, and Percy was well aware that many versions of them existed. He prepared what he thought was the best version in each case, not only by piecing stanzas together from a number of versions, but in a few cases by omitting stanzas which he thought indecent or otherwise unfit for public reading. It is safe to say that the *Reliques* started the vogue for old traditional poems, a vogue so impressive that both Chatterton and MacPherson were led into the trap of forging ancient verses to satisfy the demand for them. Both men had talent and might even have become poets in their own right had they not yielded to temptation. But regardless of that, both found believers, and the poems of Ossian, if not those of Rowley, became the battleground of critics and antiquarians for years. The history of the ballad, the spread of certain themes through a number of cultures and languages, and the new interest in philology, all combined to stimulate theories about their authorship. The curious idea was started that they expressed a collective rather than an individual soul.

Percy owned a manuscript folio which he did not think fit to print. But in 1868, well after theories of collective authorship had achieved a vogue, Furnivall printed this as *Bishop Percy's Folio Manuscript*. The subtitle of the thin volume was "Loose and Humorous Songs." It was privately printed, though in view of the prevalent taste for such verses it might have had a wide sale. It provides a reader with an excellent example of what the People say when left to their own devices. Simple, occasionally sly or arch, the songs are what would nowadays be called bawdy. A few are satires of Puritans, but most are simply the centuries-old jokes such as appeared in more literary form in Ovid's *Amores* (III, 7): the incident of the man who suddenly becomes impotent and the consequences thereof; the seduction of apparently unwilling but really eager maidens; in short the sort of thing that adolescent boys, at least in the United States, like to repeat to their schoolmates. But these themes, though certainly dear to the Folk, are also dear to the sophisticated poets. One need only turn over the pages of such an anthology as Marcel Schwob's *Parnasse Satyrique* (1905) to read the same type of verse, collected from poems written in the seventeenth and eighteenth centuries, differing from Percy's folio manuscript only in being more complicated in stanzaic form. Another source of such poetry is *The Common Muse*, edited by Vivian de Sola Pinto and Allan Edwin Radway (1957), in the preface to which one reads: "[These verses] are vital and genuine popular art to be valued as we value the English village churches of the Middle Ages, much of the anonymous carving in the Gothic cathedrals, the work of the English caricaturists of the eighteenth century and of the 'Sunday painters' of nineteenth century France."

The poems in the volumes of both Mr. Unwin and the late Russell Lord, who did for the United States what Mr. Unwin did for England,[4] are more preoccupied with rural scenery, the round of the seasons, birds and flowers, dawn and evening, than with any of the basic biological drives. But the authors of these poems, though living in the country in some cases, were not writing the "songs of the people." Such songs are usually anonymous and there is nothing whatsoever in most of them about landscapes and rural delights. As Crabbe put it very clearly in *The Village*,

> . . . the Muses sang of happy swains,
> Because the Muses never knew their pains,
> They boast their peasants' pipes; but peasants now
> Resign their pipes and plod behind the plough;
> And few, amid the rural-tribe, have time
> To number syllables, and play with rhyme;
> Save honest Duck, what son of verse could share
> The poet's rapture, and the peasant's care? . . .
>
> O'ercome by labour, and bow'd down by time,
> Feel you the barren flattery of a rhyme?
> Can poets soothe you, when you pine for bread,
> By winding myrtles round your ruin'd shed?
> Can their light tales your weighty griefs o'erpower,
> Or glad with airy mirth the illsome hours? . . .
>
> Here joyless roam a wild amphibious race,
> With sullen wo display'd in every face;
> Who far from civil arts and social fly,
> And scowl at strangers with suspicious eye.[5]

Crabbe's observations coincide with what one might observe for oneself. To the peasant there is nothing interesting in country life except insofar as it affords a means of earning a living. To him, farming or sheep-herding is drudgery which he accepts as his lot but which has no romantic flavor whatsoever. In fact, since 1800 he has wasted no time in escaping to the city and the mill or shop.

4. See Lord's *Voices from the Fields: A Book of Country Songs by Farming People.*
5. *The Village*, Book I, lines 21–28, 57–62, 85–88.

It is very rare to find a countryman who revels in the details of the landscape as John Clare did, or who dwells nostalgically on his life on the farm as Bloomfield did. But Clare did very little real work in the country and seems to have spent his time wandering about observing what there was to observe; and Bloomfield, after his boyhood, was a shoemaker in London. It is almost always the distance from the country that stirs such men to poetry about it, the very fact that they are removed from what they call Nature that stimulates them. They are at most homesick. Even Burns, who spent a good bit of his time in the drawing rooms of the great or in the pubs of Scotland, wrote of what he remembered, though not in tranquillity, rather than of what he saw. I have no pretensions of knowing why anyone writes anything, even historical studies such as this one, but it seems absurd to think of a poet who is sitting in a room in London or Edinburgh as a Wordsworth roaming the hills of the Lake Country. One might say something similar of Robert Frost, who did indeed know the New Hampshire countryside but who was in London when he published *North of Boston*. In any event, neither Frost nor Wordsworth was especially rustic. Wordsworth studied at Cambridge, Frost at Dartmouth and Harvard. They were hardly to be called ill-read, uneducated men speaking from instinctive compulsions.

The really uneducated poet was Walt Whitman. And his lack of education explains his use of misunderstood French expressions and neologisms that were never a part of normal English. Surely no one is prepared to say that the American *Volksseele* finds its authentic expression in terms like *Allons, camerados . . .* What such expressions indicate is precisely a lack of education which is no more of one country than of another.

Along with the geniuses like Burns there were other poets whose identity has been lost in the obscurity of the past. I am not speaking merely of the ballad writers, but of the authors of short nonnarrative poems. Such men would be the poets whose works

are in the Percy folio manuscript, and a number of others, some
of whom have been given names and others of whom are no more
than legendary poets. With Walter Mapes, one finds a diversity
of *jongleurs* and minnesingers. According to Edmond Faral there
was a division of labor in Provence: the troubadour wrote the
songs, the *jongleur* sang them. The works of these poets are not to
be described with a single adjective, for a given public might listen
with equal pleasure to what Faral calls *un conte ordurier* or one
that preaches a moral.[6]

As far as I know, no one has ever attributed verses such as
these to the soul of the folk. But there are political songs written
and sung in England which would be properly classified as popular.
In Thomas Wright's *Political Poems and Songs*,[7] a volume frequently cited by historians for its reflection of public opinion, one
comes upon verses which are directed at the Lollards, for instance,
and are just simple abuse. Thus one called *Gens Lollardorum*
begins,

> Gens Lollardorum gens est vilis Sodomorum,
> Errores eorum sunt in mundo causa dolorum,
> Hii sunt ingrati, maledicti, daemone nati, . . .[8]

Sometime these poems, in English, turn on the clergy:

> The other side ben poore and pale,
> And people put out of Presse,
> And seems caitives sore a-cale,
> And ever in one without encrease;
> Icleped lollers and londlesse;
> Who toteth [i.e., "spies"] on hem, they ben untall,
> They ben araied all for the peace,
> But falshed foule mote it befall . . .
>
> With pride punished they [i.e., the clergy] the poore,
> And some they sustaine with sale;

6. Edmond Faral, *Les Jongleurs en France au Moyen-Age*, pp. 76 and 207.
7. London, 1861.
8. This in prose translation would read: "The tribe of Lollards is the vile
tribe of Sodomites, their errors are the cause of the world's ills. Thankless
are they, cursed and born of devils . . ." (*ibid.*, p. 13).

> Of holy church make they an hore,
>   And filleth her wombe with wine and ale;
> With money fill they many a male,
> And chaffran [i.e., "barter"] churches when they fall,
>   And telleth the people a learned tale;
> Such false traitors foule hem befall.[9]

Frequently all the ills of the time are blamed on the Lollards. Such poems are known to all students of English literature, and the verses I quote will suffice to recall the themes and manner of the poets. How far they represent the People as a whole or what section of the People they represent I shall not attempt to say, but it is clear that anyone who could write even the mediocre Latin of the *Gens Lollardorum* must have been a clerk. And I doubt that even the English poems would be attributed to shepherds, cobblers, and artisans in general.

It was what we call folksongs rather than scurrilous and satirical verses that first attracted the attention of lovers of poetry to popular verse. They were appreciated for their beauty as early as the sixteenth century. In 1581 Sir Philip Sidney had said in his *Defence of Poetry* that poetry was the oldest form of literature, no book being older than the poems of Musaeus, Homer, or Hesiod; that each nation produced poets before it produced writers of prose; that even the earliest Greek philosophers expressed their ideas in verse, "so that truly, neither philosopher nor historiographer could at the first have entered into the gates of popular judgements, if they had not taken a great disport of poetry." At about the same time (in 1589) George Puttenham had written in *The Arte of English Poesie*:

> It appeareth, that our vulgar running Poesie was common to all the nations of the world besides, whom the Latines and Greekes in speciall called barbarous. So as it was notwithstanding the first and most ancient Poesie, and the most universall, which two points do otherwise give to all humane inventions and affaires no small credit.

9. *Ibid.*, pp. 305 and 307, respectively. Cf. pp. 304, 312, 346, 347, for similar verses against the clergy.

This is proved by certificate of marchants and travellers, who by late navigations have surveyed the whole world, and discovered large countries and strange peoples wild and savage, affirming that the American, the Perusine and the very Canniball, do sing and also say, their highest and holiest matters in certaine riming versicles and not in prose, which proves also that our manner of vulgar Poesie is more ancient than the artificiall of the Greeks and Latines, ours coming by instinct of nature, which was before Art or observation, and used with the savage and uncivill, who were before all science or civilitie, even as the naked by priority of time is before the clothed, and the ignorant before the learned.[10]

It is obvious that if the literature of the savage is primordial literature, then the savage is literally primitive. But there is no evidence that this is so, and even the use of the word "primitive" is deprecated now by ethnologists. Be that as it may, its use has been widespread, and even the Greeks, who were not after all influenced by Herbert Spencer, thought of the savages whom they knew as men in a state of nature. But if poetry was, as argued by Puttenham, the most ancient form of literature, and if it was made by the People, not by individual authors, it could be envisioned under the guise of a literal vox populi. Such ideas gained plausibility in the eighteenth century when discovering the pattern of history became the dominant pastime of certain philosophers. Among such writers the most influential was Herder, but the idea that primitive literature was poetry had been anticipated in philosophic circles by Vico, and in Germany itself by Hamann.

There is, however, one more witness to the "naturalness" of poetry to whom we should refer before moving on to Vico. That witness is Montaigne in his essay "Des vaines subtilitez." There we find him saying in Florio's English translation:

Popular and merely natural Poetry has certain Graces, and inbred liveliness, whereby it concurs and compares itself unto the principal beauty of perfect and artificial Poetry, as may plainly be seen in the Villanelles, homely gigs, and country songs of Gascony, which are brought unto us from Nations that have no knowledge at all, neither

10. Ed. Gladys Doidge Willcock and Alice Walker, p. 10.

of any learning, or so much as of writing. Mean and indifferent Poetry, and that consists between both, is scorned and contemned, and passes without honor or esteem.[11]

The theory that primordial literature was poetry was systematized by Vico. Although he had little influence in his own time, his opinions have been studied assiduously in the twentieth century. Michelet's edition of the *Oeuvres choisies* in 1835 surely must have been read by philosophers of history, for there are echoes of Vico in others. Few philosophers of the nineteenth century seem to have read Italian, and probably the traces of Vico's ideas that one finds in them entered their thought indirectly.

In his *Scienza nuova*[12] Vico sets up three stages in history: the poetic, the heroic, and the human. These correspond to childhood, youth, and maturity. In the first period men express themselves in myth, which arises from childlike insight and is expounded in poetry. Clearly a man who believes this must next decide whether childhood is inherently nobler than youth or maturity, if he is going to appraise civilization. Vico is almost unique in opting for the negative. Primitive man is simply primitive, Vico thinks, and though he appreciates the poems of Homer and, of course, the Bible, it is not because they express the thoughts and feelings of a childlike mind but because they are beautiful.[13] They are in essence, he believes, religious poems, and

11. *Essays*, Book 1, 54 (spelling modernized). The French runs, "La Poësie populaire et purement naturelle a des naïvetez et des graces par où elle se compare à la principale beauté de la poësie parfaite selon l'art; comme il se void és villannelles de Gascoigne et aux chansons qu'on nous rapporte des nations qui n'ont congoissance d'aucune science, ny mesme d'escriture. La poësie mediocre qui s'arreste entre deux, est desdaignée, sans honneur et sans prix." The distinction between natural and artificial poetry was also to be made by Jakob Grimm.

12. I use the edition of Paolo Rossi (Milan, 1959), abbreviated as *S.N.*

13. Anyone interested in the development of the cult of childhood might consult my book *The Cult of Childhood*.

he identifies the wisdom of the pagan sages with that of the ancient Hebrews (S.N., p. 402).

The second age of history is the heroic, to which "natural theology" corresponds. In this age the supernatural forces of mythology and poetry are concentrated in the soul of a man. The heroic nature gives rise to a special type of culture and hence of religion. But it is still a period in which most people must be governed by one or by a few; the mass, it is clear, cannot be expected to govern itself. For that to occur, the Human Age must come into being, an age that combines the supernaturalism of the Age of Gods with the Age of Heroes and its cult of the great man. For human nature, says Vico (S.N., p. 742), being intelligent, is therefore modest, benign, and reasonable, and recognizes as law the demands of conscience, reason, and duty. In spite of these generalizations about ages, Vico does not believe in collective minds. He still can write, for instance, of individual culture-heroes who confer blessings on their fellows (S.N., p. 277): Cadmus bringing letters to the Greeks (p. 296); Orpheus "reducing the savagery of the Greeks to humanity" (p. 298). In short—at least in the Heroic Age—the whole people do not act as one spontaneously, as if the force of evolution pushed them on. They acquire new ways of thinking and feeling through the influence of Heroes. Yet Vico wrote of common sense as "a judgment made without any reflection, commonly felt [as true] by an entire class, an entire people, an entire nation, and all mankind." As Rossi points out in a footnote to this passage, common sense is similar to custom and forms a criterion of truth and action. One might explain its power as analogous to the compulsive force of habit in childhood, but for Vico it was instilled in human beings by Providence.[14]

14. From the Elementi. I number these by the Roman numerals assigned them by their author, adding the pages. This particular remark on common sense is xii, p. 329.

Primitive human beings, as Auguste Comte was also to say, project their natures into the non-human world (xxxii, p. 341). They attribute to the will of God the causes of things "without considering the means which the divine will makes use of" (xxxiii, p. 341). But primitive anthropomorphism leads to sublime poetry (xxxvii, p. 342). It leads to it, however, through individual "theological" poets whose writings made the transition into the Heroic Age (xliv, p. 345). If this is so, then the idea of historical determinism is still further weakened, though Vico himself seems to waver between the belief that human nature inevitably matures, as a child does, and that the process of maturation is the result of education. He lays it down as a law (liii, p. 349) that "men first have feelings without awareness, then they become aware with minds perturbed and moved, and finally they reflect pure mentality." This sequence corresponds, it turns out, to the three ages: gods—sensations, heroes—fantasy, men—reason.

In view of this one might imagine Vico to be optimistic about human history. For many eighteenth-century thinkers believed that once the rule of reason obtained, all problems would be solved in the best possible fashion. But quite the contrary was the case according to him. His conclusion was that all history shows the corruption of nations in their rise, progress, stability, decadence, and end. Men begin by being subordinated to a family, set up an aristocratic republic on the family model, hold up the ideal of popular freedom, pass into monarchy, establish it, and finally ruin it. Each of these moments reflects a type of human character: the huge and lumbering (Polyphemus), the magnanimous and proud (Achilles), the courageous and just (Aristides), the virtuous tainted by vice (Alexander and Caesar), the gloomy and meditative (Tiberius), and finally *i furiosi e sfacciati*, madmen dissolute and shameless (Caligula and Nero). In short, as soon as Vico comes into contact with historical figures of whom there are fairly reliable records, he has to admit that degeneration is as natural as continuous improvement. No Neapolitan of the eighteenth century could be expected to be an enthusiastic admirer of his contemporary statesmen.[15]

By Herder's time the notion that poetry was older than prose was well established. Percy, in his introduction to the *Reliques*, takes this for granted and cites the American Indians, the Saxons, the ancient Britons, and the "Gothic nations," in evidence. But he believes that each of these peoples had its bards and says nothing of a collective soul of which poems are the expression. That peculiar idea, which was to become widespread later in the nineteenth century, stems perhaps from Hamann's *Aesthetica in Nuce*.[16] For in that book we find him saying:

[Poetry] is the mother-tongue of the human race, as the garden is older than the field, painting than writing, song than declamation, parables than inferences, barter than commerce. The rest of our earliest forebears was a deeper sleep; and their movement was a tumultuous dance. Seven days they sat in the silence of reflection or astonishment; and opened their mouths to utter winged words. Sense and passions speak and understand nothing but images. The first outburst of creation and the first impression of the historian, the first appearance and the first enjoyment of nature, are united in the words, "Let there be light." Herewith begins the experience of the presence of things.[17]

Hamann, as those who have tried to understand him know, had no fear of the obscure so long as it was not the obscurity of the learned or the affected. For instance, in an apology for the simple style of the Gospels he found a greater significance, as Tertullian did too, in the incredible than in the plausible. This appears with special force in his "A Clover-leaf of Hellenistic Letters."

If . . . the divine style chooses the foolish, the shallow, the ignoble, to put to shame the strength and ingenuity of all profane writers, there certainly is need of the illuminated, enthused and

---

15. For an exposition of Vico's theory of poetry as a whole, see Fr. Emilio Chicchetti, O.F.M., *La Filosofia di Giambattista Vico*, 2d essay, pp. 79 ff.

16. For an English translation of this very difficult writer, see Ronald Gregor Smith, *J. G. Hamann: A Study in Christian Existence*.

17. *Ibid.*, p. 196.

eager eyes of a friend, an intimate, a lover, in order to discern
through such a disguise the beams of heavenly glory. *Dei dialectus
soloecismus*, says a well-known commentator. Here too it holds that
vox populi, vox Dei.[18]

Most of this is reproduced in Herder, whose admiration for
Hamann needs no proof. But neither he nor Hamann made clear
just what the *Volksseele* was. Did the term mean that in a given
population there was a collection of individual souls who were all
alike, or was there a transcendent soul in which all individual souls
participated, or indeed did either of them ever face the question
as a problem worth solving? At times Herder talks as if all people
whom he thought to be primitive were alike psychologically.
Others have talked of the Medieval mind, the Renaissance spirit,
the modern temper, and even the modern mind, without mentioning the question of how such beings exist and in what ontological sphere. The matter would be trivial, in fact pedantic, were it
not that the heterogeneity of individuals has always produced
many of the intellectual, moral, and aesthetic problems that have
confronted men at any given time. Moral problems, for instance,
often arise because contemporaries disagree about what is right,
good, just, and so on, not because all accept the same criteria of
value.

Herder believed that any primitive people would be similar
to any other and that they would all have characteristics unlike
those of non-primitives. In his correspondence about Ossian, for
instance,[19] he flatly asserts that the American Five Nations have
everything in common with Ossian: death songs, battle songs,
dirges, hymns about and to ancestors. Therefore Ossian must be
authentically primitive. But he had also said a few pages earlier

18. *Ibid.*, p. 186. Note how the voice of the People here is foolish, ignoble,
shallow, but at the same time divine. This derives no doubt from Saint Paul's
"being a fool in God."

19. *Auszug aus einem Briefwechsel über Ossian und die Lieder alter Völker.*
Ed. Suphan, Vol. 5, p. 166.

(p. 160) that Ossian's poems were those of an untaught "perceptual" (*sinnlichen*) Folk, and that their genuineness could be proved only if one responded to the "spirit"; it is grasped by an *inneres Zeugniss*. Why anything perceptual could be known only by inner testimony is strange, since the senses are our main contact with the external, not the internal, world. But the Soul of the Folk is "after all little more than perceptual understanding [*Verstand*] and imagination" (p. 185). Here he is probably repeating the commonplace that primitive people, like children, are below the rational level; that is why they think in sensory images. Yet at another time, when he was more concerned with national as contrasted with common characters, he wrote that only climatic and historical data could define a national character.[20] It may well be that he was thinking of national traits, Italian, French, German, as modern emergents from primitive homogeneity. There may have been in the back of his mind vestiges of his biblical training, according to which at some early period, before Babel, all men were shepherds, leading peaceful patriarchal lives (p. 483). For in one passage he does describe conditions as if they were common to all mankind and at the same time peculiar to Asia Minor. Here at any rate men lived like children under the benevolent despotism of their fathers, in whose likeness they conceived God (p. 484). If he thought that these men had counterparts elsewhere—in India or China, for example—he says nothing of such a thought.

History, as in the works of so many other writers, seems to be a sort of vermiform creature which moves about and, having left one location, is followed by a historical void. For in a manner that is found in other writers too, history for Herder, after the infancy of the race, next turns up in Egypt and Phoenicia where its boyhood is passed and where the pastoral life yields to the

20. *Auch eine Philosophie der Geschichte zur Bildung der Menschheit* (1779), Vol. 5, p. 503.

agricultural, wherefore property, law, order, the police, are all established (p. 487). Next, obviously, comes Greece, where the "fairest youth" of mankind is lived in freedom (p. 496); Greece became the "cradle of humanity, of fellow feeling, legislation, and of that which is most agreeable in religion, customs, literature, poetry, practices, and arts—all was youthful joy, grace, sport, and love" (p. 496).

It would be futile to attempt a reconciliation between this and the idea that poetry belongs to the childhood of the race. A man who had read the Greek tragic poets must have become aware of their emotional and rational maturity, to say nothing of their strong individuality. It was not merely the number of actors required by a play of Euripides that distinguished him from Aeschylus. Nor is either much given to youthful joy, grace, sport, and love. But a man who can see an identity between the Ossianic and Homeric epics, or who can write of Hebrew poetry as particularly appealing to youth,[21] could not have sharpened his powers of discrimination. He addressed himself here especially to the young who "are particularly sensitive to times before the Mosaic servitude, who have not been oppressed by the yoke of rules, to whom the dawn of the world is as the dawn of the soul" (p. 221). He is certain in such passages that Homer, Ossian, and the pre-Mosaic poets all lived the same sort of lives and wrote the same sort of poetry (p. 225). Yet he is capable of insisting that to understand the poetry of a people one must study their climate (*Luft, Himmel*), their corporeal constitution, their music and their dances (p. 226). He knew that northern peoples had a different climate from that of the Mediterranean peoples, and when he wanted to preach cultural nationalism he emphasized this. In fact, in this same study of Hebrew poetry (p. 231) he described the Nordic languages as "close to the sounds of nature, but hoarse, as if only externally [related]. They croak, roar, hiss,

21. See the introduction to *Vom Geist der Ebräischen Poesie*, Vol. 2, p. 221.

creak like the objects [they name] themselves. Wise poets make use of this with great economy." [22] But since in this passage he wanted to extol Greek and Hebrew, he added that in the south the proximity to Nature is closer than it is in the north. (But just what is Nature here? Nature, one might think, was as close to a man in one place as in another.) The pulse of Nature, he says (p. 237), is the rhythm of poetry, and poetry is "the speech of feeling," saying nothing to the *Verstand*. Thus the language of poetry expresses "the primitive logic of the senses," "the oldest history of the human spirit and heart."

To make much sense out of this is very difficult. But perhaps enough has been said to show that according to Herder, poetry is the primordial form of literature, that it expresses the Folk-Soul, and that it is emotional, not rational, speech. The nebulosity of such ideas is the source of their power and from it emerges such a famous phrase as Jakob Grimm's *Das Volk dichtet*, a sentiment shared by A. W. Schlegel and Uhland.[23]

In English-speaking countries the most influential spokesman for the People as Poet was obviously Wordsworth. His importance

22. Here, I confess, I am in doubt whether Herder meant that Nordic tongues have more onomatopoeia or that in some way their words resemble the objects they name, objects that are natural rather than artificial. That the word "*Baum*" resembles a tree more than "*arbor*" or "*dendron*" does not seem arguable. And are "*mugire*," "*clamare*," "*fremere*" less onomatopoetic than "*brüllen*" or "*roar*"?

23. There is doubt, however, that Grimm ever said the words attributed to him. See P. B[arry], "Das Volk Dichtet Nichts," *Bulletin of the Folk-Song Society of the North East*, no. 7 (1934), p. 4. A more thorough account of Herder's notion of the source of popular poetry will probably be found in Erwin Kircher's *Volkslied und Volkspoesie in der Sturm und Drangzeit*, a Strasbourg dissertation which I have not been able to use. My remarks in the body of the text should be supplemented by Schlegel's *Geschichte der romantischen Literatur*, particularly the chapter called "Romanzen und andere Volkslieder," and by Uhland's *Alte hoch- und niederdeutsche Volkslieder*, in his *Schriften*, Vol. 3, pp. 10–13. See also Albert B. Friedman, *The Ballad Revival*, pp. 249 ff.; and L. A. Willoughby, *The Romantic Movement in Germany*, chaps. 1–3.

here lies in his conscious attempt to use the language of the People and incidents in their lives as the diction and subject-matter of his poetry. He identified the People with men whose lives were "low and rustic," but by "low" he clearly meant "poor," not "criminal" or "immoral." Wordsworth seems to have been more concerned with the kind of language he would use than with his subject-matter, but they were closely related in his mind.[24] For, as he says, "low and rustic life was generally chosen, because in that condition, the essential passions of the heart find a better soil in which they can attain their maturity, are less under restraint, and speak a plainer and more emphatic language; because in that condition of life our elementary feelings co-exist in a state of greater simplicity, and, consequently, may be more accurately contemplated, and more forcibly communicated; because the manners of rural life germinate from those elementary feelings; and, from the necessary character of rural occupations, are more easily comprehended; and are more durable; and lastly, because in that condition the passions of men are incorporated with the beautiful and permanent forms of nature" (p. 9).

Just why the rural population was to be so characterized is left mysterious. All people, rural or urban, have "elementary passions"; some express them with less restraint than others, but this is irrelevant to rural or urban environments. One need but walk along Piccadilly or Fifth Avenue to hear expressions of elementary feelings as forcible as any Wordsworth might have heard in the Lake Country in 1798. Nor are these feelings less elementary because they are experienced and expressed in a city. To the Greek Cynic, the closer one approached the life of the animals (rather than that of the peasant), the closer one drew to Nature. For to the Cynic the animals were self-sufficient, unbound by social conventions, and unburdened by possessions. The rustic is indeed less burdened by possessions, and few rustics in eighteenth-

24. All quotations are from the preface to the *Lyrical Ballads*, edited by George Sampson.

century England were even freeholders. Poverty has always been distasteful and the ability to endure it has often, though far from always, been praised. It may be that the shepherd, the plowman, the serving maid, the idiot, are more pitiable than the coachman, the street sweeper, the butcher's boy, or the policeman, all of whom are also poor. But what is less natural in the latter group? To Wordsworth men who earn their living in the country have passions that "are incorporated with the beautiful and permanent forms of nature." That the Lake Country is more beautiful than Hyde Park will be granted without a moment's hesitation; but that its inhabitants feel its beauty, as an incorporation of their passions, is less certain.

As for rural language, Wordsworth believed that rustics "convey their feelings and notions in simple and unelaborated expressions." That may well be so. But so do newsboys, shopkeepers, bus conductors, and all others who are not conscious of the intricacies of motivation and emotion. That Nature is simple, that it always follows the simplest course, is a venerable tradition, and it may be true that the simplifications of science have given rise to the idea that the simple is more "natural" than the complex. In actual fact, Wordsworth was merely disgusted with the elaborate and highly ritualized diction of his contemporaries. It seemed, and probably was, insincere. To avoid it, he proposed eliminating all personifications of abstract ideas, and most poetic diction, and modifying prose only by meter (p. 14). The argument may be condensed as follows: poetry appeals to all men, prose only to some; hence the language of poetry must be universal, that is, the language of humanity as a whole. Such language is the language of the emotions, not of reason (p. 25). And feeling is more characteristic of the rustic than of the urban man. Therefore the language of the rustic is more natural than that of the city dweller. The sacred word "natural" does its usual duty here. It is both descriptive and normative, meaning now "rural," now "instinctive." There is undeniably an implication of anti-intellectualism in Wordsworth which appears not only in his theory of poetic diction but also in his poetic practice. As early as *Tintern Abbey* we find him

> . . . well pleased to recognize
> In nature and the language of the sense,
> The anchor of my purest thoughts, the nurse,
> The guide, the guardian of my heart, and soul
> Of all my moral being.

The People, then, are more natural than the non-People; they are rustics, and speak, as both Vico and Herder thought, the "language of the sense." [25]

This may have come about as a reaction from his youthful fervor for the French Revolution. For one group of revolutionists, as is well known, found the essence of humanity in reason. It was, unfortunately for Wordsworth, Robespierre, the self-styled disciple of Rousseau, who found it in feeling.

The admiration for folksongs and ballads did not follow merely from theories about collective minds or *Volksseelen*. Such poems are simple and naïve and thus seem less contrived than the verses of recognized poets. It must be admitted, however, that sometimes a very sophisticated poet will contrive verses as simple in appearance as hymn tunes—Emily Dickinson and A. E. Housman, for example. But simplicity and naïveté are given the highest praise only by the cultural primitivist. Neither Sir Philip Sidney nor Montaigne attributed to them a beauty higher than the beauty

25. Compare what Wordsworth has to say of the speech of the People with what Zola says on the same subject in the preface to *l'Assommoir*, which dates from 1877, three quarters of a century after the preface to the *Lyrical Ballads*. But Zola's people in this novel, which he himself in the same preface has called "le premier roman sur le peuple, qui ne mente pas et qui ait l'odeur du peuple," were urban people, not rustics. Yet it was their ancestors who made the revolution and for whom the revolution was made. It may be worth adding that even the Jews of the *Shtetl*, the small towns in Poland and Russia, who had no cause to admire the peasants, yet had a saying, "A peasant proverb is as true as Torah." See Mark Zborowski and Elizabeth Herzog, *Life Is with People*, p. 144.

of the classics. That sort of praise had to wait for the eighteenth century to close; then anything medieval or apparently medieval took on a new charm. Just as Gothic architecture, ruins, chivalry, forests, and mountains began to lose their ugly traits, so what were believed to be the songs of the *jongleurs* and *trouvères* were revived and speculation over their authorship arose. It is interesting that it does not seem to have occurred to Percy to ascribe any authorship to his ballads other than that of an individual bard employed by a king or local potentate for purposes of entertainment. It was this against which the folklorist protested, even when he did not go so far as Herder or Grimm in inventing a collective soul to create these songs. We are all indebted to the folklorists for collecting an amazing mass of material from all over the world which showed that certain themes appeared everywhere in fables, songs, ballads, as in games, myths, and religious rites. The inference was that the ancestors of the human race, not merely of one people, who had lived before the dispersion consequent upon the destruction of the Tower of Babel, had passed on this material to their descendants. A second hypothesis was that by the process of diffusion from some central point, the same things had been accomplished. A third was that certain themes, rites, myths, and so on, were inherent in human psychology and would be found wherever human beings were found. Diffusion would seem to be the theory most congenial to the empirically minded, for there were always some details which were not really universal. Even useful instruments are not universal, witness the wheel. On the other hand, when it was a question of "basic biological drives," there was reason to believe that geographical location would not cause their satisfaction to be thwarted. Thus love songs, banqueting songs, dirges, hymns, to take a few examples mentioned by Herder, might be expected to exist everywhere and not to vary essentially from people to people. If folksongs are of this nature, then the fact that those of the Nordics resemble those of the Mediterranean peoples would not entail a belief in a collective soul at all. The fact that two poets were human beings would suffice to explain their similarities.

Unfortunately, Percy's *Reliques*, as I have said, contained poems touched up by their editor, so they cannot be taken as representative of anything of ethnological interest. It was Francis James Child with his *English and Scottish Ballads* (1857–58), published later in a revised and more complete edition as *The English and Scottish Popular Ballads* (1882–98), who did most to collect the data from which generalizations could be drawn. In Francis B. Gummere's *The Popular Ballad*, first published in 1907, conclusions about the authorship of the ballads were presented in a reasonable manner without any metaphysical underpinning. Gummere pointed out that the continuity of balladry was dependent upon the stability of language. "Poetry made in the vernacular," he said, "and orally transmitted, depends for its preservation upon such linguistic stability as will enable it to pass from generation to generation without the changes of word and form that make it both unintelligible as language and impossible as verse." [26]

Such stability in English began roughly in the fourteenth century. At the same time Gummere realized that human beings, flesh and blood men and women, transmitted these verses and that such variants as are found in them can be explained as normal. When any simple sentence is repeated from person to person, changes will be made in it.[27] There is, however, one bit of speculation in which Gummere indulges, but one that has a degree of plausibility. That is that the ballad was "a narrative lyric made

26. In the Dover reprint of 1959, p. 31.

27. Since Gummere's book is now easily procurable, I refer to p. 6, where he gives an interesting example of how even a printed poem can be modified when quoted from memory. The poem in question is Henley's *Invictus*, the authorship of which was asked by a reader of the *Philadelphia Bulletin*, November 16, 1906. It is well worth looking up.

and sung at a dance and handed down in popular tradition" (p. 75). That there are narrative lyrics made and sung at dances cannot be disputed. They are found—or were found forty years ago—all over the European countryside. But that all ballads had this origin could in the nature of the case be no more than a hypothesis. Still, hypotheses are clearly needed when explanations are sought.

Admiration for folk-poetry thus has several roots. (1) It may spring from simple antiquarianism—the desire to discover, collect, and preserve everything of the past. This in itself does not endow folk-poetry with any special aesthetic value. But since whatever is antiquated takes on some kind of value, that value may easily change from whatever it originally was to the aesthetic. So unbelievers in either Judaism or Christianity may still highly regard the Bible as literature. (2) It may also spring from a historical interest in what themes were celebrated by the People, what battles, deaths, religious events, were thought worthy of celebration. (3) It may spring from the feeling that Herder seems to have had, that the popular origin of folk-poetry conferred higher value upon it than individual authorship would have done. This was consonant with Herder's growing nationalism and his rebellion against the cultural hegemony of the French. The argument seems to be that if one is a German, then German art must be better than French art or Italian art or any other national art. But Herder would probably have qualified the adjective "better" by the phrase, "for the German." Linguistic chauvinism is too common at the present time for us to do more than point to the example of the Irish, the Israelis, the Icelanders, the Flemings, and for that matter, the impatience of Americans with Anglicisms or of Englishmen with Americanisms. It would be of advantage to all of us to speak a widely disseminated language, if it had a great literature, but that would appear to be unpatriotic, even if one's mother tongue is read and spoken by only a few of one's compatriots.

To take an extreme example, should a Breton refuse to speak and read French? I doubt that any Breton would answer in the affirmative, but he would nevertheless feel moved by songs sung in Breton and would prefer to give his estate a Breton name, even if it meant nothing more beautiful than *Mon Désir*.

What now were the folk-poems like?

Gummere sums up some of the characteristics of the ballads. First, he says, "it is only in very recent development that the humble or common man is put into the foreground of story or play" (p. 82). The ballads deal with the upper classes. Not only that, but they recognize the privileges of rank, sometimes to a laughable extent. For instance, and this is my example, not Gummere's, in the ballads edited by Percy, there is a poem called "The Beggar's Daughter of Bednall Green." The Beggar turns out to be Henry, son of Simon de Montfort, and thus his daughter is of noble birth in spite of appearances. In "The King of Scots and Andrew Browne," the reward of Browne's bravery is a knighthood and "lands and livings great." And in the last stanza of "Little Musgrave and Lady Barnard," a ballad of adultery, the lovers, murdered by Lord Barnard, are buried together, but rank is duly preserved in the grave:

> A grave, a grave, Lord Barnard cryed,
>   To put these lovers in;
> But lay my ladye o' the upper hande,
>   For she comes of the better kin.

In "The Knight and the Shepherd's Daughter," which plays upon the theme of Bednall Green, the girl turns out to be the daughter of a duke. In short, for these are only a few examples of rewarding virtue by bestowing rank, the People seem to have seen no particular value in their own station in life and to have retained the idea that worldly privilege and riches were given by God to those whom he thought worthy of them. One might cite in objection one ballad called "The Bitter Withy," referred to by Gummere (pp.

228–29) on the ground that its tone is different. The Child Jesus is snubbed by "three jolly jerdins."

> Oh, we are lords' and ladies' sons,
> Born in bower or in hall,
> And You are but some poor maid's child
> Born'd in an ox's stall.

But this is not said in protest against rank and its privileges at all. The case is unique and the attitude of the jolly jerdins is characteristic not only of the fifteenth century but of all times. Indeed recognition of rank is one of the persistent themes of folk-poetry. If the People were the author of such verses, they were expressing an ambition to rise above their station. The situation is very much like that in some of the fairy tales collected by the Brothers Grimm. The poor boy wants to become rich, to marry the king's daughter; the poor mistreated girl wants to marry a prince. Puss-in-Boots does not persuade his unfortunate master to subside and be contented with his lot; on the contrary, he manages by obvious trickery to turn the master into a marquis and to help him carry off the beautiful princess. So Cinderella is not portrayed as a willing servant to her cruel stepmother and stepsisters, saying to herself that she must accept whatever fate God has assigned her. Unless such stories were satires on the current aspirations of society, they voice a philosophy of life antithetical to the teachings of the Church. One of the most amusing cases of "the People's" snobbery is the transformation of the outlaw Robin Hood into the Earl of Huntington. One might conclude that, as the revolts at the end of the fourteenth century showed, the People were none too anxious to remain the People. And as the social history of the United States has shown, once the People are liberated from the autocracy of their masters they follow the same struggle for prestige as those from whom they sought liberation.

Gummere also says that "the ballad muse is cleanly," that "only a few [ballads] are distinctly coarse" (p. 338). Chaucer, it will be recalled, puts the coarsest of his tales into the mouths of the lower orders. We have already referred to Furnivall's edition of Percy's folio manuscript of "loose and humorous songs." [28]

Mention has been made in passing of some of the poets discussed in Rayner Unwin's *The Rural Muse*, but there were others who should at least be named. They include weavers, booksellers, millers, bricklayers, a laundress, a milkwoman (who called herself Lactilla), a sailor, and a pipemaker. Reading quotations from their works, one concludes that these men and women had in mind a poetic prototype which they tried to exemplify. A man like Clare was clearly a poet in his own right, as Chatterton was. But on the whole the poems of James Woodhouse, Robert Dosley, Robert Tatersal, Mary Collier, and their fellows, are pretty dreary and obviously derivative. But their emergence from the great undifferentiated populace does signify a change in the social structure. Robert Bloomfield, shoemaker, author of *The Farmer's Boy*, is quoted as saying,

> The commone people . . . are a rough set no doubt, but I dislike the doctrine of keeping them in their dirt, for though it holds good as to the preservation of potatoes, it would be no grateful reflection to good minds to know that a man's natural abilities had been smother'd for want of beeing able to read and write. How can we consistently praise the inestimable blessings of letters and not wish to extend it? Or why should the Great and Wealthy confine the probable production of intellectual excellence to their own class, and exclude, by withholding the polish, all that might amongst the poor by nature be intended to be Newton's and Locke's? [29]

28. As samples, see "Walking in a Meadowe Greene" (p. 31); "It was a puritanical ladd" (p. 35); "Bee not affrayd" (p. 47); "Doe you meane to overthrowe me?" (p. 49); "A man and a younge maid that loved a long time" (p. 51); "A creature for feature I never saw a fairer" (p. 53); "Can any one tell what I ayle?" (p. 55). These will suffice; I have already cited *The Common Muse* and the *Parnasse Satyrique*. If more is needed, see the poems called Goliardic and some of the *fabliaux*. Anonymous and "folk" poetry are no worse in this respect than most poetry of which the authorship is known. And if one shrinks from the coarse, one would do well to avoid the Old Testament.

29. Unwin, *The Rural Muse*, p. 105.

The answer was given, as Mr. Unwin points out, in Mandeville's essay on *Charity and Charity Schools*. Mandeville began by saying that where slavery is not permitted,

> the surest Wealth consists in a Multitude of labourious Poor; for besides that they are the never failing nursery of Fleets and Armies, without them there could be no Enjoyment, and no Product of any Country would be valuable. To make the Society happy and People easy under the meanest Circumstances, it is requisite that great Numbers of them should be ignorant as well as Poor. Knowledge both enlarges and multiplies our Desires, and the fewer things a Man wishes for, the more easily his Necessities may be supply'd. The Welfare and Felicity therefore of every State and Kingdom, require that the Knowledge of the Working Poor should be confin'd within the Verge of their Occupations, and never extended (as to things visible) beyond what related to their calling. The most a Shepherd, a Plowman or any other Peasant knows of this World, and the things that are foreign to his Labour or Employment, the less fit he'll be to go through the Fatigues and Hardships of it with Cheerfulness and Content. Reading, Writing and Arithmetick, are very necessary to those, whose Business require such Qualifications, but where People's livelihood has no dependence on these Arts, they are very perniciois to the Poor, who are forc'd to get their Daily Bread by their Daily Labour . . . Abundance of hard and dirty Labour is to be done, and coarse Living is to be complied with: Where shall we find a better nursery for these Necessities than the Children of the Poor? none certainly are nearer to it or fitter for it. Besides that the things I call Hardships, neither seem nor are such to those who have been brought up to 'em, and know no better. There is not a more contented People among us, than those who work the hardest and are the least acquainted with the Pomp and Delicacies of the World.[30]

Hideous as such a view seems to a modern reader softened by humanitarianism, it would be well if we could tell in advance whom God had chosen to be lettered. There is certainly little sense in wasting a college education on anyone predestined to be an ass or an ox. The pages of history contain some names of men who read as they plowed or studied by the light of the hearth, and they are not the least worthy of our forebears. The problem

30. Bernard Mandeville, *The Fable of the Bees*, ed. Kaye, pp. 253 ff.

is like that of the Elect and the Damned in Saint Augustine: the Church, not knowing who is who, prays for all. That may be the wiser course for human beings too. One thing seems true: in the United States it was not the rural Muse who gave an American intonation to poetry; it was William Carlos Williams, Robert Frost, Carl Sandburg, Alfred Kreymborg, Amy Lowell and the Imagists, Edwin Arlington Robinson, and their associates. The farming folk, on the other hand, who contributed their verses to *Voices from the Fields*, wrote as the standard poets wrote, in the traditional meters and about the traditional themes.

THE PEOPLE IN ART

By "art" in this essay I shall mean only the visual arts, for though there have always been popular dances and other festivals, such manifestations of feelings about the People can hardly be given in a book. Literature has an essay to itself; and whatever mention there may be of music will be given separately.

Insofar as the People are identified with the working class they hold an ambiguous position in the Bible. In the first chapter of Genesis Adam has nothing to do beyond enjoying the pleasures of Eden, the company of Eve, and, of course, observing the commandment not to eat of the Tree of Knowledge. In the second chapter we are told that he was put in the Garden to tend it—surely nothing too arduous. But the Fathers were puzzled about Adam's life before the Fall.[1] They had in fact little to say about it in the beginning, though later they were to expatiate on the evils which were nonexistent at that time. Whatever the details, the pre-lapsarian condition corresponded to the State of Nature in philosophy and to the Golden Age or the *Saturnia regna* in mythology. On the one hand, it was a purely hedonistic state; on the other, it involved some work, but work of a very delightful kind.

In the essay on "The People in Literature" I have shown, I hope, that very little was said about the urban artisan until recent times. And that little was said in ridicule, in condemnation of his behavior, in attempts to keep him in his place. He was but an atom of the mob. But by the thirteenth century and the formation of the gilds, the skilled artisan took on a kind of social power which had not been seen since the rise of the Plebeians in Rome.

1. See George Boas, *Primitivism* . . . *in the Middle Ages*, the essays on "The Original Condition of Man."

For now Western Europe was becoming a proto-industrial community, and the organization of the gilds created a sociopolitical class which was later to become the bourgeoisie. The differences between the modern middle-class man and the medieval artisan cannot be denied, but the members of the gilds had precisely that middle position between, let us say, the nobility and the serf that the bourgeoisie has between the rich entrepreneur and the proletariat. The People as they figured in art were more likely to be rural workers than artisans, though here too there were exceptions.

Machiavelli, writing about the influence of Christianity in the *Discorsi*,[2] tries to show that modern religion does not favor freedom. In contrast to paganism, Christianity, he says,

> has set up as the greatest good humility, abjectness, and contempt for human things; the other [paganism] put it in grandeur of mind, strength of body, and in all the other things apt to make men exceeding vigorous. Though our religion asks that you have fortitude within you, it prefers that you be adapted to suffering rather than to doing anything vigorous. This way of living, then, has made the world weak and turned it over as prey to wicked men, who can in security control it, since the generality of men, in order to go to Heaven, think more about enduring their injuries than about avenging them.

No more than a word is needed to see Machiavelli's anticipation of Gobineau and Nietzsche. Whatever may have been the intention of the Church, the outcome of her practices agreed with Machiavelli's diagnosis. Though it has often been said that the Church condemned slavery, abbeys held slaves and nothing effective was done to uproot slavery as a system.

As for freedom of person, according to which a man might enter the trade or profession he liked and educate himself as he would, that was not only difficult but, in England after 1388, impossible, for by royal statute all after the age of twelve should continue in the same state of bondage or serfage, and the House of Commons "even petitioned against sending of villeins' sons to

2. Trans. Allan Gilbert, Vol. 2, pp. 330–31.

school." [3] But, as Coulton says, that was too odious to be enforced.

The man who is not free but subject to the will and caprice of a master, whether he is technically a slave or simply a villein, is not likely to acquire the respect of his superiors. One might pity such a person but one would not hold him up to admiration; the marks of inferiority would be upon him, and in art they would be exaggerated to make him either ludicrous or ugly. Now it was never the program of the Church to divide men into a large number of the powerless and a small number of the powerful, but that has been the usual situation both before and after the Redemption. It is also true that beginning with Saint Paul the Church has urged her members to accept the government God has given them, except—and the exception is essential to the teaching —when that government orders them to violate the laws of religion.[4] Hence the Church did everything it could to cooperate with the State in putting down popular rebellions. Consequently, whoever was in power was likely to be assisted by the Church, and he knew enough to assist her in return. Hence when we see at Chartres for instance, the windows donated by a gild, we have no evidence that any group of artisans was held in esteem because of their labor or their art. The gild-masters were just as much potentates as today's industrial entrepreneurs or labor-union leaders. They did not rank so high in the social hierarchy, but they had power. It is interesting to see how a movement like Lollardry began at the end of the fourteenth century by including members of the House of Commons and did not develop its proletarian character until the fifteenth century, by the middle of which it became the faith of tradesmen and artisans, with here and there

3. G. G. Coulton, *Medieval Panorama*, p. 81.
4. Though this is a commonplace, it may be as well to refer to Romans 13. The best introduction to the Church's position on obedience to authority is *The Church Speaks to the Modern World*, edited and with an introduction by Etienne Gilson (pp. 11–12), and the whole of the encyclical, *Diuturnum* (1881).

a few priests, merchants, and professional men. But by the early sixteenth century "all save a few belonged to the common people —weavers, wheelwrights, smiths, carpenters, tailors, and other tradesmen." [5]

In short, the rise of the proletariat was delayed until modern times, and power was retained in the hands of owners of real property. When one finds that Parliament ruled that no one under the degree of freeholders should keep a dog or that villeins should not send their sons to school, one begins to think it absurd to maintain that the People had much voice in any political decisions.[6]

Does what I have just said conflict with the fact that every trade or art had its patron saint? Can one argue that because a type of labor was patronized by a special saint, it must also have enjoyed terrestrial esteem? That seems unlikely. The archers had four patrons, Saints George, Gilles, Sebastian, and Ursula, but this side of Paradise they took the same chances as barbers who could appeal only to Cosmas and Damian, or washerwomen who were protected by Blanchard, Marguerite, and Veronica. The cooks were almost overpatronized, for six saints watched over them, whereas gold-beaters could look only to one, Saint Eloi. Maybe it was thought that economic groups with celestial advocates needed none on earth and, conversely, that men who had power on earth needed no heavenly patrons except their particular guardian angels. The Thrones, Dominations, and Powers looked out for potentates, and that may have given them special prestige, if any was needed. But once one had gained rank in the nobility, one had only one's personal patron to appeal to. In any event there is no evidence that the prestige of one's patron saint conferred

5. Quoted from A. G. Dickens, *The English Reformation*, pp. 24–30. It will be recalled that the *petite noblesse* played an important role in the early days of the French Revolution. The mob took over later.

6. See A. L. Smith, "The Constitution under Lancastrian Rule," in Traill's *Social England*, Vol. 2, p. 310.

any prestige on one's trade. Saint Veronica certainly stands high in the rank of saints, but she shed little glory on washerwomen.

If one now looks to early Christian legend for themes which might be utilized by painters for the glorification of the common people, one comes upon only two: the Annunciation to the Shepherds together with their Adoration of the Infant Jesus, and Saint Joseph as Carpenter. I have not been able to find early illustrations of the latter theme, which one might imagine to be the more important. In fact, Saint Joseph shared the patronage of carpenters and builders with a number of other and lesser saints: Blaise, Julian the Hospitaler, Mattias, Wolfgang, even Anne and Colette, so that there was no compelling reason to accentuate his calling as something noble. He was, moreover, reduced in rank during the Middle Ages as the Blessed Virgin was elevated. His role in the Mysteries is often comic. Réau, who goes into some detail about his iconographical fate, quotes a stanza by Eustache Deschamps which pretty well shows how low his fortunes fell at one time:

> En Egypte s'en est allé,
> Tout lassé, et troussé
> D'une cotte et d'un baril.
> Vieil, usé,
> C'est Joseph le rassoté.[7]

It was apparently not until the fifteenth century that Joseph began to take on greater stature. And the first church in Rome dedicated to him, S. Giuseppe dei Falegnani, was dated as late as 1522. Yet among the Apocrypha is an Arabic *History of Joseph*

---

7. Louis Réau, *Iconographie de l'Art Chrétien*, Vol. 3, p. 754. Réau adds: "Véritable 'tête de Turc,' c'est une cible pour les rimailleurs de Mystères qui le lardent de quolibets irrévérencieux, ainsi qu'un autre personnage de l'Evangile: Nicodème, le 'dépendeur' du Christ, dont le nom abrégé a donné nigaud." Cf. *The Cherry Tree* and the Coventry Play of *The Miraculous Birth* and *the Midwives*, in which Joseph expresses a certain petulance at his wife's desire to eat some cherries. The text can be easily found in A. L. Lloyd's *Folk Song in England*, p. 119.

the Carpenter, which might have been used to enhance the prestige not only of the *virgineus sponsus Virginis* ("the virgin spouse of the Virgin") but also of the carpenter's art which he was said to have practiced to the day of his death.[8] Quite the contrary took place, however. To the average man of the Middle Ages, fond of satire and indeed of buffoonery, an old man married to a girl of fourteen, a man moreover voluntarily chaste, a person who seemed to be simply a supernumerary in the great events in which he vaguely figured, was inevitably absurd. Carpenters continued to be of low rank in spite of Saint Joseph.

Of even less importance was the occupation of four of the Apostles. Though fishermen figured in fairly early art—scenes depicting the miraculous draught of fishes, for example—there was no special sanctity attached to fishing itself. The fish, there is no need to point out, was another matter. As a symbol of Christ it requires no more than passing mention. Much might have been made of it, but fishing as an occupation had no special status in art. Fishermen did get into poetry, if not into painting, in the piscatory eclogue; but I have spoken of this in an earlier essay. The odd feature of the piscatory eclogue is that, unlike the pastoral, it did not glorify its subjects. Sannazaro seems to have been the first to bring the genre to perfection, though scenes of piscatorial life had been introduced into literature much earlier. In Sannazaro lines from Vergil's eclogues were taken over bodily and modified only to the extent that the sea is not the land. But all this dates from the Italian Renaissance, not from the Middle Ages.[9]

8. See *The Apocryphal Gospels*, trans. B. Harris Cowper, p. 124.
9. See Henry Marion Hall, *Idylls of Fishermen: A History of the Literary Species*, pp. 45 ff. This study traces the fortunes of the genre through the eighteenth century and shows how a hard and painful occupation turned into a gentleman's sport. But whereas the Shepherd was always something pretty, the Fisherman became an English Gentleman, fond of the rural life and of the outdoors. The last of the "fisher idylls" treated by Dr. Hall is Thomas Scott's "The Anglers—Eight Dialogues in Verse." "The purpose of the

The one outstanding honorable peasant calling was that of the shepherd. Shepherds were in a special category. They figured largely in both Testaments, and their occupation furnished metaphors in terms of which ecclesiastical organization was built. The priest became a pastor; the faithful became a flock; the head of the Church was ordered to "feed My sheep"; Christ became the Lamb of God, an object of adoration *qui tollit peccata mundi*; and the Savior is represented from very early times as the Good Shepherd. In the Third Gospel the angels announce the Nativity to shepherds, and the shepherds present themselves before the manger to adore the Christ Child. Here they balance the Three Kings (literally Magi), thus showing, I imagine, that both the high and the low join in acknowledging Him. And if the Kings bring Him precious gifts, the Shepherds give Him a lamb, a crook, or a pipe. They are sometimes accompanied by a rustic musician playing bagpipe or flute. The *Annonce aux Pastoureaux* is illustrated at least as early as the tenth century (Codex Egberti in Trier) and the Adoration as early as the twelfth (Capital of St. Pierre de Chauvigny).[10]

There is no longer any way of discovering just why shepherds, instead of sowers and reapers, or carpenters and weavers, were introduced into religious legend, but it may derive from their importance in the lives of the early Israelites. They were undoubtedly a pastoral and nomadic people; the three Patriarchs were shepherds. And when the Old Testament came to be thought of

pieces," he says (p. 184) ". . . is to emulate the glories of [*The Compleat Angler*]." I have not attempted to read these idylls myself, but judging from the sections quoted by Dr. Hall, they would be the delight of lovers or didactic poetry.

10. Réau (*Iconographie de l'Art Chrétien*, Vol. 2, p. 234) in discussing this says: "L'art byzantin n'avait illustré que le thème de l'Annonce aux Bergers et jusqu'au XVe siècle, sauf de très rares exceptions, l'Occident s'en tiendra là. C'est seulement à partir de cette époque qu'on voit les trois pâtres s'agenouiller devant l'Enfant pour lui offrir l'agneau, la houlette et le flageolet et que les artistes créent, sur le modèle de l'Adoration des Mages, le thème de l'Adoration des Bergers."

as a prefiguration of the New, the eminence of the shepherds may have been raised in man's imagination to the status of a sacred symbol. As early as Philo Judaeus, the Bible had become allegory as well as history. To interpret every text in the Book as symbolic was customary almost from the very beginning of Christian exegesis. Yet in Mark, which is usually considered to be the earliest of the Gospels, nothing whatsoever is made of the Shepherds. Maybe—though this is purely conjectural—the same sentiment that inspired the pastorals and idylls of Theocritus and Vergil had some influence in setting the Goatherd and Shepherd as a type apart from all other working men. There is nothing especially beautiful in herding sheep, nothing outstandingly noble. But one who has never engaged in this task might romanticize it: its loneliness, the outdoor life under benevolent skies, sleeping in the open air, playing a rustic flute on a flowered hillside, all this may have played a part in forming the pastoral spirit among the Pagans. At any rate, by the first century that spirit was well formed. The hardships of a shepherd's life never entered the picture. It is likely that all writers of pastorals were urban dwellers whose boredom with bricks, stones, cement, crowds, markets, tumult, and quarreling drove them to imagine a more congenial regimen. Neither Theocritus nor Vergil was a rustic, nor were any of the authors of Renaissance or modern pastorals. It would be absurd to read into Spenser's Shepherd's Calendar, with its sharp criticism of contemporary issues and movements, any idealization of its author's pastoral life.[11]

This bucolic tradition then was simply a literary convention

11. In another Shepherd's Calender, Le Grant Kalendrier et Compost des Bergiers, first published in Troyes some time during the fifteenth or possibly early sixteenth century, and reprinted in Paris in 1924, there is a chapter De l'Honneur et estat de bergerie which lists all the Ancients, Kings of Israel, and prophets—and adds even Cyrus—who were shepherds. By the time this was issued sheep herding was no longer the main occupation of the People, and it is clear from the matter printed in the Almanach that it was addressed to the general reader, whoever he might be.

by the time the Gospels were written. It indicates, as I have suggested, no appreciation of the real shepherd's life. The medieval shepherd was a serf and could escape ignominy only by entering the religious community. That, however, did not prevent anyone higher in the social scale from thinking of pastors, the Lamb of God, and accompanying tropes without reference to their literal significance. In short, as far as Romanesque and Gothic art were concerned, the Shepherd was a religious symbol and had neither social nor political reference. Similar remarks are in order about scenes of working life, such as the labors of the months. Cultivating the vine, sowing wheat, cutting the meadows, harvesting, threshing, the vintage, such themes are found in Books of Hours and in part woven into tapestries.[12] The monthly labors are accompanied by monthly sports on some calendars and we are shown ladies and gentlemen hawking or busy at other diversions according to the season. The work, as was to be expected, is being done by peasants; the sports and other pleasures are carried on by the upper classes. But then, even in our humanitarian day, it would hardly be likely to find a farmer depicted yachting or a mechanic playing polo, though both might in reality enjoy such pleasures.

The pastoral theme was continued well down into the eighteenth century in painting as well as in literature. Just as nostalgia for the simple life was expressed in poems that were in no sense serious attempts to depict the lives of shepherds and shepherdesses, so it was expressed in songs—the *bergerettes*—and in paintings. These paintings were imaginary and charming fantasies and it would be foolish to take them seriously. But Le Hameau, the little farm in the Parc de Versailles, was also a fantasy, and Marie-Antoinette when she played at being a dairy-maid had no thought, one supposes, that she was doing anything other than play. What is interesting about all this is not the desire to simplify life and to seek some way of escaping from courtly ceremonial and what

12. See Emile Mâle, *L'Art religieux du XIIIe siècle*, pp. 85 ff. See especially Figures 32–41. But what I say is common knowledge.

has been called the artificiality of the drawing room, but rather the image by which the happier time was symbolized. Why the pastoral life, rather than the life of the small shopkeeper or artisan? Why not turn, as William Morris did, to an imaginary Middle Ages with its goldsmiths, scribes, illuminators, and other craftsmen? The momentum of custom may explain this better than any other one cause, but it is questionable whether it is a sufficient cause. For the fact remains that the custom itself goes back at least to Theocritus and Vergil, and, though the latter may have copied the former, the former attracted him or he would not have copied. Men have always liked masquerades, it is true, but they could have masqueraded as something other than shepherds.[13]

The People in Painting

It may now be well to mention a few works of visual art in which the People are represented. One of the most interesting is the twelfth century *Hortus deliciarum* of Herrad von Landsberg, Abbess of Hohenberg (d. 1195).[14] Here one has drawings of the reaper, the miller, and the plowman; scenes of builders mixing mortar, squaring stones, carrying mortar, together with military

13. Honesty compels me to point out that sometimes the occupation of shepherd is not admirable. One finds that the noble Griseldis is reduced to the level of shepherdess, as Nicollete, though in reality a princess, is also a shepherdess. One also finds, as Grace Frank points out in *The Medieval French Drama*, that shepherds sometimes provide comic relief, as in *L'Incarnation et la Nativité*. And in *Le Jeu de Robin et de Marion* "the speech of these peasants is coarse." Robin is a peasant *miles gloriosus*, and the play is both bergerie and pastourelle (*Medieval French Drama*, p. 233). Mrs. Frank also says that "in the religious and serious plays . . . realistic shepherds abound" (p. 234, n. 1). There are similar conflicts in any period: we have romances of chivalry and *Don Quixote*; the novels of Ouida contemporary with those of Henry James.

14. See Dahlmann-Waitz, *Quellenkunde*, no. 5723. The original illustrations of the *Hortus* were burned, but facsimiles have been reproduced in a modern publication in Strasbourg (1901?) by the Editions Oberlin.

events, scenes of princely life, religious rites such as baptism, incidents from the New Testament, and allegories such as the Wheel of Fortune. In fifteenth-century tapestries one comes upon woodcutters (Musée des Arts Décoratifs) and hunters of boar and bear (Victoria and Albert Museum); in the sixteenth century there are vintage scenes (Cluny), shepherds (Gobelins), and typical pastoral in the *Noble Pastoral* of the Louvre.[15] Scenes of rural life in tapestries are of no more nor less significance than those found in the miniatures of the Limbourgs. They serve a decorative and picturesque purpose and make no comment on joy or sorrow. In Etienne Chevalier's *Book of Hours* there is a Nativity in which three unidealized shepherds are pictured accompanied by a bagpiper.[16] One may guess, but no more, that the artist's realism was deliberate, but whether it had any religious significance is impossible to guess. Was it, for instance, a reminder to Chevalier of the vanity of worldly goods, of the universality of the Redemption, of the necessity of all ranks to adore the incarnate God? The significance of visual symbols frequently, indeed always, varies with the eye that sees them. But one thing is certain. No one took the shepherds of the pastorals seriously; most people until the time of Bruegel thought of real peasants as clumsy louts.[17]

Bruegel (ca. 1525–68?)

With Bruegel, however, there comes a definite change in point of view. I obviously cannot take up each painter who followed the

15. These are all reproduced in Roger-Armand Weigert, *French Tapestry*, trans. Donald and Monique King.
16. Easily found in Paul Wescher, *Jean Fouquet and His Time*, Plate 3.
17. Cf., for example, Dürer's drawing *Three Peasants*, Jorg Brey's *October*, and Urs Graf's *Peasant Couple Dancing*, nos. 26, 119, and 145, respectively, in the catalogue of the exhibition *Dürer and His Time*, circulated by the Smithsonian Institution, 1965–66. These drawings date from the sixteenth century. See also in Franzepp Würtembeyer's *Mannerism*, "Portraits of People of the Lower Classes," p. 212.

sixteenth century and shall therefore be satisfied with those who seem to me to be influential in changing the public's mind. Though no one is sure of the exact date of Bruegel's birth, no one denies that he lived during the second half of the sixteenth century, at least a generation later than Dürer. He did most of his work in Flanders during a period which was one of the unhappiest in the history of that troubled region. The Netherlands revolted against Philip II of Spain in 1568, and by 1581 it had declared the independence of the seven provinces under William the Silent. The Duke of Alba, who had been sent there with a large force, having as his mission the extermination of heresy, proceeded to check religious deviation by the most extreme measures. But he also exasperated the orthodox by imposing on the country the Spanish *alcabala*, a tax of five per cent on all sales. The inhabitants had meanwhile fitted out a fleet and defeated the fleet of their Spanish rulers which gave them mastery of North Holland. By 1573 the Duke of Alba was recalled, but he left behind him the memory of 18,000 persons whom, he boasted, he had executed. Anyone who has read Motley's *Rise of the Dutch Republic* will recall scenes of invasion, of devastation, of the capture of cities, of treachery and revenge, which haunt one for years, the siege of Saint Quentin being one of the most terrible. This is the background against which Bruegel's work must be viewed. The nightmares of Bosch and his school are a prelude to Bruegel's paintings, which are a sadder but calmer commentary on the state of his mutilated country. The conflict was not merely between two nations, but between religious creeds and practices as well. This brought it down to the level of a civil war.

At the same time, this period saw the activity of men like Stevenius, Mercator, and Ortellius; it was then that Janssen either invented or developed the compound microscope; a time when Orlando di Lasso, Philippe de Monte, Cipriano de Rore, were composing. Hence alongside of the destructive forces men were able to exert constructive forces, and science and the arts seemed capable of resisting anarchy. When one remembers that this was the time of Titian, Veronese, and Tintoretto; of Palestrina, the two Gabrielli, and Peri; and finally, for there is no need to overload our text, of Shakespeare and Marlowe, one is amazed at such a collection of geniuses. When one adds the names of the great scientists to those already listed, one has the feeling that warfare, devastation, bigotry, and tyranny are powerless to crush the creative spirit. Who knows what might have been accomplished if peace and harmony had prevailed?

The late Ludwig Münz maintains that one of the most potent influences on Bruegel was the geographer Ortellius. In his book *Bruegel, the Drawings*,[18] Münz points out (p. 11) that though the widely sweeping landscape had been initiated by Patinier in the twenties, a new development had occurred by 1550, which led to the production of panoramas for manuals of geography. To make such drawings obviously requires keen powers of observation and a willingness to accept subservience to Nature as a guiding principle. The age was one in which in Italy as well as in the Low Countries the natural sciences were as lively as the arts. The relations between the two fields are worth a moment's consideration. For the new science prided itself on controlled observation rather than on deduction, and the new movement in painting also prided itself on what was later to be called naturalism. One no longer knows in what direction the influence ran, whether it was from the arts to the sciences or the reverse. In any event, if an artist sets out to paint what he thinks is Nature, then he will have to choose what is natural in some sense of that word and reject what is unnatural. It is a commonplace that the tradition had been to identify the natural with that least modified by man. Thus the rural landscape is supposed to be more natural than the urban; forests more natural than such gardens as those of the Villa d'Este or Versailles; and peasants more natural than members of the upper classes. Instinct or intuition is more natural than learning

18. Trans. Luke Hermann (Greenwich, Conn., 1961).

or reason, and, if one can find persons in whom instinct predominates, then one can devote one's powers of expression and interpretation to them.

However weak this may be as an argument, it is one that has been maintained throughout Western history. It is a form of cultural primitivism which has sometimes lauded the child and the animal as exemplars. Bruegel illustrates this point of view to perfection and both his landscapes and his larger compositions point to the country and the peasant as subjects of greatest interest to the artist. Others must have shared his interest, for peasants are not usually patrons of artists. In view of this it is understandable that Bruegel should have used the local rural scene in his religious paintings. To represent the Slaughter of the Innocents as taking place in a Flemish village might seem ignorance on the part of a sixteenth-century painter. But to emphasize the contemporaneity of biblical events is also to insist on their timelessness. If we crucify Christ every day, so we sacrifice Isaac daily, stone the Woman taken in Adultery, and try to comfort Job. And in this case Herod's soldiers are dressed like Spaniards and there undoubtedly lies behind the painting an attack on the Occupation.[19] Even in such paintings as *The Fall of Icarus, The Battle of Lent and Carnival, The Triumph of Death,* or *The Carrying of the Cross,* the setting is Flanders. Any one of these, except *The Road to Calvary,* could have been painted with characters taken from the upper classes, but just as Caravaggio was to transform his biblical personages into Italian peasants or paupers, so Bruegel seems to have thought of all themes as best embodied in peasant life. *The Proverbs* or even *The Children's Games* could have been just as well represented with little royal personages. Any theme of general human applicability must be illustrated with some kind of human beings. Social class will be apparent in any

19. This painting now exists only in a copy in the Kunsthistorisches Museum in Vienna. See Charles de Tolnay, *Pierre Bruegel l'Ancien,* Vol. 2, Plate 89.

choice, for the costumes and backgrounds will inevitably be associated with social status. One hardly needs the title *Mrs. Siddons as the Tragic Muse* to know that the woman depicted was not a washerwoman. That Bruegel chose peasants with all their grossness of figure and heaviness of posture would seem to mean only that he chose them as most truly representative of universal human problems.

Such a statement can be only speculative, for the one way we have of knowing what an artist intends is by looking at his pictures. Nor have we any certain way of knowing what his public saw in his pictures. Moreover, in Bruegel's case we have no diaries or magazine interviews or treatises on painting or manifestos associated with him. All we know is what we see; and what we see in, for example, his drawings of the Vices or Virtues is their rural background with windmills, waterwheels, sheds, cottages, little streams, country animals, wine barrels, and so on. But there are significant exceptions. The personages who incarnate Avarice, Lust, Pride, Envy, and Sloth are ladies clothed not as peasants but as members of the leisure class. Lust is of course naked, and I should prefer not to judge to what class a naked woman belongs, though this one is not the bulky peasant type who appear in the other drawings. She is slim, with elegant rippling hair. It is hard to believe that this was not intentional on Bruegel's part. No proof was needed then nor is any needed now that a peasant could be just as avaricious, lustful, envious, and so on, as a duke. Amusingly enough, when it was a question of doing a series on the Virtues, he turned from realism to allegory: Charity being a woman with a pelican on her head, Hope a woman standing on an anchor in a stormy sea with a sickle in one hand and a spade in the other. Just as a blindfolded female with sword and scales stands for Justice, so the other virtues are depicted in greater or less fidelity to traditional iconography. Whereas the Vices could be embodied in the upper classes, the Virtues are embodied only in emblems. But in both series of drawings, the settings are rural and the victims of the Vices are peasants or fantastic beasts. Thus just as the Fall of Icarus takes place in Flanders, so does all morality. The general is in this way made concrete. The universal is shrunken to a narrowly localized event or group of events. Hence the outcome is definition by demonstration. It comes about as if one were to say, "You ask what was the Slaughter of the Innocents, the Conversion of St. Paul, Prudence, Avarice? This is it." Such a procedure, which rejects all but the most recent elements of tradition, is a rejection of abstract ethics. Bruegel's paintings resemble the *exempla* used in sermons. But they are relatively new *exempla*. "Relatively," because a good bit of the material in them comes from Bosch.

Münz points out (*Bruegel, the Drawings*, p. 29) how Bruegel stands in what he calls the tradition of the Stoic humanists, who

. . . strove to see the world clearly, without for one moment letting their criticism be limited by a dogma. They all see with open eyes that there is no paradise on earth, and recognize the world for what it is, with all its mistakes. They see the world as something that man must experience, they feel that a deeper faith must exist, which stands higher than any of the dogmatically entrenched Christian creeds. Thus in order not to lose their inner freedom in these times of religious and social conflict, they find a means of escape in stoicism, in which, as one can not always have good luck, misfortune is often almost sought after as something good, as a means of purification; and the value of the individual ego in retirement from the world is recognized.

This clearly is an interpretation of the total work of Bruegel, not derived from anything left by way of verbal testimony. That what Münz calls stoic humanism was a widely held philosophy of life in the sixteenth century need not be disputed. But when it is a question of finding a philosophy in a picture or series of pictures, the problem is not one of verbal but of visual exegesis. The ancient stoic did indeed withdraw from involvement in the world's work. He wished to free himself from all external bonds. But it would be difficult to find such detachment in Bruegel. In fact, what would reliable evidence of detachment be? Possibly devoting one's talents to still lifes, if one were talking of the nineteenth century, and abstractions, if one were talking of our own times. A painter like Delaroche was more detached from the social problems of the nineteenth century than Courbet was, and yet, if one were to judge from subject matter alone, knowing nothing of the ideals of each, one would be hard put to it to decide. Of course, neither was a stoic in any usual sense of that word. As soon as a painter expresses his ideas and emotions via recognizable visual objects, accurately drawn from nature, he is forced to look upon the world as if its visual aspect "mattered." He cannot maintain that the look of things is of no importance. To take that point of view is to become a painter so "abstract" that one will put upon one's canvas only geometric shapes, lines, masses, and possibly indications of movement. But that was not Bruegel's way. How could he possibly have drawn the pictures which are called *Lern-und Lesebilder* if he was at all detached from human concerns? Of what importance is it to a stoic whether others learn anything whatsoever so long as he himself has learned?

The relevance of Bruegel's paintings to our theme comes out in the figures he chose to teach his lessons. He was not teaching the heavy peasants he drew, but those who were exerting power over them. And yet there have been those who thought this man was a comic painter.[20] It seems strange to think that anyone could see humor in *The Blind Leading the Blind* in Naples, in *The Magpie on the Gibbet* in Darmstadt, or in the two paintings of the hay and the corn harvest, or, so far as my personal judgment goes, in *The Wedding Breakfast*. Far from being comic, such

---

20. For instance, the author of the eleven-line article on Bruegel in the *Encyclopaedia Britannica* (11th ed.). As a sample of his judgment, I quote the following: "The subjects of his pictures are chiefly humorous figures like those of D. Teniers; and if he wants the delicate touch and silvery clearness of that master, he has abundant spirit and comic power." A fairer estimate of the same date is that of Karl Woermann in his *Geschichte der Kunst aller Zeiten und Völker* (Vol. 3, pp. 172–73), where Bruegel is said to be in many respects the great artist of the Low Countries in the sixteenth century.

paintings now seem to be bathed in an atmosphere of melancholy suffused with charity. What they seemed to Bruegel's contemporaries is another story.[21] But the fact that some critics saw them as comic shows how recent is our sympathy for the poor and exploited. If I am right in thinking of Bruegel's peasants as surrogates for the People as a whole, then the painter felt nothing but pity for us all.

Caravaggio (1573–1610)

What Bruegel was doing in the Low Countries was being done in an entirely different manner in Italy by Michelangelo Caravaggio. The manner was different, since Caravaggio's People were not simple peasants. They were card-sharpers, fortune tellers, inhabitants of the Roman slums, in short, urban low life for the most part. And because he reduced the social status of saints and martyrs, his works, even when commissioned by cardinals to be installed as altar pieces, were sometimes refused. Several of his paintings caused trouble. The constant charge was that his figures were indecorous. Saint Matthew and the Angel was rejected "on the ground that it was not proper, nor like a saint, sitting there with his legs crossed, and his feet rudely exposed to the public." [22] As Hinks puts it, Caravaggio's "pictures were not edifying: far from inviting us to aspire towards the Communion of

21. Since writing this essay I have read Otto Kurz's article, "Four Tapestries after Hieronymus Bosch," in the Journal of the Warburg and Courtauld Institutes, Vol. 30 (1967). See especially pp. 156–57.

22. Cardinal Bellori, as quoted in Roger Hinks, Michelangelo Merisi da Caravaggio (p. 102). For Bellori's ideas on what a painting should be, the most easily procured source in English is Elizabeth Gilmore Holt, Literary Sources of Art History (pp. 320 ff.). But Walter Friedländer in his Caravaggio Studies has shown—at least to my satisfaction—that "the democratization of saints like Matthew on the part of Lombard artists probably was rooted in a general religious disposition to return to the supposed simplicity of the early Christian apostles." So also in regard to the dirty feet of the kneeling peasants in the Madonna di Loreto, Friedländer points out that this

Saints, he brought the Saints down to our everyday life, and showed us the Magdalene as a common girl drying her hair, St. Matthew as a little workman surprised to find himself writing beautiful Hebrew letters in a large empty book, and the Blessed Virgin as a victim of an accident in Trastevere" (p. 87). One might argue whether or not this practice is edifying. Friedländer has pointed out the similarity between this and the teaching of Saint Philip Neri who was a contemporary of the painter. And as for the realistic detail of the paintings, that was precisely in line with what Saint Ignatius Loyola had preached in his *Spiritual Exercises*.

It is indubitable that Caravaggio was fascinated by horror. He painted at least three canvases in which men are decapitated— a Judith, a Salome, and a David and Goliath, one sacrifice of Isaac, and a Medusa, all of which are about as repulsive as he could make them. And what is more interesting, psychologically speaking, the heads of Holofernes and of Goliath, and perhaps of John the Baptist as well, are said to be self-portraits. If this is true, then it looks as if he had also seen himself as a horrified witness of the martyrdom of Saint Matthew as well as of the crucifixion of Saint Peter, for the same head appears in them all. It is also possible that his head was in the lost painting of the *Betrayal*, as Judas, for the same features are in the four of them. The question of why he should have so despised himself can no longer be answered. But a censorious critic might point to his numerous paintings of naked boys, as well as to his scandalous career as tavern brawler, duelist, ruffian, and murderer. Certainly a critic like Bellori would maintain that the man had reason not to be self-satisfied. But today, in spite of his unsavory character —indeed perhaps because of it—he has become more sympathetic.

had been anticipated in Antonio Campi's *Nativity* in San Paolo (1580). Plates 51–53 in his volume show that Flemish painters before Caravaggio had painted "loose company," money changers, drunkards, lecherous old men, and whores.

For in our time the man who rejects society, who is a rebel against law and custom, is admired for his independent spirit; and the pederast is no longer driven to suicide. Because of our greater tolerance, we are not blinded to the beauty of Caravaggio's paintings or to what he has to say of himself.

For we too can ask the question he appears to have asked: What would these scenes look like if they happened today? This, we have assumed, was also Bruegel's question. There are dozens of Renaissance paintings of the themes Caravaggio was called upon to illustrate. But in no other *Judith and Holofernes*, for example, does Judith clutch her victim by the back hair, tug his head to one side, and slice well into it, while her aged companion, a wrinkled crone holding the bag in which the severed head is to be carried, looks on as any contemporary Roman hag might have looked on. If the call to Saint Matthew is witnessed by the same boys who were painted in *The Card Sharpers* and *La Zingara*, that is probably because Caravaggio thought them to be the type which would have frequented publicans. In fact, one of them seems to be a witness to the martyrdom of the saint, though well in the background. Again, the figures with old clothes and soiled feet who kneel before the Virgin in the *Madonna of Loretto* certainly add to the pathos of the scene, just as the complete nakedness of the young Jesus in the *Madonna dei Palafrenieri* strengthens the impact of what is depicted. One of those ingeniously suspended *cache-sexes* which were in vogue at the time might have protected the decency of the Son of God, but it would also have been absurd. It is to be expected that in a time of unbridled lubricity purity of thought must be preserved at all costs.

When one meditates over the paintings of the Italian Renaissance, showing the patriarchs and martyrs, the saints and prophets, richly clothed, wearing jeweled crowns, of immaculate grooming, and of beautiful corporeal appearance, one wonders what was going on in the minds of the painters. Were they simply painting beautiful pictures or illustrating the Bible and the Golden

Legend? If the former, there is no question of their success. If the latter, then the word "illustrate" must be interpreted etymologically. But whatever their motivation, artists of the next generation seemed to have suffered a change of heart. For not only Caravaggio, but before him both Tintoretto and Bassano, brought the supernatural into Nature. I refer, as one possible cause of this, to the innovations in natural science. In an article published in 1938, the late Professor John Tull Baker spoke of "naturalistic explanation" as the belief that "what happens around us can . . . be made clear to us in terms found within these happenings. It is not necessary for us to look beyond." [23] But to look for naturalistic explanations of what are inherently supernatural events is to reject, whether one knows it or not, the intervention of God in human history. The very heart of both Judaism and Christianity is anti-historical. To give a naturalistic account of the Creation, the Sacrifice of Isaac, the Giving of the Law, the Incarnation, Vicarious Atonement, the Virgin Birth, the miracles, the Resurrection, assuming this to be possible, is to be rational, no doubt, but also to be neither Jew nor Christian. But there is another side to the question. As I suggested in writing of Bruegel, such dogmas reflect the timelessness of moral and theological principles. To a man like Caravaggio, as to any thoughtful person, sacrifice, martyrdom, repentance, are as much of today as of biblical times. Each has a double location: in a historical series and in an ideological pattern. The Crucifixion may be both a historical event and also a symbol of every man's denial of God. That the only way to express the latter is to say it "in the language of the People" might be disputed, but that the People participate in religious history should not be disputed. In both literature and painting they have usually been relegated to the background. They might adore the Infant Jesus as shepherds, but they were also the Roman

23. In *Courbet and the Naturalistic Movement*, ed. George Boas, p. 36. My friend, Dr. E. H. Gombrich, also reminds me that the influence of Savonarola should not be underestimated.

soldiers who tortured Christ on the road to Calvary. Whatever happened, as it was given to us in art, happened only to the Best People. In England at the time of Caravaggio's activity, the greatest dramatic poets were staging scenes more horrible, if possible, than any depicted by Caravaggio. The murder of the Duchess of Malfi and of Desdemona are more of a nightmare than anything in the "indecorous" pictures of Caravaggio. But Webster and Shakespeare kept such events in a nobler milieu.

Hinks points out that just as the Reformers translated the Bible into the vernacular, so Caravaggio "transposed the personages of sacred legend into the terms of ordinary experience" (p. 88). This is true enough. But it might be added that this rips the veil of mystery off sacred legend. When this is done, what happens to awe and reverence? For purposes of religious discipline it may be better to keep the arcana veiled. If, after all, the death of the Blessed Virgin is simply the death of anyone's wife or daughter, would it not be more prudent to substitute for death the magic of a corporeal assumption?

In spite of this apparent "leveling" of the most exalted human experience, something approaching the beatific vision, there was a tradition in Christianity dating back to the thirteenth century at least, which would justify at a minimum an attenuated naturalism. I refer to the Franciscan doctrine that the first step on the road to God is the sight of His handiwork in the beauty of Nature.[24] This appeared in a primitive form in the writings of Saint Francis of Assisi, and later it became the center of natural theology. One of the most famous examples of this is in Montaigne's *Apology for Raimond Sebonde*. But up to this point, Nature referred to extra-human nature. Mankind had always been thought of as something added to the natural order. The natural order had been created for the use of man; he was therefore no integral part of it. One could fit him into it with rural folk, on the ground that they are more natural than urban dwellers, and then go on to

24. In St. Bonaventura's *Itinerarium mentis in Deum*.

including all men among animate beings, beings like beasts and vegetables. At this point the usual distinctions between higher and lower orders are eliminated. A cat may then look at a king and the king may count himself lucky if a cat pays any attention to him whatsoever.

Louis Le Nain (1593–1648)

Louis Le Nain fits into the pattern we are sketching at this point. But to interpret his work is mainly a lyrical enterprise. For whereas Bruegel stands in a tradition that is well known and painted amid scenes of devastation which are reflected in his work, Le Nain stands apart, as far as anyone knows, from all political and social turmoil and, except for one or two paintings of religious themes, does not seem to take sides in the battles that were dividing Christendom. One of three brothers, all of whom were painters, his work was not distinguished from that of his associates until 1929 when Paul Jamot was able to identify the canvases which were his.[25] He was thus, to all intents and purposes, neglected by art historians until our own century, and though several of his paintings were in important collections, those collections were not open to the public.[26] All three brothers were known and were members of the Académie royale des Beaux-Arts, but

25. In Les Le Nain. Jamot had as early as 1922 published "Etudes sur les frères Le Nain" in the Gazette des Beaux-Arts. In 1862 Champfleury had written about the brothers in Les Peintres de la Réalité sous Louis XIV, les frères Le Nain, on which Sainte-Beuve had commented in his essay on Champfleury in Nouveaux Lundis, Vol. 4. But the individual works of the three brothers had not been differentiated.

26. La Forge was in the collection of the Duc de Choiseul, then in that of the Prince de Conti, and finally in that of Louis XVI. The Visite à la Grand'mère was bought by the Baron de Crozat in 1772 for Catherine II of Russia. Other paintings had been commissioned by and hung in churches. See the catalogue of the 1934 Le Nain exhibition at the Petit Palais drawn up by Mlle Germaine Batnaud. But the history of the greater number of the paintings is still obscure.

since Louis died on May 23, 1648, and had entered the Academy on March 1 of the same year, he did not have much influence as an academician. The fact is that as the *Roi Soleil* rose to greater and greater effulgence, naturalistic painting sank below the horizon. Now when one looks at the dates of Le Nain's birth and death and reflects that, though he was born in Laon, he did his work in Paris, those canvases of his which represent peasant life seem more and more puzzling. His younger contemporaries, Adrian van Ostade (1610–87) and Brouwer (1608–40), and his older contemporary, David Teniers (1582–1649), were all given to painting peasants, but their peasants were the rollicking, drinking, dancing peasants who were later to form the opening choruses of comic operas. Le Nain's peasants have a noticeable dignity and sobriety. They are seated in groups, often looking straight out of the canvas as if the spectator had surprised them at their simple meals or during a brief moment of rest. They are the peasants of whom La Bruyère was to write, "They spare other men the toil of sowing, plowing, and reaping in order to live, and they thus do not deserve to lack the bread which they have grown." [27] In short, Louis Le Nain's People are neither the peasants of Bruegel nor the urban ruffians of Caravaggio. The former have taken on symbolic meaning and the latter, paradoxically enough, have become saints and martyrs. Le Nain's peasants are simply themselves and carry no allegorical charge. They are a challenge to the spectator who can view them as he would view a part of the natural landscape, a group of trees or rocks. And it may well be this that gives them the dignity which their admirers have seen in them. They are, it should be observed, always at a standstill. Even in *La Forge*,

---

27. "Ils épargnent aux autres hommes la peine de semer, de labourer et de recueillir pour vivre, et méritent ainsi de ne pas manquer de ce pain qu'ils ont semé." *Les Caractères*, ed. Gaston Cayrou, pp. 428–29. Cf. Paul Jamot, *La Peinture en France*, p. 33: "Les paysans de Louis Le Nain tiennent souvent un verre où miroite le sombre rougeur du vin. Mais dans ces intérieurs rustiques, chez ces hommes dont les vêtements sont grossiers et rapiécés, que de gravité, que de dignité paisible, que de distinction naturelle!"

the smith has dropped his tools. All action has ceased, has been frozen at a given moment. They thus become an invitation to look and meditate, not to laugh or to paste a moral sentiment upon a spectacle. Small wonder that Félibien found Le Nain's style *peu noble*. Félibien was no more capable than Sir Josuah Reynolds of appreciating that kind of nobility that requires no applied ornament to label it as such. Le Nain was, as far as I have been able to discover, the first painter to see beneath the rags and squalor what has sententiously been called the dignity of man.

Paul Jamot[28] has objected to an interpretation of these paintings which is close to that given in this essay—that "the work of the Le Nain brothers is a protest against the harsh treatment of the landlord and the poverty of the peasant." [29] If that were the case, he says, who would be there to hear the protest? The peasants had neither the money to buy paintings nor any interest in them. The *bourgeoisie* was satisfied with things as they were, and the nobility was far from indulging in that form of liberalism which was later to wreck their society.[30]

I doubt very much that such paintings were a protest in any literal sense. I see no way of injecting into the minds of painters whose biographies are almost entirely obscure any intentions whatsoever. But it can hardly be denied, and certainly is not denied by Jamot, that Louis Le Nain's peasants have a kind of inherent nobility and that they are neither ridiculed nor prettified. Jamot himself admits in that part of his book given over to Louis Le Nain (p. 32) that he was a man animated with a new spirit

28. In *Les Le Nain*, p. 112.
29. "L'Oeuvre des Le Nain proteste contre la dureté du seigneur et la misère du paysan."
30. "Auprès de qui un peintre pouvait-il en espérer du succès? Les paysans qu'il est supposé défendre n'avaient ni écus ni regards pour la peinture, la bourgeoisie était satisfaite et la noblesse était loin encore de ce dilettantisme libéral qui, un siècle et demi plus tard, applaudissait aux entreprises des démolisseurs de la société établie et prenait tant de plaisir à être battu qu'il fournissait lui-même les verges."

which nothing foretold either in the works of his brothers or in that of his time and country.[31] It is precisely in Le Nain's sober presentation of his peasants that this new spirit consists, a spirit that is found neither in the paintings of his Flemish and Dutch contemporaries nor in the poets of this period.

The early seventeenth century saw other painters who were interested in the poorer classes. Velázquez (1599–1660) and Murillo (1618–82), with the former's *Forge of Vulcan*, to take but one example, may have kept alive the notion that the People were of some aesthetic interest if of no other. So with Murillo's numerous paintings of street urchins. There was neither social satire nor moral comment in these canvases, and indeed Murillo's youngsters seem happy enough, soliciting neither pity nor relief. They will grow up to resemble Lazarillo and Sancho Panza. For more acid comment on society one must turn to Jacques Callot (1592–1635), whose prints of the miseries of war were not to be equaled until Goya published his *Desastros*. The period was one in which war was a horrible actuality. The Wars of Religion in France had no sooner subsided than the Thirty Years War began. Its generalized slaughter and devastation carried the religious disputes into the political arena, and while the generals earned medals, the People reaped death. Few centuries have witnessed more of human callousness, for along with the cruelty, deceit, and large-scale mendacity were magnificence and unrivalled splendor. It is to the unending credit of artists like Louis Le Nain and Callot that they saw the rot beneath the surface. And yet their patrons were princes and dukes, the very men most responsible for the evils portrayed. One wonders whether these patrons ever looked at the works of art they paid for.

The eighteenth century was one in which the People figure in amusing scenes on the *piazze* of Venice, in the streets of Paris,

31. "Un homme animé d'un esprit nouveau que rien n'annoncait, ni dans les productions de ses propres frères ni dans celles de son temps et de son pays."

the taverns of London, and at the races, in the rough and tumble life below the strata of the salons. Such paintings are seldom serious, though they conceal serious implications. The sketches of Giovanni Domenico Tiepolo are charming and so are the oils of Longhi, but they are hardly a direct comment on life, as the moralities of Hogarth are. One has to wait for the nineteenth century before another Bruegel or Le Nain appears. Such an artist was Daumier.

Daumier (1808–79)

It is a falsification of historical causation to assign credit for popular movements to any one man, but as far as the nineteenth century is concerned, major credit must be given to Daumier for making the People, at least in France, sympathetic. Though his lithographs and paintings did not resemble the world of those artists whom we have been writing about, they were similar to them in the dignity with which they depicted the poor. Daumier was surely one of the important cultural forces of his time. He probably did more than any other artist in France—I am not speaking of poets or novelists—of Hugo or Lamartine—to change men's minds. With an uncanny insight into those hidden powers that control society, he was able to ridicule ideas whose destruction was essential if a new social order was ever to be built. As examples one can take his caricatures of lawyers, of the classical drama, of neoclassical art, of the Bourgeois Monarchy, and of the triumphant middle class in general. One might almost say that he had discovered the middle class with all its timidity, ignorance, self-satisfaction. He seemed to understand that in a constitutional monarchy the bar would take the place of the army. Whereas under the Ancien Régime it was the soldier who was in control and whose virtues were the ideal, under a regime where statute took the place of a personal monarch, the man who could untangle the intricacies of the law would rule society. The chicanery and double-dealing of the sophist would become bit by bit the ideals of the citizen. There are about seventy caricatures of lawyers in Daumier's work, and not one seeks to portray the profession of the law as other than contemptible. He saw the citizen as the victim of both the legalist and the King-General. And whereas the revolution of 1789 had dethroned Louis XVI, a pitiful warrior, those of the 18th Brumaire, of 1814, of 1830, and of 1848 had replaced one evil with another. In Daumier's eyes logical manipulation had replaced bravery. Men who live in countries with written constitutions know with what legerdemain the intention of their authors can be transformed to "fit the times."

The association of neoclassicism with the *Ancien Régime* was only a historical accident.[32] But its association with the Terror and with Napoleon was as logical as any rationalization of art can be. For the men of the Terror seemed to believe that they were reviving the Roman Republic, just as Napoleon thought he was reviving the Empire. All that was revived or could be revived were the trappings of the periods in question, classical names for children (Achille, Jules, Emile), and for institutions (the Senate, for instance), costume, subject matter for pictures and poems, details of furniture and architectural design. The Arc de Triomphe de l'Etoile did not turn Napoleon into Augustus Caesar, nor did election to the Senate turn its members into Roman patricians. David's nudes did not look like Romans, and Canova's *Napoleon* was merely ridiculous and not Augustan at all.[33] It was Daumier who saw the absurdity of such stupid pretense and who understood that making French eighteenth-century academicism grotesque was to direct taste toward more reasonable themes. Hence in his series on the public swimming baths he showed what the naked human body actually looked like.

He was at his most cruel in his caricatures of Louis-Philippe

32. For a quite different interpretation of this aspect of Daumier, see the authoritative book by Raymond Escholier on this artist, p. 8.
33. I refer to the nude Napoleon in the courtyard of the Brera in Milan.

and the statesmen of the Bourgeois Monarchy. Some of these lithographs are mere caricatures in the same way that *graffiti* on walls might be, with oversized heads and wizened legs. But in such drawings as the *Rue Transnonain* he achieved a kind of pathos which was on a level with tragedy. He took his position as artist seriously; he was not working to delight or to titillate the taste of the dilettanti but to comment on life in the society of which he was a spectator. And his comment was far from being uniformly hostile. His drawings of the Third-Class Carriages, of the Third-Class Waiting Room, of the Washerwomen, the Beggars, the Street Singers, were direct and very simple presentations of the endurance of poverty and of hard work. While he tried to destroy respect for the regime under which he was living, he also tried to arouse some pity for those who bore the burdens of that regime. His lithographs were not programs. They fixed moments in history about which the spectator could make up his own mind. Though the legends under his caricatures are often very funny, they could be dispensed with in the majority of cases and the residue would be just as funny. Of course it is true that his sheer artistic talent was very rare. Only a Hokusai, perhaps a Picasso, could vivify a line as he could. His sense of bodily expression was unequaled. The gestures of his figures ceased being those of the academic manuals which in the long run were choreographic attitudes ritualized over the years. His were instantaneous glimpses of emotion caught alive and preserved in all their vitality. But such skill is based upon an uncanny power of observation. Daumier, we are told by those who have studied his career in detail, never drew from a model after his student days, but always relied on his visual memory. To observe so closely and remember so faithfully demands a sympathy, indeed an affection, for what one is looking at. And it is fair to say that though his caricatures of officials are acid, those of *Les Parisiens aux Champs*, or the Five Senses, are softened with good humor. The irony of his career is that it terminated in blindness. But he had given to the French public about four thousand drawings that were the creation of a social class low in prestige but essential to a democratic government. He did not foresee its future and, in fact, one of his most moving drawings is of *The Future* lying muffled and blindfolded.

Daumier, like Caravaggio, was interested above all in urban people. But when one is discussing French painting of the nineteenth century, one cannot forget that by 1850 the French had for sixty years been living through social turmoil, occurring mainly in their cities, turmoil which embraced the hopes and catastrophes of the Revolution, the Terror, the Consulate, the Empire, the First Restoration, the Hundred Days, the second reign of Louis XVIII and the advent of Charles X, the July Revolution of 1830, the Bourgeois Monarchy, and the Revolution of 1848. Out of all this emerged nothing more satisfactory than the Second Empire and the fake Renaissance of Louis Napoleon. The arts of those sixty years show the effects of such a situation, for at one extreme there were those who sought a refuge from reality in neoclassicism and the *beau idéal*, and at the other, the various types of romantic fantasy, some men fleeing into the Middle Ages, some idolizing Shakespeare, Ossian, Byron, Scott. It was a period when each kind of art issued a manifesto which it hoped would justify its existence in the eyes of the public. Thus a tradition was initiated which has lasted into our own times when it is taken for granted that no picture or poem can be understood until explained. The painter and the poet became alienated from the rest of society, demanded privileges which mankind in general refused to grant, and, as if to glory in their alienation, adopted vestimentary eccentricities to mark them off from the bourgeoisie.

Jean-François Millet (1814–75)

The penetrating vision of Daumier saw through these follies and, as I have tried to suggest, enabled men to see for themselves the regnant absurdities. His contemporary, the French Jean-François Millet, was born a peasant, was miserable in town, and found what happiness he had—and it was not very much—only in the country. In his case we are lucky to have available a number of letters which he wrote to his intimate friend, Alfred Sensier, and which were published in part in 1881.[34] These letters give us an idea of his purpose in art as well as an insight into his character. Hence what follows is not wholly conjecture.

The paintings and some of the drawings of Millet are so well known that they need no description. Though harshly criticized as ugly and brutal, indeed as repulsive, by the art critics of the time, paintings like *The Gleaners, The Angelus, The Sower, The Man with the Hoe*, became so popular, especially in the United States, that reproductions of them hung in numerous homes and school rooms and were used on calendars. Only Guido Reni's *Aurora*, the *Sistine Madonna*, and Holman Hunt's *Light of the World* have captured the taste of the general public to the same extent.

Millet's are not pretty or sentimental pictures, but stark representations of a painful existence lived at the mercy of wind, cold, excessive heat, drought—an existence that is an uninterrupted battle. When Millet painted a shepherdess, she had no resemblance to the shepherdesses of the pastorals or of the *bergerettes;* she was a peasant, coarsely dressed and shod in sabots, as much an integral part of the landscape as the earth on which she stood. When he painted a farmhand resting on his mattock, the man was gaunt, exhausted, sweating, and as unlike the reapers of Léopold Robert as Jeanne d'Arc was unlike Agnès Sorel. "Millet's shepherd," says Sensier, "is not a vulgar peasant cast in the image of the ploughman or the field hand. He is enigmatic, a mysterious being living alone. His sole companions are his dog and his flock. . . . In the winter he wanders over the damp earth seeking the slightest signs of vegetation. Come spring, he brings aid to the

34. Alfred Sensier, *La Vie et l'Oeuvre de J.-F. Millet*, edited by Paul Mantz.

ewes at lambing time. He is their caretaker. He is the flock's friend, the friend and the doctor. He watches the stars, he probes the skies, and he predicts the weather." [35] Whether one agrees with all that Sensier says or not, Millet's peasants were unlike those of tradition. As Paul Brandt, whose studies of the working class in art are authoritative, puts it,

> What had the peasant become if we disregard the ever-typical pictures of the months [the labors of the months], until his appearance in art? A drunken, quarrelsome clown among the Dutch, a perfumed Céladon among the French—never taken seriously as his dignity and sacred position gave him the right, struggling with clods for his beloved bread, at work. Even with the struggle of the fourth estate against the third, which had secured the lion's share of the booty of the Revolution, the artists had seen this only as an occasion to depict him as a "suffering agrarian" and to arouse pity for him—they did not seek him in his work.[36]

This tradition of the clumsy lout as the typical peasant was, according to Brandt, entirely changed by Millet's *Winnower*. But realism of Millet's sort, unlike Courbet's, was based on no political doctrine whatsoever, though it seemed to some of his critics to be

35. "Le berger n'est pas un campagnard fait à l'image des laboureurs ou des autres travailleurs des champs; c'est un personnage énigmatique, un être mystérieux; il vit seul, il n'a pour compagne que son chien et son troupeau. . . . L'hiver, il va sur la terre encore humide à la découverte des moindres végétations. Au printemps, il aide les mères brebis dans la venue des agneaux. Il les soigne, il est le guide, l'ami, le médecin du troupeau. De plus, c'est un contemplateur; il examine les astres, il sonde les cieux et prédit le temps" (p. 167).
36. Paul Brandt, *Schaffende Arbeit und Bildende Kunst*, Vol. 2, p. 221. "Was wäre der Bauer, wenn wir von den immer noch üblichen typischen Monatsbildern absehen, bisher in der Kunst gewesen? Ein betrunkener, streitsüchtiger Rüpel bei den Holländern, ein salbenduftender—Seladon bei den Franzosen,—ernst hatte ihn in dem, was ihm seine Würde und seine geheiligte Stellung verleiht, im Ringen mit der Scholle ums liebe Brot, in seiner Arbeit, niemand genommen. Selbst die Kämpfe des vierten Standes gegen den dritten, der sich von der Beute der Revolution den Löwenteil gesichert hatte, waren für die Künstler nur ein Anlass geworden, ihn als 'notleidenden Agrarier' hinzustellen und Mitleid für ihn so wecken—bei seiner Arbeit hatten sie ihn nicht aufgesucht."

a visual expression of an undefined sort of socialism. Quite the contrary was true. Millet was too innocent or too ignorant to know what socialism was. He was a simple peasant himself, whose religious ideas were all gathered from the Vulgate and whose literary taste was formed by reading Vergil.[37] As for politics, he knew nothing of them. His moral standards were those of the Decalogue and he was totally uninterested in moral casuistry. In keeping with this one is not surprised to find him saying, "Boucher did not paint nudes, but rather little sluts without any clothes. His was not the lavish exhibition of Titian's women, proud of their beauty to the point of making a show of it, to the point of showing themselves in their nudity, so sure were they of their power." [38] Boucher's women, he thought, were "artificial," Titian's "natural," and that settled the matter. But when he came to ask himself what natural human life was, he answered in the words of Genesis 3:19: "In the sweat of thy brow shalt thou eat bread, till thou return unto the ground; for out of it wast thou taken: for dust thou art, and unto dust shalt thou return." Life to him was expiation for a primordial sin; and the most that one could hope for was calm and silence. [39]

37. He had been drilled in Latin as a boy by his parish priest, Father Jean Lebrisseaux. See Sensier, *La Vie et l'Oeuvre*, p. 26.

38. "Boucher ne faisait pas des femmes nues, mais des petites créatures deshabillées: ce n'était pas les plantureuses exhibitions de Titien, fières de leur beauté jusqu'à en faire parade, jusqu'à se montrer nues tant elles étaient sûres de leur puissance." *Ibid.*, p. 55.

39. See a letter to Sensier (*ibid.*, p. 157): "Work is my motto, for man is doomed to labor. 'Thou shalt live by the sweat of thy brow.'" ("Mon programme, c'est le travail, car tout homme est voué à la peine du corps. 'Tu vivras à la sueur de ton front.'") Again (*ibid.*, p. 130): "The human aspect is what interests me most in art, and if I were able to do what I wish, or at least attempt it, I would only carry out the result of impressions made upon me either by landscapes or figures. Never is it the gay aspect which I notice. I do not know where to find it and have never seen it. The happiest things I know are tranquility and silence." ("C'est le côté humain qui me touche le plus en art, et si je pouvais faire ce que je voudrais, ou tout au moins le tenter, je ne ferais rien qui ne fût le résultat d'une impression reçue par

The critics of his time would not or could not see things in this light. *Le Semeur*, they said (Sensier, p. 156), expressed a curse upon the condition of the rich, since the man was depicted casting his seeds toward the heavens in anger. There could be no other way to sow seeds by hand than to cast them upwards so that they could be widely scattered; and the anger in question was supplied by the critics; but to depict suffering humanity, even if the suffering was no more than inferred, was held to be a protest. Similarly the critics of Courbet saw him as a socialist even before he came under the influence of Proudhon.[40] As a matter of fact, Millet's peasants are far from being in a state of agony. *The Gleaners* and the couple in *The Angelus* are dignified and, if anything, resigned to their lot. They are symbols of pain only if one has already presupposed that to work is disagreeable. But since official art did presuppose that and wanted pictures, if they represented anything, to represent the pleasures of the leisure class, painters like Millet were doomed from the outset to be rejected as troublemakers. But the trouble the troublemakers make is to point to things which the arbiters of taste had rather not see. To see sawyers, woodcutters, charcoal burners, quarry workers, stone breakers, road menders, and the like would be disageeable only if one preferred not to admit one's dependence on the proletariat. The dependence is to be sure reciprocal, but the middle classes get greater returns for what they invest in labor than the laborers do for what they invest in production. This was the basis of the proposed reforms of St. Simon, Fourier, Proudhon, and to some extent of Marx. When an economist announces that labor is not a commodity or that property is theft, he is not noting any facts whatsoever. For labor has been bought and sold at prices

---

l'aspect de la nature soit en paysage, soit en figures. Ce n'est jamais le côté joyeux qui m'apparaît; je ne sais où il est, je ne l'ai jamais vu. Ce que je connais de plus gai, c'est le calme, le silence.")

40. See George Boas, "Courbet and his Critics," and Charles H. Sawyer, "Naturalism in America," in *Courbet and the Naturalistic Movement*, pp. 45 ff. and 110 ff., respectively.

fluctuating in the labor market just as wheat or cotton are bought and sold at fluctuating prices. And property is theft only if you assume, with Saint Ambrose, that God intended all things to be owned in common. But this assumption could hardly be substantiated. To confuse economic with moral ends is, like all confusion, misleading. The *laisser faire* school of economics guided the thought of early nineteenth-century economists, for it was based on what was supposed to be the scientific thesis of general determinism. Hence the correct attitude to take was at most to give a penny to the beggar at the risk (a) of pauperizing him and (b) of making a foolish, because futile, gesture. Peasants were peasants because there had to be all sorts of people in the human panorama. They either did not suffer, being less sensitive to privation than ladies and gentlemen, or, if they did suffer, that was also part of Nature's plan. Meredith's army of unalterable law was an appropriate symbol for this philosophy, though it was already obsolete by the time Meredith invented it. The only excuse for trying to ameliorate the lot of the peasant or laborer was that to do so was pleasant.

Millet's initiative was carried on by Van Gogh, a great admirer of his who frequently copied his works. Later, in the United States, one finds the same tendency to use the workman, the farmer, the beggar, in general the man who is down and out or simply poor, as a serious subject of painting in members of the Ashcan School. What serious intentions lay behind this and how much was just due to a desire for novelty or a new picturesqueness is a matter of argument. It is impossible to tell whether a painting of a man in rags is an expression of any social idea or simply a painting with ideological reference. Murillo's street urchins are similarly ambiguous. Was he trying to attract the attention of the rich to the poverty of their fellows or was he noting an element of visual interest that had not been emphasized before? The "meaning" of a pictorial subject is often supplied by the spectator. Though Millet disallowed any doctrine in his paintings, yet it is hard to disagree with Arnold Hauser when he says, "Millet paints the apotheosis of physical work and makes the peasant the hero of a new epic." [41] And he continues by saying, "It is unmistakably clear that the choice of motifs is here conditioned more by political than by artistic considerations." In the cases of Daumier and Courbet, who are combined by Hauser with Millet, there is little doubt. But in Millet's case the distinction between an artistic and a political motif is less clear. For it would never have occurred to Millet to paint something without social reference, even though he would not have been willing to phrase the reference in philosophic terms. In short, the fusion between subject matter or motif and artistry was complete. So in Van Gogh, we find from his letters that the very colors he used were chosen for their moral symbolism, not for their harmonious visual relationships. But that was part of his art. He was not merely making a beautiful pattern of colors and shapes but an ethical symbol embodied in colors. Few persons looking at Van Gogh's paintings think of this symbolism, but he thought of it, unless he was a greater hypocrite than one has any reason to believe.

As the nineteenth century moved on, a growing interest in popular life is noticeable, an interest that runs parallel to the development of naturalism (or realism) in the novel and on the stage. In the United States one has only to think of William Sidney Mount, Eastman Johnson, even Winslow Homer, to see this, of the Currier and Ives prints, of the Rogers groups. Later we come upon the Ashcan School. In Europe the names of the sculptor Meunier, of Käthe Kollwitz, of the young Picasso, come to mind, names that no longer stand for a special technique of drawing or painting, but for a warmer sympathy with the unfortunate, the exploited. Homely scenes, sometimes simple middle-class interiors (in Vuillard, for instance) take the place of elegance, splendor, mythology, or sensuality.

41. *The Social History of Art*, Vol. 2, p. 776.

This is perhaps more clearly seen in the United States than in Europe and more in the North than in the South. Northerners, in general, were not descended from landed proprietors and had few pretensions to be *grands seigneurs*. Their culture was a village culture, not a plantation culture, and the cobbler, the carpenter, the farmhand, the woodcutter, voted in townmeeting along with the squire and the minister. As the rural background receded and the city took its place in the lives of northern Americans, it was perhaps inevitable, or at least explicable, that a nostalgia for the farm should take over. Such a nostalgia today is obvious in the fad for Early American decoration, furniture, prints, and pewter, regardless of their intrinsic value. It is truistic to say that one cannot be nostalgic for what one has never experienced, but many a man has substituted dreams of grandeur for longing for his youth. The grandeur which the average American, if he comes from the North, seems to want is the grandeur of the man who has risen from the soil by his own efforts. The liberality of those men who have realized their dream checks one's tendency to attribute their careers exclusively to the love of possessions. It is more likely that they have been motivated by the desire to meet a challenge, to "succeed."

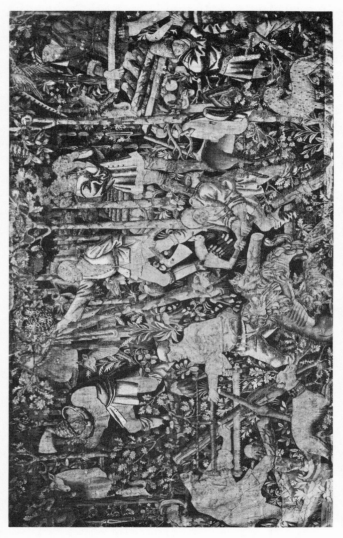

The Woodcutters. Tournai tapestry with the arms of Nicolas Rollin, Chancellor of the Ducs de Bourgogne. Courtesy of the Musée des Arts Décoratifs, Paris.

Urs Graf, *Peasant Couple Dancing.* Courtesy of the Staatliche Museen Kupferstichkabinett, Berlin.

Pieter Bruegel the Elder, *The Blind Leading the Blind*. Galleria Nazionale di Capodimonte, Naples. Photograph by Alinari–Art Reference Bureau.

Adriaen Brouwer, *Woman Making Pancakes.* Courtesy of the John G. Johnson Collection, Philadelphia.

Pieter Bruegel the Elder, *The Wedding Dance.* Courtesy of The Detroit Institute of Arts.

Michelangelo da Caravaggio, *The Madonna of Loretto.* Church of Sant'Agostino, Rome. Photograph by Alinari–Art Reference Bureau.

Louis Le Nain, *Peasant Meal*. Musée du Louvre,
Paris. Photograph by Archives Photographiques.

Louis Le Nain, *Peasant Family.* Musée du Louvre, Paris. Photograph by Archives Photographiques.

Jean-François Millet, *The Sower*. Courtesy of the Museum of Fine Arts, Boston, Shaw Collection.

Jean-François Millet, *The Man with the Hoe.* Crocker Collection, San Francisco. Photograph by Marburg–Art Reference Bureau.

Anonymous, *Equestrian Portrait of President William Henry Harrison*. Courtesy of The Baltimore Museum of Art.

Vincent van Gogh, *The Potato Eaters.* Courtesy of the Rijksmuseum Kröller-Müller, Otterloo, Holland.

André Bauchant, *Peasant Scene.* Courtesy of The Baltimore Museum of Art, Cone Collection.

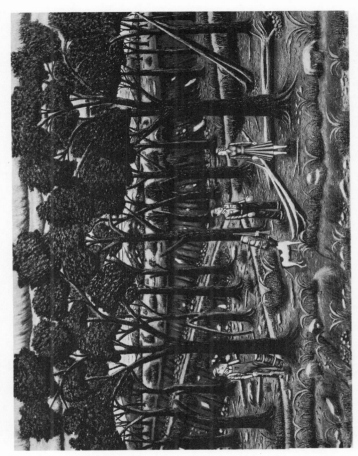

Patrick J. Sullivan, A-Hunting He Would Go. Courtesy of The Museum of Modern Art, New York.

THE PEOPLE AS ARTIST

Histories of art, like all histories, have to be selective. They cannot include everyone who ever held a brush or chisel in his hand and have, as a rule, excluded those artists who are called modern primitives, Sunday painters, self-taught artists, and popular masters. One reason for this may be that their works of art have a high degree of similarity. Another may be that by definition they are amateurs not professionals and have been recognized as of equal aesthetic interest only in recent years, that is, from about 1915. If they painted in the eighteenth century, their status is different and antiquarianism alone gives them a page or so in the standardized histories of painting. The same is true of the Italian painters of the early fourteenth century; they were first recognized as historically important, though aesthetically uninteresting. At a time when evolution in all fields of culture was accepted as a dogma, they were the germs of modern, that is, Renaissance and post-Renaissance art.

The case of the French and American self-taught painters is different. Anything American, as distinguished from European, was highly prized. Emerson's American Scholar was an American scholar, independent of the traditions of the Old World and contriving a new kind of learning. The truth is that no one has ever been entirely independent of anything. The problems that faced the American scholar were the same problems that had faced all scholars, and when a serious American university was founded in Baltimore in 1876, it took over the methods and problems of German universities. Similarly, the American painters of the eighteenth century followed the methods of the European painters, and two of them, Copley and West, returned to Europe

—England in this case—and adjusted with ease to the demands of the European world of art. The limners who hawked their skills from village to village carried canvases already decorated with handsome gowns upon which they fitted the heads of the sitters. The poses and the gowns were all in the tradition of the English portraitists; and when one comes to the landscape painters of the nineteenth century, Thomas Cole and Frederick E. Church follow the tradition of Claude, and the self-taught painters follow the tradition of Cole and Church.

It is doubtful that a person who had never seen a painting or a reproduction of a painting would ever develop the idea of making one. In the academies copying was recommended as an early step in instruction, and many an artist has spent fruitful hours in a museum copying the masters. A man like Manet may have been more assiduous in copying Velázquez and Goya than Monet was in copying anyone. But the way to become an artist was first of all to enter someone's studio, in which case one copied the master, and then to go to the Louvre or Uffizi and copy the better-known painters, the celebrities. The self-taught painters were not ignorant of other painters. If they had not seen originals, they had seen various types of reproductions. Almost any house in the United States had a lithograph or chromolithograph or steel engraving on its walls. If there was nothing better, there was a Currier and Ives print. So today the households which would be those of peasants in Europe hang at least a calendar-picture on their walls.

The vogue for the works of the autodidacts belongs to the history of taste rather than to the history of painting, though the distinction is artificial. It is artificial because the interaction between taste and works of art is reciprocal. What the critics praise or dispraise will determine to some extent what artists will paint, but critics obviously would have nothing to praise if artists were not there to turn over works of art for comment. Since we are dealing with the history of an idea, we are forced to turn to the reasons that critics have given for praising the works of the *maîtres populaires*. The main reason, to put it very briefly, is that such painters express the spirit of their people, or of The People. Now it is clearly much more difficult, if indeed possible, to imagine that the collective People could paint a picture than it is to imagine their writing a poem. A picture may be copied or imitated, but the original remains unchanged except insofar as chemical or physical deterioration have changed it or as our manner of looking at and interpreting visual objects shifts. Words, on the other hand, as they pass from mouth to ear to mouth again, leave no trace except on the memory of those who hear them. The best, then, that one could do in order to make pictures the product of the collective soul was to switch from the word "creation" to the word "expression." Whereas there could be no Folk-picture as there could be a Folk-song, there might be a picture which expressed the *Volksseele*, the collective soul, though it was painted by an individual artist.[1]

As in Herder, the idea of the People's art might sometimes mean art created for the People rather than by them. In 1860 Henry Ward Beecher made a speech in Philadelphia to the effect that until modern times all paintings had been made not for the People but for the nobility, the priesthood, or the government. It was the Puritan who rebelled against this custom. But as his speech is hard to find and contains most of the reasons which later appeared in praise of the self-taught painters, I give it in full.

> They [the Puritans] are charged with indifference to beauty, and wanton destruction of art. But what was the art which they beheld? Not harmonious lines and wealth of color. Art is a language. It came to them speaking all the abominable doctrines of oppression. The more beautiful, the more dangerous. It was a syren. Its beauty was a lure. Did not the Puritans tread in the very steps of the Primitive Christians? Was not Art, in the early day, but heathenism

1. An exception might be the "exquisite corpse" of the early Surrealists, but each part was drawn by an individual.

in its most potent and attractive form? The legend might be forgotten; the perilous mythology, let alone by one generation, would perish. But Art stood aloft, gleaming in the tempest, radiant from thousands of pictures, silently fascinating and poisoning the soul through its most potent faculty—the imagination! And when the early Christian turned away from art, it was not because it was beautiful, but wicked. It embalmed corruption—it enshrined lies! And the Puritan lived in an age when the priest, the aristocrat, the king, had long and long been served by art. I doubt if in Cromwell's day there was a picture on the globe that had in it anything for the common people! The world's victories had all been king's victories—warrior's victories. Art was busy crowning monarchs, robing priests, or giving to the passions a garment of light in which to walk forth for mischief! Will any man point me to the picture of the wonderful number that Raphael painted or designed that had in it a sympathy for the common people? They are all hierarchic or monarchic. But Michael Angelo was at heart a Republican. He loved the people's liberty, and hated oppression. Yet what single work records these sentiments? The gentle Correggio filled Church, Convent, and Cathedral dome with wondrous riches of graceful forms. But common life found no sign of love, no help, no champion in him. The Venetian school, illustrious and marvelous, has left in art few signs of liberty, and yet where might we expect some recognition of the simple dignity of human life, if not in this Republic? But her rich men had artists, her priests had artists, her common people had none. In all the Italian schools not a picture had ever probably been painted that carried a welcome to the common people. To be sure, there were angels endless, and Madonnas and Holy Families without number; there were monkish liquids turned into color. Then there were heathen divinities enough to bring back the court of Olympia and put Jupiter again in place of Jehovah. But in this immense fertility—in this prodigious wealth of pictures, statues, canvas, and fresco—I know of nothing that served the common people. In Art, as in Literature, Government, Government, GOVERNMENT was all, and people nothing! [Applause.] I know not that the Romantic World of Art ever produced a democratic picture.

The Germanic World, from whence came all our personal and popular liberties, had a strong development in their schools of Art of popular subjects. Their pictures teem with natural objects, with birds and cattle, with husbandry, with personals, and their life with domestic scenes and interiors.

What had an Englishman, if a commoner, to thank art for? Not a painter in England, from 1500 to 1700, until the days of Hogarth, ever expressed an idea which was not inspired by the aristocracy or the monarchy!

While, then, the Puritan stood forth under the inspiration of a new life in the State—the life of the common people—he had no thanks to render to art in the past. On the contrary, it stood against him. It plead for the oppressor. It deified the hierarchy, it clothed vice in radiant glory. It left homely industry, sterling integrity and democratic ethics without a line or hue. Every cathedral was a door to Rome. Every carved statue beckoned the superstitious soul to some pernicious error. Every altar piece was a golden lie. Every window suborned the sun, and sent his rays to bear on a painted lie or a legendary superstition. With few exceptions, at that time of little influence, the art of all the world was the minion of monarchy, the servant of corrupted religion or the mistress of lust. It had brought nothing to the common people and much to their oppressors. [Applause.] When the Puritan broke the altar, it was not the carving that he hated, but the *idea carved*. It was not the window that he shattered, but the lie which it held in its gorgeous blazonries. [Applause.] [2]

If I read this speech correctly, Beecher was thinking exclusively of subject matter when he spoke of art for the common people. I base this opinion on his contrast between the genre painting of the Germanic peoples and the religious and mythological paintings of the Italians. But when it is a question of art made by, rather than for, the People, one finds very few genre paintings. The People as a whole prefer, as the ballads and folksongs show, intimations of the life of the Great, illustrations to the Bible, portraits of national heroes, or the customary emotional pictures like Sacred Hearts and Marterln. It was the traditionalistic painters, Eastman Johnson, for instance, or Mount, who painted scenes of everyday life, not the autodidacts. The miraculous, the strange, the heroic have always appealed to popular taste, not the explicable, the ordinary, the commonplace.

In fact, the assumption that art should be made for that section of the population known as the People may not have been an original thought in 1860; it was relatively novel outside of the United States. The tradition within the States had been

2. From the *New York Times*, Saturday, December 22, 1860, p. 8.

twofold: there had always been professional painters who did portraits of the rich in the European manner,[3] and there had also been journeyman itinerant limners. Until recent times such portraits were thought of as merely quaint. Very few critics would have taken them seriously. But they were incontestably paintings made for the People, in the sense of the working class, both rural and urban, and were made usually, though not always, by persons who were self-taught. The "self-taught artist" would be a much more accurate label for such painters than adjectives like "primitive" or "folk." In fact, when the Museum of Art of the Carnegie Institute of Pittsburgh held an exhibition of the works of Hicks, Kane, and Pippin in 1966, they called it "Three Self-taught Pennsylvania Artists," and made no attempt in the catalogue to identify their spirit with that of America, Pennsylvania, Pittsburgh, or the working class. They treated the artists as self-representative, as individuals, each with his own program.

The tradition in the United States has been that the self-made man or the self-taught man is to be admired. The reason for admiration is probably simple enough: it is harder to learn something by oneself than through instruction. But in the case of the self-taught artist, it was not his dogged Spartan persistence that brought him renown, but certain aesthetic achievements that were absent in the work of the professionals. Such traits were "lost," in the sense that they were supposed to be inherent in primitive art, both in the art of men who lived in caves millennia ago and in that of some men living in modern times, like the Polynesians and the African Negroes, who were assumed to remain in what was qualitatively a culture less developed than our own. Thus we find Holger Cahill praising the folk-artist for his simplicity, lack of affectation, and childlike quality (p. 5); Leon Anthony Arkus praising his three Pennsylvanians for their "poetical

---

3. Holger Cahill says that there were 400 known portraits of people born in the colonies before 1701. See *American Folk Art: The Art of the Common Man in America, 1750–1900*, p. 4.

sensitivity," "vitality," and the creation of "a personal imagery
rather than a stereotyped academic rendering"; Jean Lipman
speaking of the folk-artists as having a "unique freedom from
realism," of the "purely aesthetic qualities of abstract design" to
be seen in their paintings;[4] and Raymond Escholier in a book by
Maximilien Gauthier, who calls the French equivalent of our
self-taught painters *les maîtres populaires de la réalité*, saying that
their outstanding quality is a combination of naïveté, sincerity,
and candor (*franchise*). Gauthier himself, in his introduction to
this brochure, writes a paragraph which is an essential document
in the history of this idea.

> True artists [he says], are so endowed that they remain a bit
> pastoral in spite of all the knowledge that can be acquired, of all
> the vain conquests of intelligence. If this were not so, art would
> have died out long ago. . . . The pastoral spirit, which can neither
> be learned nor taught, is the antithesis of the academic spirit. Hav-
> ing no knowledge or rather . . . believing that it has none, it is
> its task to question everything. And questioning everything amounts
> to opposing to fixed theory the moving reality, to open to liberated
> art all life's possibilities.[5]

No one would be likely to deny the charm of such works of
art. They do indeed have the charm of children's drawings, but
by no stretch of the imagination can they be likened to the
highly skillful work of the African or Oceanic sculptor or the men

4. Arkus, Catalogue for "Three Self-Taught Pennsylvania Artists (Carnegie
Institute, 1966); Lipman, *American Primitive Painting*, p. 5.
5. "Les vrais artistes sont ainsi doués, pour demeurer un peu bergers en
dépit de tout le savoir qui s'acquiert, de toutes les vaines conquêtes de l'intelligence. Simon, il y a longtemps que l'art serait mort . . . L'esprit berger, qui
ne s'apprend ni s'enseigne, est le contraire de l'esprit académique. Ne sachant
rien, ou plutôt . . . croyant ne rien savoir, il est celui qui remet tout en
question. Et remettre tout en question, c'est, spontanément, opposer à la
théorie fixée le réel en mouvement, ouvrir à l'art libéré toutes les possibilités
de la vie." From the catalogue of *Les Maîtres Populaires de la Réalité*, an
exhibition held in Paris in 1937. The echoes of Bergsonian epistemology are
clear. The shepherd is again used as a symbol of the innocent childlike rustic
who has no "intelligence" but plenty of "insight."

who made the rock-paintings of North Africa or the cave paintings in the Valley of the Vézère. This latter group of works of art, when they are "realistic," as the paintings of animals in the caves, are as lifelike and unschematic as the animals of Pisanello's sketchbooks or those of Dürer. In fact, that is what excited the admiration of the critics when they were discovered. It seemed almost impossible that savages living twenty-five thousand years ago, without benefit of an art school, could achieve such extraordinary truth to life. It should also be pointed out in a parenthesis that more of their admirers had seen them in reproductions than *in situ* where they are overlapped with numerous other drawings and give no evidence of any general composition. But even when they are seen in the caves themselves, they take on a character of vitality which is startling.

The African and Oceanic sculpture seldom goes in for that kind of realism, but it has a sense of form which gives it a perfect unity. This is not true of it all, and sometimes feathers, hair, shells, and other extraneous bits and pieces are stuck to the figures for reasons which the Occidental usually does not understand. But no one with an eye for sculptural form would deny the excellence of a Benin head or Gabon mask. We cannot see these things as members of the tribe would see them; we cannot read into them whatever symbolism may be there, for even if we are ethnologists, we have to bring an outsider's knowledge to their interpretation. They are not, so to speak, written in our mother tongue. But that in itself liberates us, so that we can, if we wish, look at them as if they were plastic objects and nothing more.

It is precisely this which transforms American folk-art in the eyes of some critics. Mrs. Lipman is frank enough to say that the American primitive is to be praised because his "technical liabilities made way for a compensating emphasis on pure design" (p. 6). But the African sculptor had no technical liabilities. His control of his carving tool was masterly, his surfaces subtly rhythmical, the passage from plane to plane anything but obvious.

Simply running one's palm over the surface of an imitation will show the great difference between the old original and the modern fake made for the tourist trade. If the sculptor had a sense of pure design which his work was an attempt to gratify, he was working within a tradition and not in rebellion to it. His knowledge, pace Gauthier, was precisely the kind that is acquired. The general similarity of style that is to be seen in the arts of the various sections of Africa is seen also in the sculptures of India, China, and Japan, not to mention Egypt and Greece. Yet within each of these regions there are also variation and individuality enough. And though, to take an obvious example, a seated Buddha from Grandhara must have the same pose as one from China, there is no difficulty in telling which is which. In certain places, in Siam, for instance, the purpose of the sculptor has been to reproduce as faithfully as possible an earlier work; what is now known as self-expression was not highly esteemed there.[6] In fact, self-expression is a modern value, dating roughly from the end of the eighteenth century and emphasized during the Romantic period.[7] But if one's aim is to speak for the Tribe as a whole, or for the Race or Nation or Folk, then clearly individual differences must be eliminated. If, to take another interpretation of "Folk-art," it is art for the People, rather than by them, then again to please a whole group will necessitate the erasing of any artist's idosyncrasies. For the history of taste is enough to show that even today outstanding peculiarities are not tolerated by the general public. The most popular painter in the United States at the time of writing is Andrew Wyeth and he is the most faithful to traditional realism. And when a very individualistic stylist, like Van Gogh, is admired, his paintings become "Van Goghs."

6. See A. B. Griswold, *The Arts of Thailand*, handbook to an exhibition held in 1960–61–62, pp. 32 ff.

7. Not that the Romantics were willing to let anyone express himself in any way he pleased. They had their own rules of deportment and, though the latitude they offered was extensive, Classicists were excluded from the school, however sincere.

The individuality of the artist takes the place of the individuality of the work of art.

When then Mr. Cahill writes of "the art of the Common Man," as "an honest and straightforward expression of the spirit of the people" (p. 3), the question of just what is meant by the phrase cannot be avoided as pedantry. He lists in the same paragraph the trades of the artists with whom he is concerned as those of house painter, sign painter, portrait limner, carpenter, cabinetmaker, shipwright, woodcarver, stonecutter, metalworker, blacksmith, and the like, and such men could in some lexicons be identified with the People. But when one looks at their works of art, one finds, as was true of the popular poets also, that they all aspire to the condition of the traditional painters. The portraits, though stiff and angular and without depth, are nevertheless posed in the traditional manner with drapery or landscape in the background, emblems of the sitter's occupation nearby, and, in the case of the limners, settings all prepared beforehand regardless of the subject's status in life. The still lifes are baskets of fruit or vases of flowers, in some instances painted from stencils. The landscapes differ from traditional landscapes only in the absence of perspective—the space is flat. It would be thought Philistine of me to insist that it is the inadequacy of their technical skill that gives the pictures a genuine charm, a charm which almost all critics have called childlike. When Mr. Cahill says that such works are "folk art because [they are] the expression of the common people, made by them and intended for their use and enjoyment" (p. 6), it is of course historically true that these works were made by the common people, if common people are the artisan class, but it must also be remembered that when they could get good reproductions of the famous academic pictures they bought them too. Engravings of Raphael and Rubens were advertised and presumably found a market, just as in the latter part of the nineteenth century Millet's *Angelus* or Holman Hunt's *Light of the World* were purchased by the thousands.[8] Schools at the time when the folk-artist was painting may not have acquired the habit of hanging carbon prints of famous pictures on the class-room walls, and it is also possible that the artists in question had never seen any reproductions of more well-known artists' works. But they certainly derived from somewhere or other not only the idea that pictures existed and that they could make them as well as anyone else but also the idea of what a "real" painting looked like.

M. René Huyghe is quoted by Gauthier as saying that "Popular painting" comes from the "most lasting depths of human nature" (*du fond le plus permanent de l'homme*). This in a sense might be true of all painting whatsoever, for it is as permanent a trait of human nature to copy the work of others as to project one's dreams and fantasies out of oneself. In fact the latter has to be learned as much as the former, for what is in dreams is usually what one has learned to suppress. I may be doing an injustice to M. Huyghe in insisting on a clearer statement of his meaning, but the pathos of the permanent is so compelling that one accepts the word and presumably its denotation without stopping to think of whether the permanent is really any better than the temporary. Any general trait is often thought to be better than one which is limited to an individual or a small group, and yet there is also the point of view that the rare is more valuable than the common. How to reconcile these attitudes, while maintaining that value is correlated with frequency, is be-

8. Though this is no place for autobiography, the house in which I was born and grew up was decorated by an enormous steel engraving of *The Death of Webster at Marshfield*, another of Landseer's *The Stag at Bay*, another reproduction, probably lithographic, of something by Thomas Cole which remains vague in my memory, a colored lithograph of a still life of fruits, flowers, wine, glassware, napery, and there is perhaps no need to say, an enlarged photograph of Burne-Jones's *Angels Descending a Staircase* and *The Pot of Basil* by John Alexander. There was not to the best of my knowledge a single original oil in the house.

yond the power of logic. They show as a matter of fact that the assignment of value should be based on a decision that has nothing to do with frequency. One cannot insist that the universal is better than the particular and also insist that crime or some other evil predominates in a society. It would seem more reasonable to define good and evil by some other means. Or perhaps it would be better to follow an alternative course and maintain their indefinability. Even if we adopt a simple hedonism and identify good with pleasure and evil with pain, we have at least something detectable as the token of our sins and virtues.

If, then, we hold that the untutored mind is inherently wiser than the trained mind we should also hold that its pronouncements are likely to be sounder than those of scholars, including psychologists, sociologists, and aestheticians. But "likely" is a weasel word, and when one uses it one can always squirm out of the cases which on their face refute our assumptions, by saying (1) that they are rare exceptions or (2) that "in a deeper sense" they are "really" corroborative rather than the antithesis. Thus if we come upon a picture made by a self-taught artist that we find downright ugly or trivial or otherwise inadequate, we can say that it is not really representative of his work, or that it is the exception which proves the rule (overlooking what "proves" means in this context), or that the artist has surreptitiously been influenced by some academic critic to modify his normal style. If Hicks, Kane, and Pippin do express the common soul of the American People, then whatever they make ought logically to be a form of such expression. The American People's soul may slip from rectitude to an occasional misdemeanor. But if we praise an artist for expressing his nation's soul, then we have to stick to our guns and praise whatever he turns out. In cold fact, that is about what happened in the case of Grand'ma Moses. The rules of academic drawing were abandoned as rules, once she was praised. Her colors were flat and their combination lacked any degree of subtlety. There were no criteria for appraising her work other than the feelings of the men and women who saw them. They apparently pleased some people and, though one can theoretically explain the causes for pleasure, one cannot give reasons for it. I mean by this the banality that one may admire something because it exhibits certain principles of design, correct perspective, invention, imagination, and still not find any pleasure in looking at it. Contrariwise, one may find great pleasure in the enjoyment of a work of art without "understanding" anything about it—an experience common in the enjoyment of music. But it is as relevant to our appreciation of people as it is to our appreciation of works of art. The Lord Chesterfield may be perfectly correct, like Castiglione's Courtier, and yet we may find him unpleasant—indeed, the "yet" might well be replaced by "therefore." But though the paintings of the self-taught artist may be incorrect according to all the rules we can find in the history of criticism, the combination of all the forms of incorrection may strike us pleasantly. We do not like the picture in spite of its crudities but because in combination they hit us with the delightful feeling that we have when we listen to a child's account of something that happened in school.

A cultural primitivist is almost honor bound to admire the naïve. Usually he will substitute "childlike" for the adjective "naïve." If he admires the childlike, it is usually because he is repelled by the mature, though this is not inevitable. In the United States this state of mind is almost endemic. We have taken the word "cute" as an all-purpose term of praise and anything cute will have overtones of the childlike. I find in the examples of the use of this word as given in the dictionary that little girls are cute and so are little bungalows. I imagine that the doll's house would be a perfect example of cute architecture. There is, however, something here which on the surface is paradoxical. We are a large nation and should like to use our power only for noble ends. We are also a rich nation and willing to spend our money on schemes that would be unimaginable if they did not exist. No other population has so many murderers, and once a particularly revolting crime is reported in the newspapers, we find that it is immediately emulated here and there. If a man in Chicago strangles nine student nurses, a man in Austin feels that he must shoot five beauty-parlor attendants. When asked why, his answer is that he wants his name to be remembered. All this is childlike. And so is the desire to build up great collections of shaving mugs, matchboxes, and other inherently worthless objects. To admire such activity on the ground that it is naïve and that its aims are cute is cultural primitivism with a vengeance. But it should be remembered that there was once a belief, shared by few but voiced by none other than Clement of Alexandria, that Adam before the Fall skipped about the Garden like a child.[9] This, it must be recognized, was far from being the usual patristic point of view. The child as such is held to be innocent, free from all personal sin, though incapable of some sins for obvious reasons. Yet even the newborn baby is tainted by inherited guilt, and it is not an inherent part of the Christian tradition to hold up the child as anything more than pure. A blind man can see no evil and a man whose arms are amputated cannot play a false note on the violin.

The combination of brutality and naïveté which is so characteristic of us may indicate a form of compensation, the one balancing the other. As to that I am unable to judge. But those who believe in the homogeneity of ages, times, cultures, and so on, might wonder whether it would not be expected that a great nation whose triumphs are of a technological order would be more likely to admire technically excellent works of art than those that are admittedly inadequate technically. When Mr. Cahill speaks of the paintings of his artisans and craftsmen as expressing the spirit of a people in an honest and straightforward way, the most he can mean is that the People consists of artisans

9. See my *Essays on Primitivism* . . . *in the Middle Ages*, p. 24.

and craftsmen. But one cannot help asking how pictures without academic perspective, combined with flat areas of color, are any more expressive of artisans and craftsmen than the pictures of Trumbull or Copley. Craftsmen and artisans are bound to measure accurately if nothing more. Copley and Trumbull conform more closely to the rules of the academy than Kane and Hicks do, but surely they are as honest and straightforward. It is, to be sure, questionable how relevant such ethical terms are to painting. Is Raphael more or less honest and straightforward than Ingres? Rubens in some of his paintings might be said not to be straightforward, in the sense that much is allegorical, but that would not imply dishonesty. Spenser's *Faerie Queene* and the *Pilgrim's Progress* are not straightforward, for that matter, nor can any allegory exist without tortuous evasions of fact. The probability is that these so-called primitives did the best they could to approximate the manner and subject matter of the traditional masters and failed to come very close to their goal. But their failure turned out to be a success in an unanticipated way: they produced pictures that were aesthetically charming while technically childlike. That is what Jean Lipman means when she speaks of their technical liabilities making for compensating emphasis on pure design.

Among these self-taught painters is one who is strangely alien to the prevailing mode. I refer to Patrick J. Sullivan. In the exhibition "Masters of Popular Painting" he showed three oils. The titles alone, with his comments on them, are enough to set him apart from his fellow autodidacts. One called "Man's Procrastinating Pastime" shows three more or less human beings in a wood, with the head of a corpse barely showing above his grave. One of the anthropoids has large splay feet which seem to grow out of his knees. Sullivan said of this painting, "The forest is the subconscious mind of man. . . . The man kneeling over the grave symbolizes mankind in general burying the evil part of himself deep in the mind. The tall formidable-looking man is urging mankind to get out into the conscious or clear light of day. . . .

The grotesque creature to the right is my personification of sin. . . . Man is always procrastinating, trying to hide his evil self instead of courageously showing his good part and performing good deeds—hence the title." [10] The second of these paintings is called "An Historical Event." The canvas is divided in two by a flag pole on which is flying a flag which has a heart pierced by an arrow and a bow and arrow. To the observer's left is a flowerlike structure in which is a full face portrait of the then Mrs. Simpson. To the observer's right is a lion with a man's head, bearing a royal crown on its back. In front of it stands Cupid pointing off the frame. In Sullivan's own words, "The picture as a whole is the heart of the ex-king . . ." from which "Cupid is ordering the lion with its empire representation." Actually this is a throwback to Renaissance allegorical painting. The technique is crude from the academic point of view, but the details, had they been depicted in the correct manner, would have thrown the picture into line with those canvases which the members of the Warburg Institute have done so much to interpret. There is nothing here expressive of the spirit of America or of any other country. What is expressed is a set of ideas originating in the artist himself. Not even the most articulate of the self-taught painters, except possibly Hicks, expressed himself in this way, and all Hicks did was to repeat over and over again the biblical idea of the Peaceable Kingdom, as given in Isaiah. That was hardly specially American.[11] That the lion will lie down with the lamb needs no

10. Quoted from the catalogue *Masters of Popular Painting* (New York, 1938), p. 137.

11. A collection of animals similar to that of Hicks will be found in the drinking trough of Giovanni da Bologna in the gardens of the Villa Medici, Città di Castello, dating from the middle of the sixteenth century. Cf. also Velvet Bruegel's *La Terre* in the Louvre. As a matter of fact Julius S. Held has shown in "Edward Hicks and the Tradition" (*Art Quarterly*, 1951, Vol. 14) how Hicks copied "the typical products" of the "academic tradition." As he puts it; "His method of work seems to have been the assembling, in ever new variations, of certain stock figures and poses. He repeated them over and over again and it seems probable that he took them from a pattern book

exegesis here, unless, and this is highly improbable, the former stands for Judah and the latter for Christendom. With the exception of Mr. Sullivan, then, most popular paintings have been extremely literal. They may not have represented what their makers saw—though that was the aim—but the outcome was a flat landscape, a stiff portrait, a bowl of flowers or fruits, all derivative from the tradition. It may be that the divergence from the academic in the painting of academic subjects is precisely the detail that gives some of these pictures their attraction.

The illustrations to this chapter will do more than argument to show how unoriginal most autodidacts have been. Their works have frequently been compared to those of children.[12] And the child usually has an idea that there is a standardized way of representing people and things. "How do you draw a man?" "How do you make a tree?" Such questions arise from the assumption that there is one correct way of drawing a man or a tree. The picture is a hieroglyph. This is approximately true of the pictures made by savages or, if one prefers, of preliterate man. It is even true up to a point of Egyptian frescoes. The Egyptian profile with the eyes and shoulders in a frontal position is typical. Each primitive tribe in Africa represents things in so standardized a fashion that students can identify the locality from which the work emanates by its appearance. As a matter of fact, it is true, though to a smaller degree, of all art, even that of today. The styles of the Renaissance, the Baroque, the Rococo, the Neoclassic period, are too well known to need more than passing reference. Nor would anyone date a painting by Kline or Rothko or Mondriaan before the twentieth century. It was during and after the Romantic movement that individual styles became pronounced, though it goes

which he had made for himself as the typical craftsman that he was" (p. 126). I owe this reference to Held's article to E. H. Gombrich. It shows that at least one folk-painter did exactly what the folk-poets did—imitate the tradition.

12. See George Boas, The Cult of Childhood, pp. 91 ff.

without saying that artists of all times, whether deliberately or not, had what the Germans call their own handwriting. But there is a great difference between the unavoidable individual style of a man and the style that is cultivated consciously as a mark of individuality. One may lump together the styles of Rubens, Fragonard, and Delacroix as similar in their brushwork, for example, but no one, to the best of my knowledge, ever mistook a Delacroix for a Rubens. No one ever confused a Manet with a Velázquez in spite of their obvious similarities. But the similarities between children's drawings and those of the self-taught artists on the one hand and of real primitives on the other in most cases arise from the same assumption that painting is a ritual. I cannot pretend to prove this in any scientific manner, for the simple reason that I cannot question primitives and that there are too many children and self-taught artists whom I have never been able to talk to. But I have followed children's work with some assiduity and have tried to answer their questions when they were troubled over some technical problem, and I am fairly convinced of what I am asserting. It is only lately that anyone, whether trained in an art school or not, whether a child or not, has produced works which run from doodles to carefully planned and prepared compositions and which are all treated equally as serious works of art. The person who sits before three or four cans of paint and pours them on a canvas letting accident take over at this point may unquestionably turn out a painting that has beauty. So a stone which has been weathered by sand and wind and rain may have as beautiful a shape as anything carved in a studio. A human being may be beautiful without any artificial aids. But neither the stone nor the beautiful human being is supposed to be a work of art. And a painter who abdicates and lets gravity or accident carry on is not painting in the same manner or with the same purpose, to say nothing of the same results, as Botticelli, Montegna, Poussin, Rubens, Ingres, Delacroix, Matisse, or Picasso. I am not saying that his works of art are not more beautiful, for that has nothing to do with the question. A mocking-bird's song may be more beautiful than a flute sonata by Bach. A polished slab of calcareous metamorphic rock may be more beautiful than a fresco by Piero della Francesca. But is that because one is a work of nature and the other a work of art? Does one express something which the other fails to express?

A more important question is why in a time of great technological advances, scientific victories over tough problems, sophistication in psychology, the public should want a return to autodidacticism. Cultural primitivism of one or another species has been a frequent enough attitude in the history of the Occident to cause no surprise when it recurs. The "return to Nature," the "simple life," the "reliance on instinct," or intuition, rather than reason, the need for some unexamined, unanalyzed, uncriticized way of living that seems to spring from "the heart of things" is probably justified psychologically, however unjustified it may be logically. A man simply cannot question the springs of every one of his daily acts. He has to develop certain habits on which he can rely to give him time to think over problems which are not those of daily life. Habits, whether of muscular behavior or of thinking, are compulsive and are not always recognized as habits. That which is compulsive will be called right by the person who is its victim.

Now we have learned in the last fifty years that most of our behavior emerges from unconscious motivation, and because it is unconscious it seems more natural than the motivation of which we are aware. In view of the sanctity with which the adjective "natural" is invested, we tend to appraise what it qualifies more highly than we do the unnatural, that is, the artificial or learned. Yet, as some of the Greek Cynics saw, in one sense of that multivalent word "unnatural," eating cooked food rather than raw, wearing clothes, living in houses, all are unnatural. Adam was not created fully clothed, and what he devised as his first raiment was a sign of his Fall. There are dozens of examples that a historian could exhibit to show how we always return to Nature, instinct, faith, when we want to do something that we cannot justify rationally. But though we know that this happens, we do not know why. For, if we were to speak in teleological terms, we would say that evidence exists for the sake of answering questions. And in the long run evidence consists in what always occurs as a cause of the problematic effect. We do reverence causes; we even speak of God as the First Cause. But though causes are instructive, are necessary as adjuncts to explanation, and though their discovery is a great delight, in themselves they are important only as a means to prediction and control. Hydrochloric acid is the main agent in digesting food, but we do not write hymns to HCl; we do not swallow it in large doses to aid digestion; we do not give up food and drink it instead. Analogously, though all sorts of childhood repressions may be the causes of action, we need not behave like children for that reason.

None of this is an argument against admiring anything that seems admirable.[13] If a child's painting or a dribble over a canvas is beautiful, by all means let us admire it. But if we then say, "It is beautiful because it expresses the soul of a child," or, "It is beautiful because it proves the liberation of the painter," we are in a state of confusion. Instead of admiring the effect (the picture), we are admiring its cause. One cannot see the soul of a child or the liberation of a painter; they are not visible objects. They are inferred as the source of what is visible. All that is on the paper or canvas is colors and shapes. The rest is read out of them.[14] But this cannot be avoided if we are to say anything about a picture other than to announce our feelings of pleasure or dis-

13. I should prefer to write, "that is admirable," but that would involve us in disputes about the status and origin of value-judgments.

14. See E. H. Gombrich, *Art and Illusion*. Until one knows clearly what "express" means, it might even be argued that to express nature is to copy her as exactly as possible. A *trompe-l'oeil* would then be the most perfect expression in question. But that obviously is not what the admirers of "popular painting" do mean.

pleasure at the sight of what we see. We do not see a tree on a canvas; we see a picture of a tree. The two things are not only existentially two but qualitatively different. Some aestheticians would say that we do not even see a picture of a tree; we see a colored shape which we interpret to be a picture of a tree. But omitting that as an unnecessary complication, let us suppose that we have before us the pictures of two trees, one in full leaf, the other withered, as they appear in Piero della Francesca's "Resurrection." Are they just trees, or are they symbols of the Old Law and the New? If they are the latter, then we have moved far from the simple visual pattern with which we were primarily confronted. Should we have remained in our primordial state of mind or should we have allowed all that we happen to know to enter into our interpretation of the picture? The answer to this brings us back to the question with which we started, that of the value of cultural primitivism.

Cultural primitivism is an easy way of solving many of our puzzles. Just as in Spinoza's words, "The will of God is the refuge of the ignorant," so we can say, "Instinct is the refuge of the lazy." When you cannot solve a problem, you can always conclude that it is not worth solving: the grapes are sour . . . ignorance is bliss . . . "Gie me ae spark o' Nature's fire,/That's a' the learning I desire . . ." "Follow your animal instincts . . ." There are scores of proverbs and well-known quotations which tend in this direction. When all is said and done, in a body they are the foundation of that attitude which abhors machines, science, and any form of efficiency. It is very simple to ridicule this attitude, to point out that if we adopted it we would still be living in caves, eating raw meat, and all the rest. But when a philosophy of life has been accepted by great numbers of people, and they no less intelligent than we are, it is wiser to infer that it gives them some deep satisfaction. There happen to be occasions when one's emotional reactions, if that phrase means anything, to a problem are better than one's reasoning. Why, after all, should anyone love anyone else? Why for that matter should anyone bother to stay alive? Why not, as Lawrence said, follow your animal instincts and live like beasts? I doubt that anyone could give convincing answers to these questions if he relied on reasoning alone. Nobody ever fell in love with a woman because of reasons, though one might make a *mariage de raison* and give the world the illusion of seeing a loving couple. Similarly, no one ever had a religious experience because of reasons, though he might believe in God's existence because he was convinced of it from the various proofs given by Saint Thomas Aquinas. But the belief that your grandmother existed is not the experience of knowing your grandmother by direct association.[15] Do we require direct experience or can we get along on purely rational proofs? The truth is that we cannot dispense with either. We cannot live without some anticipation of the future or belief in the real existence of the past as a minimum. Consequently, it is not a matter of choosing between instinct and reason but of harmonizing the two. And that is not easy.

The notion that any work of art expresses the spirit of the People may be true, but even if it is true it is not a proof of the work's value. This is as relevant to judging the paintings of Daumier, for example, in which the subject matter is popular, as it is in judging the works of Kane, the Douanier Rousseau, or Bauchant. The aesthetic values may be intensified by our knowledge of technical problems adequately met, of traditions of representation clearly perceived, of truth to Nature exemplified, and the like, but one cannot substitute such knowledge for the immediate impact of a work of art. If now only the canvases of the autodidact or the primitive painter express the spirit of the People, then two inferences may be made: (1) that the People are limited

---

15. It might, however, be the impetus to search for photographs, diaries, letters, and so on, in order to approximate a direct acquaintance with your grandmother. Cf. Pascal, *Pensees* (ed. Pléiade, p. 1215): "C'est en faisant tout comme s'ils croyaient, en prenant de l'eau bénite, en faisant dire des messes," etc.

to what the unschooled part of the population says about them; and (2) that a spectator must restrict himself to the enjoyment of their works if he wishes to have the purest appreciation of the aesthetic. But both of these inferences seem unwarranted when tested by fact. The learned members of the population are just as much part of the People as the uneducated, and what they say has as much validity. There is no reason why one should not feel the beauty of Eakins' portraits because he studied under Gérôme and Bonnat. Works of art have many aspects and one may deeply appreciate one or more of them without being sensitive to them all. Or again, some rare connoisseurs may be able to be affected by them all welded together into a unity. A master like Rubens has nothing childlike or naïve about him; a master like Henri Rousseau has all the charm and candor of young innocence. It would appear more reasonable to grant this even if it lands one in eclecticism—a bad word for catholicity of taste.[16]

16. To round out this essay there should be some discussion of the decorative arts of the peasant, which in the United States usually means the Pennsylvania Dutch; also of early American pewter, silver, iron weathervanes, pine furniture, earthenware plates, jugs, and platters, blown glass and pressed glass, hooked rugs, ships' figureheads. The whole Arts and Crafts Movement should be introduced, since the important thing about it was the supposed beauty contributed by the human hands as contrasted with things made by machinery, though the machine caters to masses of people, not to the individual, and might therefore seem more "democratic." Lately—i.e., in the sixties —there has been a cult of *objets trouvés* and of three-dimensional objects which are assembled from bits and pieces of old furniture, machinery, junk, which may or may not resemble animals and other natural objects, as they do in Picasso's work of this type. The relevance of all this to our subject is that of the art of the autodidact: It is not tainted by academicism. This does not imply that it is more popular than traditional art, though there was a touch of demophilia in William Morris' plea to return to the crafts of the guilds. The People's contribution comes out more clearly in the fad for modern folk-songs. For where a picture or a piece of sculpture is seldom made cooperatively, this is not true of songs, dances, and music, which are performed before an audience and presumably with an audience in mind. For this see my next essay.

For a full discussion of Folk Art in all its complexity, see the *Encyclopedia of World Art*, s.v. "Folk Art.". This article has a very extensive bibliography.

VII

THE PEOPLE AS MUSICIAN

The theorists of the French Revolution based their program on what they took to be the nature of man as man. There were even members of the clergy who could accept this program with equanimity. Abbé Joli, for instance, vicar of the parish of Limoux in Languedoc, found it possible to make the following statement from his pulpit.

> Christians, you know that we are born all equal in our rights; we are today a nation of brothers; we no longer expect distinctions other than those that are assured by our merits, our talents, and our virtues. . . . That is the first law of the august code which our legislators are about to transmit to you. They received it themselves from God, for they found its source in the Gospels. And it is above all this happy conformity with the principles of Jesus Christ which should make it dear to us and worthy of our respect. . . . A Christian orator cried out not long ago, "Although a priest, I would abjure the Gospels if they did not contain the happiness of my fellow citizens." And I, I would abjure the Constitution, if equality were not its base.[1]

There was in those early days of the Revolution a veritable enthusiasm for the doctrine of the uniformity of human nature. As A. Sorel has pointed out in *L'Europe et la Révolution Française* (p. 538), the king under the *Ancien Régime* was the living image of France, and the love of country was identified with devotion to the king. But when sovereignty was transferred to the People, the nation took the place of the king, and the love of country in its turn became respect for the laws. But since the laws were based on reason, according to popular belief, the Revolution had as its primary task the establishment of the rule of reason, and it

1. *Moniteur*, June 25, 1790 (reprint, Vol. 4, p. 712).

was to accomplish this task not for one people alone but for humanity. Patriotism thus became identified with respect for the Rights of Man. The true patriot was a citizen of the world, but the "world" was left undefined. Whatever it meant, it was a country without frontiers, without land, *sans souvenirs et sans tombeaux*. It was, though many of the revolutionists may not have known this, both the Cosmopolis of the Stoics and the City of God of Saint Augustine.

If Humanity and not Frenchmen, Englishmen, and Germans, were one's fellow citizens, then there must be a common essence in all men and the benefits of the Revolution must be conferred on all alike. Was it not in fact the duty of the revolutionists to insure that all men have the priceless gifts of liberty, equality, and fraternity? In 1796 when Napoleon menaced Venice, he opened his proclamation to the Venetians with the words, "It was to deliver the fairest land of Europe from the iron yoke of the proud house of Austria that the French Army has braved the most difficult obstacles." (*Moniteur*, Vol. 28, p. 314). Conventional as such words have become in the mouths of conquering generals, and empty as they now seem, there can be little doubt in the mind of one who reads the writings of the time that the revolutionists felt it their mission to make the whole world republican and to treat its inhabitants as if bound to them by the link of brotherhood. Thus it was that the *Moniteur* (Vol. 27, p. 100) proclaimed Kant's *Project of Perpetual Peace* a new Gospel, particularly those parts of it which suggested that it was the destiny of a powerful republic to become the center of a federation of other states for the purpose of assuring the rights of the people.

The French maintained that all of their revolutionary wars were fought in defense of the subjugated. The Italians, the Dutch, the Germans along the Rhine were all to be freed, not conquered. These oppressed peoples had all left their Creator's hands alike; they were all the victims of tyrants; they were all to share equally in the blessings of republicanism. It was the insistence upon hu-

manity as a universal, incarnate in all men, which roused the
scorn of the Catholic opponents of the Revolution. "I see Man
nowhere," cried Joseph de Maistre, "I see Germans, Frenchmen,
Italians, but never Man." So Gobineau was to say, "There is no
ideal man. Man does not exist. If I am convinced that he will
never be discovered, it is above all because of language. On this
basis I can recognize him who possesses Finnish, him of the Arian
system, or him of Semitic compounds, but absolute Man, him I
do not know." [2] Yet the religion whose return to popularity de
Maistre, if not Gobineau, was striving to effect had long ago assumed as one of its primary axioms that racial and national differences are inessential. This meant more for Christians than it did
for its Stoic proponents. For the dogmas of inherited guilt and
vicarious atonement alone, to say nothing of the Augustinian theory of history, demanded that men be instances of Man, as tri-
angles are instances of triangularity.

Hence the federation of states under one great republic was
in spite of de Maistre's hatred of revolutionary notions of Humanity, duplicated in his plea for a theocratic empire under the
Pope. In both cases there was no question of the right of a nation to exist as a separate and distinct unit. The question in both
cases was how to keep these unit nations from straying from the
path of rectitude. The injustice which Kant seemed to be aiming
at was war, but as he insisted himself, one of the worst features
of war was the consequent placing of nations under foreign yokes
against their will. The revolutionists were liberating people to
govern themselves, for in self-government they saw the only cure
for despotism. De Maistre agreed that despotism was an evil but
maintained that the only check on the despot was the spiritual
check of the pope. In other words, de Maistre made the usual
medieval distinction between spiritual and temporal sovereignty.
He would have left the nations temporally free but spiritually
under papal control. That this was no solution to the problem

2. *L'Inégalité des races*, Vol. 1, p. 189.

had been pointed out to him, for, as he could see, the spiritual supremacy of the pope was bound to have temporal effects. However, when faced with such an objection, de Maistre evaded the issue by replying that he was not responsible for the ultimate consequences of the doctrine but that, since the pope could do no wrong, these consequences could not be evil.

Du Pape was written in 1817. The Bourbons were back on the throne. De Maistre and the Theological School, as it was called, found the king for whose return they had pleaded in no wise anxious to renounce any of his sovereign prerogatives even with papal supervision as a reward. The international theocracy was looked upon more or less as the intellectual pastime of clericals and soon it disappeared from sight.

At the same time, this theory was not without influence. One finds it appearing most noticeably in the early Lamennais. But before discussing Lamennais' ideas, it may be well to point out that the doctrines of the Revolution and those of the Counter-Revolution seemed to depreciate the importance of national boundaries. What is more curious, their reasons were not very different. The revolutionists believed that humanity was better off spiritually if protected by the ideals of liberty, equality, and fraternity. Nationalism, which to them meant monarchism, prevented the exercise of such protection. Hence it was the moral duty of men who did enjoy protection to see that their fellows in other countries enjoyed it as well. Joseph de Maistre also believed in a supernational community. But he also believed that such a community existed already in the Church. The program of the Church was neither liberty nor equality, but it was to a certain extent fraternity. Thus Christians who were not zealous adherents of the papacy saw no reason to object to the internationalism of the revolutionists.

Lamennais' fundamental postulate was that the sole test of truth lay in the reason of the race as opposed to the reason of the individual. The reason of the race is an expression of that solidarity which is so marked in Saint Augustine and in the Church dogmas mentioned above. But just as men are welded into nations by the solidarity of their common national tradition, so all mankind is welded into one by its common religious tradition. This religious tradition is found in the remnants of Catholicism remaining in the degenerate sects, including even idolatry.[3]

But, said Lamennais in his later years, what stands between the binding power of religion and humanity? What prevents a union of all peoples under God? The Seven Kings, who in his *Paroles d'un Croyant* plan for the perpetual slavery of the human race, are the answer. Slavery is opposed by religion, science, thought; it is reinforced by national boundaries, local pride, fear, and luxury. Accordingly, these things must be destroyed, and above all, national boundaries. A quotation or two may not be amiss.

> Man does not live alone. God has not destined for him this solitary existence. He neither preserves himself from death nor develops according to his nature except in society, by union with his kind. And the union of individuals forms peoples and the union of peoples forms mankind or the universal family for whose foundation we ought to labor unceasingly so that the sum of evil whose impure source is egotism may diminish also unceasingly and that of God's benefactions spread along our earthly road may increase in the same proportion.[4]

Again, after preaching the equality of man before God, he maintained that princes are the result of sin because they were appointed to help men in their war against their fellows. Thus their power comes from God and from the people and is not inherent in themselves as a group set apart.

> [God] has united men into families, and all the families are sisters; He has united them into nations, and all the nations are sisters; and whosoever separates family from family, nation from nation, divides what God has joined. He is doing the work of Satan. . . . And that which unites family to family, nation to nation, is first

3. For Lamennais at this time non-Catholic religions were more or less degenerate forms of Catholicism, just as noncivilized societies were remnants of the societies dispersed when the Tower of Babel was destroyed.

4. *Livre du Peuple*, section 6.

of all the law of God, the law of justice and of charity, and then the law of liberty, which is also a law of God.[5]

This Mennasian doctrine of internationalism was invented to preserve the liberty and solidarity of mankind. Lamennais, like Bonald and de Maistre, believed that man out of society—the individual by himself—is a mere point. Consequently, to free the individual is not to remove social ties; it is, however, to remove political ties. The only authority he thinks legitimate is the authority of duty, which in itself, though inspired and commanded by God, yet is consonant with the inner nature of man. Man is freest to develop his talents socially, but society demands no secular or political government. Hence the dream of Lammenais was a Europe which would be politically one but socially diverse —diverse as the natural talents of the various peoples demanded.[6] But how diverse the results might be was never appreciated by Lamennais. Nor did he realize the possibility that some peoples might express their talents in belligerency and depredation.

There was, then, little that was precise in Lamennais' political speculations, though in his later years (1851) he became more interested in the actualization of his plans. According to his biographer, Duine,[7] he hoped to see a federation of European nations, beginning with the Latin nations as a nucleus. His project, printed as *Comité démocratique français-espagnol-italien*, is unfortunately not available in American libraries, and nothing definite can be said about it until the plan is reprinted.

In August, 1849 a peace congress was held in Paris. Victor Hugo was elected its president, Cobden its vice-president. In the address with which Hugo opened the congress we recognize the leading ideas of his predecessor—the emphasis upon fraternity, upon the supposed fact that nations would preserve their cultural individuality through their union. In conclusion he said,

5. *Paroles d'un Croyant*, section 19.
6. Thus he believed in what was later called regionalism.
7. F. Duine, *La Mennais*, p. 291.

From now on the end of great statesmanship, of true statesmanship, will be this: to recognize all nationalities, to restore the historic unity of peoples, and to bind this unity to civilization by peace, to enlarge ceaselessly the group of civilized peoples, to set a good example to peoples still barbarous, to replace battles with votes, in short, and this sums it all up, to give the last word to justice which the old world gave to force.[8]

In a man like Victor Hugo, to whom phrases counted somewhat more than ideas, it is interesting to observe his clinging to old phrases, to old Mennasian phrases. In 1869, twenty years after the Paris Peace Congress, he was offered the honorary presidency of the Lausanne Peace Congress. Addressing his "fellow citizens of the United States of Europe" from Brussels, he penned sentences that but for their declamatory quality might have been written by the author of *Le Livre du Peuple*.

Civilization tends invincibly towards a unity of speech, of measure, of coinage, and to the fusions of the nations in humanity which is unity supreme. Concord has a synonym, simplification. So wealth and life have a synonym, circulation. The first of all servitudes is the frontier.

Who says frontier says ligature. Cut the ligature, wipe out the frontier, do away with the customs officer, do away with the soldier, in other words, be free. Peace will follow.

The cause of the frontier is royalty. Kings must divide peoples if they hope to rule over them. For defense, kings need soldiers; to live, soldiers need murder; to murder, soldiers need war. Hence frontiers produce war.[9]

The question naturally arises of the affiliations of Lamennais' doctrines of internationalism, his work on the *Comité démocratique*, with those of Ledru-Rollin, Mazzini, Ruge, and Darasz, the *Comité démocratique Européen Central*, formed about the

8. *Actes et Paroles*, I, *Avant l'Exil*, in *Oeuvres complètes* (1882), p. 485. The speech is also interesting for its anticipation of the argument, used before World War I, that "preparedness brings on war," and of the phrase, now current, *Les Etats-Unis d'Europe*.

9. *Actes et Paroles*, II, *Pendant l'Exil*, in *ibid.*, pp. 464–65.

middle of 1850 to unite all Europe in one organization of democratic governments. In the nature of the case information about the inner workings of this *Comité* is meager.[10] We know, of course, of the close personal relations between Lamennais and Ledru-Rollin, but whether their two projects were related I have not as yet been able to discover. The aims of the two were probably not different. Ledru-Rollin certainly, and presumably Lamennais as well, was anxious to form a federation of nations whose purpose would be the prevention of war and opposition to monarchy. Ledru-Rollin and Mazzini, living in exile in London, were joined by Kossuth, who with them issued a manifesto in September, 1855, calling for international action for the realization of their dream. They hailed the fall of Sebastopol as the beginning of a world war, after which European democracy would be organized, Poland, Hungary, and Italy might be freed from foreign domination, France from despotism. The war must be fought and won not by governments then existing, but by the peoples in revolt. But of this, as of all the works of this committee, nothing resulted.

The development of this plan changed its nature. Now the emphasis was no longer on the cultural result that would obtain if national frontiers were destroyed, but rather on the political

10. There is an account of Ledru-Rollin's committee in A. R. Calman's *Ledru-Rollin après 1848*. It may have been an outgrowth of Mazzini's Young Europe. The difference between Mazzini's internationalism and what was called cosmopolitanism is that the latter concerned the whole human race and its individual members, whereas the former was based on country. "For us," said Mazzini, "the starting point is Country; the object or aim is Collective Humanity. For those who call themselves cosmopolitans, the aim may be Humanity, but the starting point is Individual Man." See his *Life and Writings*, Vol. 3, p. 7. There is an account of Young Europe there also, on pp. 35 ff. Cf. "The Holy Alliance of People" (1849), *ibid.*, Vol. 5, pp. 265 ff. For the reciprocity between Country and Humanity, rights and duties, see *The Duties of Man*, chapter 4, *ibid.*, Vol. 4, p. 58. The pact of Young Europe was signed April 15, 1834, with representatives of Germany, Poland, and Italy.

result. Mazzini, Ledru-Rollin, and Kossuth were at the time more interested in democratizing Europe through the concerted action of the proletariat than in any moral effect this might have upon the welfare of mankind. In fact, what each was thinking of was the liberation of the particular nation to which he happened to belong from the particular government under which it was ruled. The situation, as it then stood, was the third of three stages of development. We have (1) de Maistre in opposition to the Revolution reviving the medieval idea of a spiritual empire under the Pope; (2) Lamennais maintaining that existing national political differences prevented the functioning of the spiritual empire, with God in the place of the pope; (3) the triumvirate of Mazzini, Ledru-Rollin, and Kossuth developing a plan of realizing this empire through a mass revolution against national governments. Out of it all the United States of Europe, a federation like those of the Western Hemisphere, would be formed.

In 1826, however, Théodore Jouffroy developed another argument for internationalism which again hoped for the cultural development of each of the nations by eliminating their political differences. His premises were different from those of Lamennais and his followers, and, since Jouffroy is a neglected figure, I shall give more space to his ideas than might be considered reasonable.

There are in the world, he believed, three civilizations, the Christian, the Muslim, the Brahmin, which in turn are located in Western Europe and America, the Near East, and the Far East, respectively. These civilizations are differentiated by the religions which they profess, for even the blacks in Haiti lead a European life because they are Christians. As for savages, they do not count, having neither religion nor civilization. They will sooner or later be won over to Christianity because their countries are in the hands of Christians. In fact, Jouffroy believed that the future was to be a Christian future. It is just as well that he died young.

Among the Christian nations there are four which are pre-eminent and which excel in different things—Germany, France,

England, and the United States. "Germany," he says (p. 129), "is that country in the world in which the sources of instruction are most opened and the most wisely governed, but she is far from the political perfection of France, England, and the United States. England is not less far from our civil order [*notre ordre civil*] and our impartiality, and we from her public spirit, industry, and several of her institutions. Finally, the European nations would have much to learn from the United States in economy and tolerance." These countries have each reached the end of their particular development.

The rest of Christian civilization will have to follow these three nations as they would follow a few chosen men themselves. It is thus the duty of these few leaders to study the needs of humanity as a whole.

But exactly what is this "humanity" of which Jouffroy speaks? It is that of which Vico and Herder had spoken before him and of which, he thought, Thomas Reid had spoken in his doctrine of common sense. But Jouffroy specifically thinks the differentia of man lies in his mutability.[11] The beasts remain what they were at creation; man has improved. But if he has improved, it is attributable to his intelligence. History, therefore, is the study of man's intelligence as applied to his natural condition. It is expressed in poetry and philosophy and develops in accordance with a definite law. This law had not been clearly defined by earlier philosophers of history, Bossuet, Vico, and Herder,[12] but at least Bossuet, unlike Herder, did see that humanity was one and that human thought developed freely and spontaneously.

The intelligence of the race was what Reid had called common sense. Everyone, says Jouffroy,[13] understands by common sense a certain number of principles or self-evident notions whence

11. See his "Réflexions sur la philosophie de l'Histoire," in *Mélanges Philosophiques*, p. 52.
12. "Bossuet, Vico, Herder," *ibid*., p. 86.
13. "De la philosophie et du Sens Commun," *ibid*., p. 157.

all men draw the conduct of their judgments and the rules of their conduct. These principles are simply "the positive solutions" of the major problems of philosophy, such as the nature of good and evil, beauty and ugliness. It is thus a philosophy anterior to the philosophies of the schools and it reconciles them. It is not, however, a "conscious" philosophy; it is manifested in our actions: we all act as if we were inspired by it. Philosophy proper is simply a clarification of its dim but reliable insights. It is the operation of common sense that is impeded by nationalism. So that the problem of internationalism in Jouffroy is a means of releasing the reason of humanity and, since that reason cannot err, of attaining truth.

The argument for internationalism was destined to be elaborated in greatest detail by Auguste Comte, though a study of the matter more thoroughgoing than this one would certainly include men like Saint-Martin, Saint-Simon, Fourier, Proudhon, and later, Marx. Comte acknowledged that his debt to Catholicism was great, for that religion alone, he believed, appreciated the full meaning of human solidarity and unity. To call Comte an inverted Catholic is now the most worn of scholarly *clichés*, but there is a good bit of truth in it. Humanity, he believed, was not only one "laterally," exhibiting a complete coherence of parts, but was one longitudinally as well, having a single life history.

The notion that mankind lived the life of an individual had been expressed most clearly in Condorcet, though he had predecessors. Since the rise of evolutionism as an explanatory technique, we have become accustomed to such phrases as "the childhood of the race," but it must not be forgotten they had a novel ring to them in the eighteenth and early nineteenth centuries. For if Catholicism had taught the solidarity of humankind, it had not believed in progress. Human beings had a logical unity, the unity of members of a single logical class which formed a family. But the family itself had no history, described no curve of growth, did not progress. Christian history was a series of events determined by man's supernatural relations and, though never consistently worked out even by Bossuet, tended to overlook the possibility that the organism which its students often said society was might have a life of its own above or apart from that of its members. That was Condorcet's contribution to Comte, and in the *Esquisse* he retraced the steps which he supposed humanity to have taken and forecast the steps which it would take in the future.

Comte's result was the famous Law of the Three Stages with its supposed implications. It would be absurd to expound the law here; it is enough to say that it was believed to describe the evolution of society-as-a-whole and to suggest to the social reformer ways of ameliorating the lot of man. Comte thought that the final stage of civilization had been opened with the French Revolution, a stage in which metaphysics had disappeared, all knowledge had become scientific, and all science positivistic. In this stage industry would take the place of warfare. It would develop into a time of universal order and peace.

But Comte did not stop with vague predictions of this sort. He had a plan for the organization of this society which was as detailed as a litany. Humanity as a unit seems a negation of nationality, but Comte did not commit the error of neglecting human differences for the sake of human similarities. Accordingly, he sharply distinguished between the spiritual and temporal interests of mankind, and whereas he considered the former to be international, he realized that the latter were national. This does not mean that he wished to preserve the national frontiers of his day. On the contrary, he recognized their viciousness and would have redrawn almost all of them. But he did see the value of keeping smaller national units for administrative purposes. In fact, even spiritually he recognized five leading civilizations, the three Latin, the British, and the German. Curiously enough, the regionalism of Comte was almost the reverse of that of Lamennais, with whom he had such close social affiliations. Lamennais' plea for regionalism was almost wholly spiritual, his plea for internationalism temporal.

The details of Comte's plan for reorganizing Europe, with its *pontifex maximus*, its 14,000 bankers, its 70 republics, and so on, can well be omitted from this essay. What is important for our purposes is that for Comte government would tend to become more and more spiritual as it facilitated the natural progress of human intercourse.[14] As it would become more spiritual, the political administration of the associated republics would become less serious. For he believed that human beings could be brought by education to act with the same pacific motives toward other nationals as they seem to have toward their fellow citizens. Just as the members of a family do not—or rather did not in the France of 1840—require governmental interference in their private affairs, or make war upon one another, so the new nations would learn to rely upon one another for mutual support.[15] A by-product of this arrangement would be universal peace, for "war could be organized only for one's native country," whereas labor becomes "systematizable" only by relating it to humanity. All the city states were naturally rivals in the military age, either by all striving simultaneously for a domination necessarily unique, or by separately resisting the forced incorporation that alone would unite them. Contrariwise, the industrial state makes them spontaneously converge by assigning to each an end which can become universal because it always remains external to any given nation. The exploitation common to the divers republics of terrestrial domains involves a partition of duties equivalent to that which coordinates the different classes of which each people is composed.[16] It is to be remembered that Comte did not believe that the harmonizing of economic interests and activities would suffice to bring about

14. *Politique Positive*, Vol. 4, p. 307.
15. "Considérations sur le Pouvoir Spirituel," *ibid.*, Vol. 4, p. 212.
16. *Ibid.*, p. 323.

universal peace but felt that it must be supplemented by a vigorous moral discipline which would translate moral standards from an individual to a social idiom.[17]

Such was the complexity of early nineteenth-century thought on nationalism and internationalism. In the main, two sets of interests were distinguished, the spiritual and the temporal. Hence one could be a cultural (or spiritual) nationalist and a temporal internationalist, a cultural and temporal nationalist, a cultural and temporal internationalist, and obviously a cultural and temporal nationalist.

The situation in the first quarter of the nineteenth century then was divided into four camps, depending on whether one was more interested in cultural or political autonomy. It is the former group that is the more important to us. That each People had its own culture had been approached from the point of view of national character, but the arts of a nation had never been considered as relevant to its character. The Germans, for instance, might be thought of as aggressive, brutal, gluttonous, and chaste, but their painting, sculpture, architecture, and music were appraised without consideration for any of these traits. Similarly the French might be thought of as capricious, amorous, arrogant, and so on, but no one ever thought of applying these adjectives to Chartres Cathedral. English poetry was not said to be perfidious nor Italian to be treacherous. The split between one's estimate of a work of art and of a people was definite and unbridged.

This may have been because during the sixteenth century the individual artist's personality came to the fore. It was the era of Michelangelo, when the individual artist's personality was emphasized and when artists were supposed to live their own lives, to gain privileges which other men could not enjoy, to exhibit eccentricities, and to win great renown. Vasari's *Lives* is full of stories illuminating this side of the artistic career. And, as everyone

17. *Ibid.*, p. 214.

knows, the idea grew until today it is accepted as dogma. "The artist sees differently"; he has an artistic temperament; he dresses differently; his morals are different and must not be judged by the standards that apply to ordinary people. If carried to its logical conclusion this ought to imply that a work of art must be judged by no common or overindividual standards of beauty or artistic excellence but by its adequacy in expressing its maker's personality, sometimes called his purpose.

The idea that a nation had an art peculiar to itself was given popularity by Herder. His aim was to show that a nation need not imitate classic or, what amounted to the same thing in his time, French art. The nation of which he was thinking was one that did not then exist—Germany—but which began to exist after the Napoleonic wars, bit by bit, until in 1938 it included every people which spoke some sort of German. If World War II had not ended in an allied victory, Germany would no doubt have included Switzerland and all of Scandinavia, northern France, and possibly even England. For it was language above all that determined national character according to Hitler, and all people whose mother tongue was Germanic were part of the German Folk. This did not apply to Jews, nor would it apply to Negroes living in any so-called Germanic country. But Hitler was superior to the Law of Contradiction. In any event, Herder's aim was to make the German language and German literature respectable, and the aim was understandable in view of the imitations of the French court which dotted the Germanic principalities.

It is obvious that a movement so powerful as the growth of national cultures could not be the work of one man. The rise of vernacular serious literature, literature as philosophic and scientific, previously written in Latin, meant that the learned world was broken up, as is true today. An American physicist, for instance, who cannot read French and German, and perhaps Russian and Chinese, does not know the literature of his subject. This was not true even as late as the seventeenth century. Newton and Descartes wrote their major works in Latin, and since every educated man could read Latin, these works quickly spread throughout the European community. Thus serious thought was international in expression and no one could speak reasonably of French mathematics or German chemistry.

Belles lettres had been national from the Middle Ages on, though Latin was occasionally used by authors for special purposes. The Latin poems of Milton are no more significant in the history of literature, though more idiomatic, than the French poems of T. S. Eliot. Similarly, painting was national, and even in the early Renaissance, Flemish painters were distinguished by style and indeed by their use of oils from Italian. Here the costume of the personages and the landscape were distinguishing marks. But the subject matter, whether taken from the Bible or classical mythology, was international, and though Cranach's *Judgment of Paris* does not resemble Raphael's,[18] anyone seeing either would know what it illustrated. Even landscapes and still lifes presented no problems of translation. No one seeing one of Caravaggio's baskets of fruit would wonder what it was all about.

The architect too was likely to be observant of certain rules, whether derived from Vitruvius or Alberti or imposed by the local materials and climate; and though there were regional variations of style in architecture, they were found more in domestic architecture, guildhalls, *hôtels-de-ville*, than in palaces and châteaux and churches. When Gothic architecture, which was almost general in Europe became recessive (the exception being Italy), Renaissance and Baroque came in; and though historians can differentiate between northern and southern Baroque, French, English, and Italian Renaissance, there is enough similarity in all these styles to make the classifications reasonable if not exact.

The only one of these arts which could prove an obstacle to comprehension is literature. A man does not need to know German to appreciate Fischer von Erlach, nor Dutch to appreciate Rem-

18. Now extant only in a drawing and an engraving by Marcantonio.

brandt. But obviously if he does not know English he cannot read Shakespeare. The one art which seemed truly international, and was called so in the books, was music. It is true that there were quarrels between the Lullists and the Ramellians, as there were between Rubensists and Poussinists, or later between Gluckists and Piccinists. But the quarrels were not due to any misunderstanding. Italian opera may have been disliked because it was Italian and not French, but the French found that they could enjoy Lully nevertheless. In fact the quarrel arose because so many of them did. The notion of a national music, a music expressing the soul of a people, is a mid-nineteenth-century notion. It is part and parcel of cultural nationalism and perhaps its weakest part. For though people in general prefer those artistic styles to which they are accustomed, they seem seldom if ever to have objected to new music on the ground that it is foreign. Their objections are to its strangeness, which they call by more abusive terms. The objections made to Beethoven, for instance, in the *Zeitung für die Elegente Welt* in 1804, were not that he was un-Austrian but that his second symphony was *"ein krasses Ungeheuer, ein angestochener, sich unbändig windender Lindwurm"* ("a crass monster, a hideously wounded dragon, that refuses to expire"). And when Fétis said that Berlioz wrote what *"n'appartient pas à l'art que j'ai l'habitude de considérer comme de la musique,"* he was not not condemning him for being un-French.[19] One can go through that admirable and indeed indispensable collection of diatribes against musicians, Slonimsky's *Lexicon of Musical Invective*, and one will look in vain for condemnation based on lack of nationalism. And contrariwise, those composers whose works were deliberately, programmatically nationalistic, of whom Grieg is an outstanding example, have been admired throughout the world by people who could have no idea what Norwegian life and culture were like.

The earliest manifestation of nationalism in music was in

19. See Nicolas Slonimsky, *Lexicon of Musical Invective*, pp. 42, 57.

Russia. There it formed part of that anti-Western propaganda that disturbed the salons in the middle nineteenth century. It is usually Glinka who is credited with initiating the movement. But Glinka's memoirs give no indication that he thought he was founding a school or initiating a movement of national music. He hated Italian singing and was pretty critical of French orchestral playing, but in spite of these possible tinges of chauvinism he was appreciative of foreign musical compositions and made arrangements of Spanish dances. In the second chapter of his *Memoirs* (p. 8) he says that "it may be" because of the Russian tunes he heard in his youth that he "dwelt primarily on Russian folk music later on." He also (p. 82) speculates on the sadness of Russian songs, attributing it to regional sources: "We are either furiously happy or weeping bitter tears"; "Love . . . is with us always linked with sadness." And he adds that while he was in Italy his nostalgia led him "step by step to think of composing like a Russian" (p. 83). He was, of course, aware of the idea of national music in the sense of Russian themes, themes from Russian songs (p. 88), but just as the operas which he wrote were based on Russian stories, so the songs were settings of Russian poems. *A Life for the Tzar* was enthusiastically applauded as a Russian opera (p. 109, n. 19), but it was also a Russian, Faddei Bulgarin, who styled it *la musique des cochers*. *Ruslan and Ludmila* was not the success that its predecessor had been, though it was surely just as Russian (pp. 149 ff.). It was probably the comments of musical critics that created the movement of nationalism. We are told, for instance, that Serov was influential in promoting Glinka's music (p. 164, n. 22), and we may guess at least that the ideology supporting the music was not the work of the composers themselves. The debate between Slavophiles and Westerners was very vigorous during this time.

In fact it is difficult, if possible, to distinguish the Russianness of Glinka's sounds from that of his libretti. One of the most appreciative notices of *A Life for the Tzar* was written by Henry

Mérimée, published in the *Revue de Paris* in 1844 (p. 183). This notice gave so much pleasure to Glinka that he reprinted part of it in his *Memoirs*. In it Mérimée says that "in its subject matter and poetry and music" the opera is "a most faithful summing up of all that Russia has suffered and sung." It is a "patriotic and religious act of solemnity," "a national epic." But it is, of course, not merely the music which is all that. It is the opera as a whole. What is Russian about the music is the 5/4 time that is occasionally used (as it was to be used later by Tchaikowsky), certain cadences, and themes from traditional Russian dances and songs.

That music could actually be national was a new idea. During the Middle Ages and indeed up to the end of the eighteenth century composers utilized any themes or tunes they wished to use, regardless of origin. Similarly, the social origin of a tune was never considered if a composer wished to use it. Paul Henry Lang, indeed, speaks of the folk song as "the fountain of youth from which music has gained new vitality whenever fatigue and over-cultivation threatened it with sterility." [20] The use of erotic dance tunes in religious compositions became customary, and some masses were identified by the popular tunes which their composers had borrowed. What is relevant here is the suggestion made by this fact that music was not held to communicate either social or national matter. Associations of a psychological nature were another matter. No one would expect to hear "Yankee Doodle" used to accompany the *Credo*, and yet "God Save the Queen" has been sung by several generations of Americans to the words, "My country, 'tis of thee, sweet land of liberty," etc. If the music were felt to be inherently English, it is doubtful that the song would have gained the popularity it enjoyed. But for that matter the United States national anthem today is sung to the tune of a drinking song, "Anacreon in Heaven."

If one were out to write national music, where was one to find examples? The obvious source was folk song. Aside from collect-

20. *Music in Western Civilization*, p. 197.

ing folk songs and arranging them in terms of traditional harmony, as Percy Grainger did, the nationalistic composer incorporated portions of them into his compositions much as Bach and Haydn did. The condemnation of this practice in the late Middle Ages and later by the Church is too well known to be more than mentioned here. But again it was associations with the tunes in question that caused the trouble. A mass that had no such basis was called a *Missa sine nomine*. But the use made by composers of such melodies or phrases was no evidence of nationalism. I have pointed out elsewhere that the opening of *Adeste fideles* is nearly identical with the opening of *Voi che sapete*, but even assuming that Mozart realized this, it does not prove that there is any identity of sentiment or "meaning" in the two. Nor would it imply that Mozart was trying to express the nationality of the person who composed *Adeste fideles*, or of him who sang the aria. Cherubino was, I suppose, a Spaniard, but no one has found a Spanish source for *Adeste fideles*. When, on the other hand, Tchaikowsky introduced the national anthems of France and Russia into the *1812 Overture*, his intention was clear and deliberate and had literary, if not musical, significance; if the French national anthem had been something else, he would have used that. But if the opening notes of a French folk song occur in a composition by Poulenc, they might be supposed to have some symbolic meaning, though they would have none to a person who did not recognize the song. Since World War II the theme of the first movement of Beethoven's C-minor Symphony has meant *Victory*, at least to those of us who went through that war. But Beethoven clearly could not have utilized the Morse Code nor did the V-sign occur to anyone until the war was well on.

If a person recognizes the folk songs of his country, as he is likely to recognize certain hymns sung in school or church or national anthems or popular songs, that recognition will carry a certain message to him. This is indubitable. But if he does not recognize them, no message will be conveyed beyond a vague mood, sadness or jollity. It has been said that the Blues "are filled with the deepest emotions of a race. They are songs of sorrow charged with satire, with that potent quality of ironic verse clothed in the raiment of the buffoon. . . . In song, the Negro expressed his true feelings, his hopes, aspirations, and ideals. . . ." [21] Whether it is the words or the tunes that convey these emotions is not clear, but when the songs are delivered on instruments alone without words, it is questionable whether the sorrow is any more connected with the Negro than with the white man. A person hearing a funeral march probably feels the air to be mournful, but he does not feel the mournfulness of any particular composer or people. This is the one sound reason for calling music a universal language. The history of musical criticism demonstrates how un-universal music is, but that we need not consider.

A given composer, then, a Bartók, a Grieg, a Vaughan Williams, may introduce folk music into his compositions with the purpose of making them sound Hungarian or Norwegian or English, but that does not give us any reason to believe that anyone other than Hungarians, Norwegians, or Englishmen will even recognize the tunes in question, to say nothing of feeling Hungarian, Norwegian, or English. When we hear Rimsky-Korsakov's *Scheherazade*, do we feel Arabian? If so, we have been tricked, for the music is no more Arabian than the music used for the hoochee-coochee dance is Egyptian. The point is that like the *alla turca* in Mozart, a convention has been established and we accept it without thinking. So we sometimes wonder at the "operatic quality" of Haydn and Mozart masses. The same comment was made of the cantatas of Bach. But if either Haydn or Mozart, to say nothing of Bach, had realized that their religious music was operatic in the irreligious sense of that word, they would not have written it. All three men were deeply religious. No art, other than architecture, is more conventional than music, though we must not

21. E. Simms Campbell, "Blues," in *Jazzmen*, ed. Frederic Ramsey, Jr., and Charles Edward Smith, p. 105.

forget poetic diction and the laws of perspective. As an extraordinary example of this, one has only to think of Gershwin's *An American in Paris*, in which the Americanism is the jazz rhythms and the Parisianism the taxicab horns, now forbidden by law.

The passion for folk songs in countries like Norway (Grieg), Hungary (Bartók), and Bohemia (Smetana and Dvořák) was allied with the desire for political independence. In England it was allied with a desire for cultural independence. Ralph Vaughan Williams, who believed that all music could be traced back to folk music, collected folk songs with the deliberate program in mind of writing English music. "We must be," he said, "our own tailors. We must cut out for ourselves, try on for ourselves, and finally wear our own home-made garments, which, even if they are homely and home-spun, will at all events fit our bodies and keep them warm." [22] The reason lying behind this was Vaughan Williams' belief that, as C. Hubert H. Parry had said "True style comes not from the individual but from the products of crowds of fellow-workers who sift and try and try again until they have found the thing that suits their native taste. . . . Style is ultimately national." [23] "Classical" music, Vaughan Williams said, is "nothing more or less than the Teutonic style." [24] And finally, the various artistic media "are symbols not of other visible and audible things, but of what lies beyond sense and knowledge." [25] What lies beyond sense and knowledge is presumably the sentiment of nationality, the feeling of being English or French, German or Italian. And to stimulate this is the object of the arts.

But if this dogma is accepted, then one must also admit a separation within the citizens of a country, primarily between those who can speak in the name of their country and those

22. "Who Wants the English Composer?" (1912), reprinted in Hubert Foss, *Ralph Vaughan Williams*, p. 197.
23. Quoted by Ralph Vaughan Williams in *National Music*, p. 4.
24. *Ibid.*, p. 50.
25. Quoted in Ursula Vaughan Williams, *R.V.W.*, p. 164.

who speak an international tongue. The national composer, when he bases his music on folk songs, must know what songs are folk and what non-folk. This problem has been spotted not only by professional students of folk music, like Lloyd, but also by writers interested in contemporary singers, like Pete Seeger or Bob Dylan. One such writer, John Greenway, in his essay "The Position of Songs of Protest in Folk Literature," faces the problem and concludes that "folk in our culture is an economic term." "The modern folk is most often the unskilled worker, less often the skilled worker in industrial occupations." [26] He turns out to belong to the CIO, not the AFL, a miner, a worker in a textile mill, and sometimes an agricultural laborer. This definition by demonstration is suggestive but hardly conclusive. We have songs that used to be sung by cow punchers, others by soldiers and sailors, and still others by rowdy undergraduates which are both old and of unknown authorship. Why are they not also folk songs?

If one of the differentiae of the folk song is its communal character, then these songs are surely folk songs. They are seldom if ever sung in solo; they are sung by groups, on the march or round the camp fire or after meals. Their longevity is a sign of their popularity. But there are few books on folk songs which include such music. On the contrary, the usual songs discussed are rural songs, as if the rustic were a more representative part of the folk than the urban dweller or factory hand. This point of view was definitely that of one of the most outspoken of musical nationalists—Grieg. As his biographer, Monrad-Johansen, said in 1877 at Hardanger, "he was carried away on an overwhelming wave of enthusiasm for the Norwegian peasant—for his manners and customs, his speech, his aristocratic nature, his feeling for art, his home craft, his dress; in short, everything to do with the peasants had something almost holy about it for him and on this

26. See *The American Folk Scene*, ed. D. A. De Turk and A. Poulin, Jr., p. 120.

subject he could not bear to hear a disparaging word." [27] But surely the Norwegian sailors and fishermen, like the Vikings, are as truly Norwegian as the peasant. Yet somehow or other the man of the soil generally seems more representative of a country than his fellowmen. So Karel Hoffmeister says of Dvořák that his *Slavonic Dances*, which are country dances, "spring directly from the soul of the people. Something of our Slavonic soul speaks in every theme we meet in them." [28] Again, "In Opera [Dvořák] tends in his loftiest work toward nationality and the poetry of the people" (p. 83). But again the people in question are the country people, or men and women of the distant past. Would one not also say that *Cavalleria Rusticana* spoke for the soul of the Italian people, or that *Louise* spoke for the soul of the French people? There are plenty of songs, sung by thousands, and since television by millions, that originate in cities—and not only in New York—which seem to be beloved by those who hear and repeat them. For that matter *Old Folks at Home* and a half dozen more of Foster's compositions have been taken to the hearts of thousands and few have the slightest idea of who Foster was.

Now the interest in folk songs is at least as old as the interest in ballads. John Parry, a blind Welsh harper (d. 1782), published a collection called *Antient British Music* as early as 1742, antedating Percy's *Reliques* by over twenty years. Edward Bunting (d. 1843) got out some Irish songs in 1796, and Joseph Cooper Walker (d. 1810) published a similar collection in 1786. Thus folk song collecting got well under way before the drive toward cultural nationalism had started. When Haydn and Beethoven were commissioned to rewrite Scottish airs, it was not because these great composers could express the Scottish or Irish soul better than a Scot or an Irishman could. The early collectors of folk songs were interested more in music than in nationalism. There

27. David Monrad-Johansen, *Edvard Grieg*, trans. Madge Robertson, p. 94.
28. Karel Hoffmeister, *Anton Dvořák*, trans. Rosa Newmarch, p. 59.

may have been the sentiment that stirs all antiquarians, a kind of nostalgia for a partly imaginary past, the sort of thing that one finds in some of the Romantics.[29] But sometimes one comes upon a writer like John Addington Symonds who actually believed, as Herder did, that there is a being called *The People*, a being that expresses itself in art. This being is not an individual; as far as one can tell, it has the arts for its special medium of communication. It "lives and acts and feels," [30] but where it is to be found, except in the arts, he does not tell us. The location and character of the folk varies with those who are interested in them. At times it has been anyone long enough in the grave, but in recent times the term has been applied to anyone who can twang a guitar and sing in a nasal voice. Jean Thomas, who made a serious study of the ballads being composed and sung in the mountains of Kentucky, identifies the folk with the mountaineers, who make ballads about recent as well as past happenings—feuds, floods, railroad disasters, murders, and the departures of friends.[31] These mountaineers are hardly a fair sample of the American people, however. They are a vestigial group from the families of early settlers, quaint, picturesque, no doubt, and worth describing, and certainly not typical.

As a matter of fact, some writers have been well aware of the problem of finding the folk. A. L. Lloyd, one of the soberest of folk-song amateurs, in the *Folk Song in England*, lists the following group: as those chosen by various writers to represent the People (1) the peasants, by Bartók and his school; (2) the common people (i.e., the unlettered), by Cecil Sharp; (3) people uninfluenced by "popular and art music"; (4) the poor as contrasted with the educated; (5) the urban proletariat plus those

29. H. G. Schenk, *The Mind of the European Romantics*, esp. p. 202.
30. See Phyllis Grosskurth, *John Addington Symonds*, p. 307.
31. See Jean Thomas, *Ballad Makin' in the Mountains of Kentucky*, p. xi. This book is a firsthand account of how ballads and hymns are actually composed by the Kentucky mountaineers.

already mentioned. He himself includes among the folk songs miners' songs and sea chanteys and is willing to differentiate folk song by the historical fact that it is "essentially an oral affair whose intrinsic character derives from the peculiarities of mouth-to-ear-to-mouth transmission." [32] Musically the normal folk song, he says (p. 36), and backs it up with plenty of examples, has a range of about an octave, though the range of the more ancient songs is narrower. The forms are of the simplest, short figures repeated. And since he is more interested in music than in nationalism he admits (p. 47) that folk tunes, even those thought of as essentially English, are international. The same tunes are found all over the world, just as folklore is, and he quotes Constantin Brailoiu as saying that the peculiarities of Hungarian music, as determined by Bartók and Kodály, are also found in the music of certain American Indians and even Papuans (p. 88).

Since the spread of Marxism the tendency has developed to identify the People with the working class. And indeed national cultures, so far as the Occident is concerned, are largely differentiated only by language. The nonliterary arts, architecture, painting, and sculpture, are almost alike in all countries. But obviously literature varies with the language in which it is written. The kind of music one hears in the concert halls no more varies from country to country than it did in the nineteenth century, indeed probably less so. Painting in Tokyo or Venice or New York has lost all national character. Building, similarly, has no regional distinction, and the same skyscrapers with the same rectangular façades can be seen wherever there is enough money to build them, whether it be Moscow or Chicago. This may be an argument in favor of the conclusion that it is the People, the people all united all over the world, whose soul has at last found a medium of expression. If so, it is a pretty weak argument, since fads and fashions shift in the arts as everywhere else.

32. *Folk Song in England*, p. 32.

Sydney Finkelstein in three books on music emphasizes the importance of general "appeal," general in an international sense, of all music. It is in fact his main criterion of excellence. He explains what he believes to be the popular appeal of "classic'" music, that is, the music of Bach, Handel, Mozart, Haydn, and Beethoven. Such composers, he maintains, had "a grasp of contemporary realities, in terms of the most humanly expressive language, functional structure, and meaningful design that were possible to the arts and best served the people of the times." [33] How music can do this is discussed in another of Finkelstein's books called *How Music Expresses Ideas*. In this work the author says that music contains "human imagery typical of human actions and relationships" (p. 6). These images are presumably intuitively grasped, felt, understood, by human beings, but the social (economic?) class dominant in a given society will determine what kind of music is acceptable. In Bach, says Mr. Finkelstein, there was a struggle between "the bourgeois artist addressing multitudes and the feudal craftsman-servant . . . one struggling to break through the shell of the other" (p. 32). In Beethoven "the fundamental reality was the cracking of feudalism, the victories of bourgeois democracy, the freeing of the individual from feudal servitude . . ." (p. 51). Modern music—that of Schoenberg, Hindemith, and Stravinsky—is the music of imperialism typifying "the total mystification of economic, social, and historical forces which imperialism spreads in people's minds." Their music shrouds the real world in mystery and declares it unreal (p. 82). Handel's oratorios written in England celebrated "the military victories of the middle-class Whigs over their feudal enemies at home and on the continent" (p. 28). But in folk music one hears "social consciousness; the experiences and thought held in common by people who labor, suffer and triumph together." [34]

33. *Art and Society*, p. 171.
34. Finkelstein, *Composer and Nation: The Folk Heritage*, p. 19.

The notes and figures that make up the famous song "God rest ye merry, gentlemen" are among the most international in the Occident, found in France, Bulgaria, Scandinavia, as well as in England and the United States.[35] The words, of course, differ. Just what are the images symbolized in this bit of music? The notes, the rhythm, the musical figures may stimulate emotions of sorrow, for instance, but what do they tell us about political and social structures? When one knows the words, naturally one can read them back into the music. But having been educated in a college the anthem of which was sung to the tune of "The Old Oaken Bucket," I have a tendency to believe that music could be translated into almost any set of words and no one would be any the wiser. Moreover, no composer is all of a piece; he varies more or less from composition to composition. One cannot speak of Bach, Mozart, and Handel as if they were always the same. The music of Handel's *Messiah* is different from that of *Rodelinda*, though there are undoubtedly Handelian marks in both. But the traditions of eighteenth-century music demanded that certain words be fitted to certain musical figures. Could one say that Mozart's G-minor Symphony "served" the people of the eighteenth century any more than it served the aristocracy or the people of the twentieth century? The Requiem, to be sure, is adjusted to a Catholic ritual and thus may be imagined to be less "demophilic" than the Jupiter Symphony or the clarinet quartette. But the words of a requiem mass in no way reflect or express a social hierarchy. The ecclesiastical hierarchy has never been said to be democratic, but surely to pray that God give rest to the deceased, whoever he may have been, is anything but "feudal." Moreover, I doubt that it is possible ever to translate music into words. A march may set one's feet tapping, but it does not say that armies are better than straggling mobs or war better than diplomacy. For that matter many a peaceful procession may well be accompanied by music that was written for entirely different processions.

35. Lloyd, *Folk Song in England*, p. 104.

Think of the wedding music from A *Midsummer Night's Dream* and *Lohengrin!* Mr. Finkelstein uses the presence of folk music as evidence of anti-aristocratic feeling on the part of the composer. It is thus almost literally the *vox populi*, though transmitted through an individual. He is, for instance, willing to say[36] that "in the music of . . . Chopin . . . the use of folk musical sources is openly bound to a proclamation of patriotism and a call to national freedom." But though Chopin was certainly patriotic, the waltz is no more a folk dance of Poland than it is of New York, and as for dancing to Chopin's waltzes, only a ballerina could do it. In fact, Mr. Finkelstein admits that Chopin "was sceptical of democracy" and had a "cynical attitude towards the democratic slogans of bourgeois politicians" (p. 114). The point is that music, like painting, sculpture, and all the other arts is multivalent, and its "meaning" will vary according to the ear that hears it. Haydn's masses may not sound religious to modern American ears, but that is because most of us identify religious music with the gloomy Protestant hymns. A boy who has grown up on hymns like

> There is a fountain filled with blood
> Drawn from Emmanuel's veins,
> And sinners plunged beneath that flood
> Lose all their guilty stains,

is not going to think of the Gloria in the Lord Nelson Mass as religious. For that matter, if the Gothic churches of Eastlake are religious, then St. Peter's is not.

One of the difficulties in discussing the nonmusical meaning of music is that we pay more attention to words than to the notes, when there are words. In an anthology of essays called *The American Folk Scene*, practically nothing is said of music. There are twenty-nine essays reprinted in this very useful volume, but they are all about the musicians and their techniques of singing, or

36. *Composers and Nation*, p. 111.

about the contents of the lyrics, or historical anecdotes. This is understandable, since the music of the folk song, like that of Tin Pan Alley, is almost as simple as the counting songs of children. When one refers to Vaughan Williams, Charles Ives, and Bartók as popular composers, in the sense that their voices are the People's voice, then one has to grant that the People are as fickle and ungrateful as they have often been accused of being. The overwhelming majority of concert-goers dislikes this kind of music and prefers that of Tchaikowsky. "What stamps a work as 'folk,' " says Mr. Finkelstein, "is that it expresses the communal mind and becomes part of communal life, not that it is collectively created." [37] Aside from the precise meaning of "to express," the common people are as diverse in their minds and lives as the upper classes. Some of them seek absorption in large groups and some shun such groups; some try to climb the social ladder and some laugh at such attempts; some spend their leisure time in the free public libraries and some stay at home watching mayhem on the television screen. It is about time that we recognized the existence of individuals and hence the irreducible heterogeneity of society.

37. *Ibid.*, p. 307.

VIII

EGALITARIANISM

The notion that mankind had once lived in a condition close to ideal and had then fallen from it was common to both classical paganism and Christianity. The myths of the Golden Age as well as of the Age of Kronos or Saturn, though they differed in their various versions, and the story of the Garden of Eden, were kept alive in one form or another throughout the Middle Ages and the Renaissance. Whatever the variants, all agreed that man in the beginning of history was happy and that modern man was miserable. This notion, which has been called chronological primitivism, was elaborated in poetry as well as in historiography, ethics, and political philosophy. It was an idea whose ramifications spread throughout European letters. It seemed to some of its proponents to imply that the earliest period or form of anything was the best, whether it was primitive Christianity, primitive art, primitive man as seen in savages, or even the child. Just why the primordial was better than the subsequent was never clearly explained, for there was no evidence in the Bible of just what the life of prelapsarian man was like, and though more details were given of life in the Golden Age and its analogues, they were obviously nothing more than dreams.

There was also no agreement over why man had lost his primeval happiness. To this day no biblical exegete has clarified in an unquestionable manner the meaning of the Tree of Knowledge and its forbidden fruit. The plain unelaborated account is simply that our primordial ancestors disobeyed a divine command. But the significance of their disobedience, the reason for giving the command, the very question of whether there was or needed to be any reason, these problems have filled hundreds of volumes.

Similarly, no one in pagan circles knew why the Golden Age should have disappeared. The temptation of Eve was more easily understood than the degeneration of the Golden Race. Both the pagan and the biblical accounts had to be accepted as descriptions of a historical event, the explanation of which was left to speculation.

Hence when the Dijon Academy in 1754 proposed a prize for the best answer to the question, "What is the origin of inequality among men and is it justified by natural law?" it seemed to be assumed that inequality had arisen in the course of history, that its origin could be discovered rationally, and that presumably it was an evil, not a good. In short, it seemed to be tacitly assumed that men had not always been unequal, though if a contestant had wished to argue that inequality was an inherent trait in human beings and part of God's scheme, he could have done so. What is of special interest is that the definition of inequality was left to the contestants to frame.

One of the most famous of medieval Latin phrases is attributed to Gregory the Great: *Omnes namque homines natura aequales sumus* ("All of us human beings are equal by nature"), a phrase in which the word *"natura"* is the locus of the argument.[1] Just what it meant to be equal by nature was never very clear; the closest one can come to an interpretation is to substitute another phrase, "in the eyes of God." The idea, however vague, has its literary origin in Cicero's *De legibus* (I, x, 28–30), in a passage expounding the natural homogeneity of mankind. For Cicero, man "in a state of nature" was of one kind, rational animality being the genus and differentia. The differences among men were either trivial or unnatural. In Christian writers these differences were differences of condition, economic status, bodily strength, and the like. They might be important in temporal affairs, but to God, who is not an *acceptor personarum*, they are

1. See A. J. Carlyle in R. W. and A. J. Carlyle, *A History of Mediaeval Political Theory in the West*, Vol. 1, p. 199.

worthless. Just as the Roman Stoic could disregard his condition as slave or emperor, so the Christian could be urged to disregard all social and economic, as well as political, differences as irrelevant to religious felicity.

Rousseau's *Discourse on Inequality*,[2] which was submitted in the competition, distinguished between obvious inequalities which are "established by nature," such as differences in age, health, bodily strength, and mental quality, and those which are established by convention, the political, the privileges of the rich, the prestigious, the powerful, the commanding (p. 140). And though it might seem as though the latter depended to some extent upon the former, Rousseau denies this. His denial entails the belief, to cite but one possibility, that the man endowed by birth with great intelligence or aggressiveness or bodily vigor is no more likely to rise to a position of political power than one who is congenitally stupid, submissive, or weak. Rousseau is convinced that the law of the state takes precedence over the law of nature and that this was not always so but came about at a specifiable moment of history. At the same time he repudiated all earlier descriptions of the state of nature as historically worthless and insisted that what was wanted was an account of primeval man based upon a hypothesis of human nature as such, of human nature as it must have been before societies and their laws had been framed.

He therefore rejected the Aristotelian principle that man was inherently a social animal. On the contrary, there is no more reason to believe that sociality is inherent in human nature than in animal nature. Man in the beginning just wandered about the forests like a beast, eating whatever he could find, naked, weaponless, inured to extremes of heat and cold, robust, and giving birth to robust children. Should any infant be too weak to survive, it was allowed to perish. In modern societies, on the contrary, "the State making children a burden to their fathers, kills them without

2. I use the C. E. Vaughan edition of *The Political Writings of Jean Jacques Rousseau*. The *Discourse* is in Vol. 1.

distinction before birth" (p. 143). Primitive strength, seen in modern savages, is hence lost.[3] Modern society preserves the unfit and propagates disease. Nature would have us live a simple life, in an unvarying regime, in solitude (p. 146). The one difference between natural man and the beasts is that man is a free agent, whereas the beasts are controlled by instinct alone. "Nature gives her orders to every animal and the beast obeys. Man experiences the same impulsion but recognizes his freedom to acquiesce or resist" (p. 149).

The detail of solitude was important to Rousseau. Like Lucretius he pictured man in a state of nature as "having neither house nor hut, nor property of any kind, each taking what shelter chance provided and remaining in it for one night only, males and females uniting fortuitously as the occasion and desire pro- vided, without the need of words to express what they might have to say. And they left each other with equal ease" (p. 154). Why then should they have formed societies? They had no more need of their fellows than wolves or monkeys have—an unfortunate example. They were not and could not be unhappy, for they lacked nothing that they needed and they were free, with hearts at peace and bodies in good health (p. 158). Instinct was all man needed to live a natural life; educated rationality (*raison cultivée*) is required only for living in society. These men were neither vir- tuous nor vicious; such adjectives are inapplicable to solitary beings.

Like Vergil (*Georgics*, I, 125 ff.) and Tibullus (*Elegies*, I, iii, 13), Rousseau believed that in a state of nature there was no private property. "The first man who enclosed a bit of land and took it upon himself to say, 'This is mine,' and found people sim- ple minded enough to believe him, was the true founder of civil society" (p. 169).[4] Private ownership of land is the cause of

---

3. Oddly enough, American Indians, the first real savages to be known by Europeans at firsthand, were thought by some writers to be weaker than Europeans. See A. Gerbi, *La Disputa del Nuovo Mondo, passim.*

4. Cf. Saint Ambrose, *De officiies ministrorum*, I, xxviii, 132 (*PL*, 16 col. 67).

inequality. And from this inequality, economic in nature, pride, superiority, power, all evolved. "From the moment," says Rousseau, "that a man needed the help of another man, as soon as he saw that it was useful to one man to have provisions for two, equality vanished, property entered the scene, and work became a necessity" (pp. 175–76). The woods were cleared and fields took their place. Crops were planted, "watered by the sweat of men, and soon slavery and poverty were born and grew with the harvests" (p. 176).

Returning once again to classical primitivism, Rousseau laments the invention of metallurgy and the use of iron, for with them man profited from those inequalities that had their roots in his natural endowments. "The stronger did more work; the shrewder profited more; the ingenious found means of diminishing their toil; the farmer needed more iron, the smith more wheat; and though one man worked as much as another, the one earned much, the other could hardly make a living" (p. 178).

Rousseau finds it a simple matter to deduce all the ills of society from this point on, while insisting at the same time that society itself is an evil. The Solitary Walker could hardly have been expected to praise social life, but he might have perceived its necessity. Yet to his way of thinking laws were intrinsically bad. They put shackles on the weak and fortified the strong, destroyed forever natural freedom, and perpetuated property rights and inequality, and "to the profit of a few men of ambition, subjected the whole human race forever to labor, servitude, and poverty" (p. 181). Life and liberty might well be natural rights, but not property. History, he believed, illustrates an evolution from the establishment of law and property rights through that of the courts to the final stage where legitimate power becomes arbitrary power (p. 190). The first period authorizes the distinction between rich and poor, the second that between powerful and weak, the third that between master and slave, the highest degree of inequality. It is not to be wondered that men like Robespierre looked back to Rousseau as their master, for there was at the heart of his speculation an anticipation of that form of neo-Darwinism which deprecated the building of hospitals, the protection of the weak, and even schooling. In a state of nature the unfit went to the wall. Only those individuals survived who were capable of meeting the challenge of primitive life. The Terror, after all, was a duplication of nature's technique. The guillotine simply removed from society those individuals who perpetrated its unnatural injustices.

The inequalities of nature then would have been smoothed out by nature, according to Rousseau, if private property had never been instituted. But there were other inequalities common to most societies which became more and more noticeable as the nineteenth century developed and the twentieth dawned. Each period and social group was characterized by injustice, if injustice is the unequal distribution of the good things in life, among which must be included esteem. It will not be irrelevant to list some of them, confining ourselves to American history.

Omitting inequalities in wealth, it became clear very early in American history that the owners of land were to be given privileges that other property owners could not enjoy. In Rhode Island, for example, the charter of 1663 and the franchise law of 1724 restricted suffrage to freeholders owning property of the minimum value of $134. It was not until 1842, after Dorr's Rebellion, that the suffrage was extended to non-freeholders. In New York the Senate was elected, in the words of Chancellor Kent, "by the free and independent lords of the soil, worth at least $250 in freehold estate, over and above all debts charged thereon." So was the Governor. In 1821 when it was proposed in the Constitutional Convention that the suffrage be extended, the Chancellor delivered himself of the following comments:

The Senate has hitherto been elected by the farmers of the state. . . . [It is now proposed] to annihilate, at one stroke, all those property distinctions and to bow before the idol of universal suffrage. That extreme democratic principle, when applied to the legislative and executive departments of government, has been regarded with terror, by the wise men of every age, because in every European republic, ancient and modern, in which it has been tried, it has terminated disastrously, and been productive of corruption, injustice, violence, tyranny. . . .

I wish to preserve our senate as the representative of the landed interest. I wish those who have an interest in the soil, to retain the exclusive possession of a branch of the legislature, as a strong hold in which they may find safety through all the vicissitudes which the state may be destined, in the course of Providence, to experience. . . .

The men of no property, together with the crowds of dependents connected with the great manufacturing and commercial establishments, may, perhaps, at some future day, under skilful management, predominate in the assembly, and yet we should be perfectly safe if no laws could pass without the free consent of the owners of the soil. That security we at present enjoy; and it is that security which I wish to retain.

The tendency of universal suffrage, is to jeopardize the rights of property, and the principles of liberty. There is a constant tendency in human society, and the history of every age proves it; there is a tendency in the poor to covet and to share the plunder of the rich; in the debtor to relax or avoid the obligation of contracts; in the majority to tyrannize over the minority and trample down their rights; in the indolent and the profligate, to cast the whole burthens of society upon the industrious and the virtuous; and *there is a tendency in ambitious and wicked men, to inflame these combustible materials.* [5]

Kent, it will be observed, seemed to be making the following assumption: the property owners were an industrious and virtuous minority group of creditors; the nonproperty owners were an indolent and profligate majority group of debtors. He was probably speaking in the heat of passion, but his feeling that freeholders

5. James Kent "Remarks to the New York Constitutional Convention, 1821," in *Report of the Proceedings . . . of the Convention of 1821,* etc. Nathaniel H. Carter and William L. Stone, Reporters, and Marcus T. C. Gould, Stenographer, pp. 220–21. Cf. the opening sentences of Carlyle's *Past and Present,* Book 3, chapter 8.

were more important to society than other men was not uncommon. After all, that great democrat, Jefferson, held an agrarian society in higher esteem than one in which trade, finance, and industry predominated. But dispraise of trade was nothing new. Kent was illustrating a prejudice that had been expressed and condemned in the United States as early as 1798 by William Manning.

> The reason why a free government has always failed is from the unreasonable demands and desires of the few. They can't bear to be on a level with their fellow creatures, or submit to the determinations of a legislature where (as they call it) the swinish multitude are fairly represented, but sicken at the idea, and are ever hankering and striving after monarchy or aristocracy where the people have nothing to do in matters of government but to support the few in luxury and idleness.[6]

In the United States the prejudice in favor of the propertied class has often been accompanied by the prestige given to old families as contrasted with new ones and, until recent times, to North European ancestry as contrasted with Mediterranean or Central European. Such social inequality was most clearly seen in our immigration quotas. Along with it, as far as prestige is involved, one's professional status determined social privileges— lawyers, physicians, and scholars ranking businessmen and laborers, the white-collar worker ranking the blue-collar worker, and in each group a pecking order well recognized by its members.

There has also been a definite social and at times political inequality determined by one's religious affiliation. Roger Williams was the first to attempt to eliminate this, but the disfranchisement of Jews and Roman Catholics was common in most of the colonies. Maryland at its foundation enfranchised Catholics, but the other colonies followed the example of England. And anti-Catholic prejudice did not die out when Catholics were permitted to vote. The war cry of "Rum, Romanism, and Rebellion"

6. William Manning, *Key of Liberty, Shewing the Causes Why a Free Government has Always Failed* (1798), ed. Samuel Eliot Morison.

was heard as late as 1884, and it was feared in 1960 that John F. Kennedy's election "would put the Pope in the White House." In fact, the realization that a Catholic could be elected president seemed to be startling news at the time. As for the Jews, their inequality to Christians used to appear in appointments to university chairs, and still appears in some cities when a Jew is looking for a house to live in. But even within Christianity there is an order of rank among the Protestant sects, though it varies from locality to locality. "All one body we" seems to do well enough in a hymn, but it is seldom carried out as a program.

The intellectual and racial inequalities have been too well publicized to be more than mentioned. But some states have disfranchised the illiterate and made it almost impossible for Negroes to vote. It is absurd to speak about equality when one penalty is meted out to a white man and another to a Negro, though both may be convicted of the same crime. Similarly, there is no equality when ingenuity is expended on ways of humiliating a man because of his color and regardless of his personal character or professional attainments. Inequalities in knowledge might be thought of as justifying inequalities in suffrage, but racial differences have been known to throw intellectual equality out of balance. In fact, when Andrew Johnson was faced with the problem of extending the franchise to the liberated slaves, he suggested that test of fitness be the ability to read the Constitution of the United States in English, to write one's name, to own real estate valued at more than $250 and pay taxes thereon. This, he said, would "completely disarm the adversary," meaning the northern members of Congress, "and set an example the other states would follow." [7] Other states did follow and with lamentable results.

Literacy tests did not suffice to exclude the would-be Negro voter. The members of the Virginia Convention of 1901–2 were frankly told that it "would not be a sufficient safeguard, because

7. See Kirk Harold Porter, A History of Suffrage in the United States, p. 163.

illiteracy is fast disappearing among the negroes." [8] Hence recourse was had to "the understanding clause." The chairman of the committee is quoted as saying, "I expect the examination with which the black man will be confronted to be inspired by the same spirit that inspires every man upon this floor and in this convention. *I do not expect an impartial administration of this clause.*" [9] The judges who administered the test of whether a man understood the Constitution were free to be as severe as they pleased, or as lenient. Their aim was to disfranchise the Negro by whatever means were available.

But Negroes were not alone in being disfranchised. To begin with, only twelve states allowed women to vote in 1918, and the Nineteenth Amendment was not adopted until 1920. Catholics could not vote in Rhode Island, in spite of Williams' liberalism, as late as 1767; in New York both Catholics and Jews were disfranchised, though it appears that the letter of the law was not always observed; and even in Maryland, founded though it was by Catholics, a Catholic was not allowed to vote in the 1770's. The Know-Nothing Party did its best to exclude the foreign-born from the polls, but its best was ineffectual, for a precedent had been set by Wisconsin as early as 1848 in permitting even aliens to vote after they had declared their intention of being naturalized. There aliens could vote before they became citizens. Some states, fifteen in number, excluded paupers, usually meaning inmates of almshouses, poor farms, and publicly supported institutions. Various types of criminals were disfranchised. But it is interesting that as of 1860 criminals could vote in Arkansas, Delaware, Georgia, Kentucky, Louisiana, Maine, Mississippi, Missouri, New Hampshire, North Carolina, Pennsylvania, South Carolina, Texas, and Vermont, though Negroes were disfranchised in many of the same states.[10]

8. *Ibid.*, p. 217.
9. *Ibid.*, p. 218. Italics in text.
10. See Table III in Porter, *History of Suffrage*, p. 148. Cf. Chilton Wil-

The main political inequality that stimulated movements for reform was economic. That voters must own a certain amount of real estate was fairly generally the case, and as states became industrialized and cities grew in population, the test eliminated a large proportion of the adult white males from the polls. But it was also believed, as John Jay is reported to have said, that those who owned the country ought to govern it.[11] In the state of Rhode Island the dispute came to a head in 1842 when Thomas W. Dorr, relying on the principle of popular sovereignty, decided that too small a fraction of the people was running the state. He and his followers organized, wrote a new constitution, set themselves up as a new government with Dorr as governor, and even attempted armed rebellion. But it came to nothing.[12] Rhode Island at that time was governed under the old colonial charter with only slight modifications. Dorr's constitution was called "The People's Constitution." It is interesting to observe that "the acquisition of property" was added to the inalienable rights of life, liberty, and the pursuit of happiness (Art. I, 2). The suffrage was granted to every white male citizen of the United States who satisfied certain residence requirements, but excluded members of the armed forces, paupers, the insane, and criminals. Moreover, only electors owning $150 worth of property who had paid their taxes could vote on any question of taxation or of the expenditure of public moneys. This no longer seems very revolutionary, but to its opponents it meant that it "would admit to the vote naturalized citizens who were often Irish Catholics," whereas the tradition at that time "upheld the standards of

---

liamson, *American Suffrage, from Property to Democracy, 1760–1860*, pp. 15 ff. and p. 277. I have omitted from this paragraph tests that were applied on the state level but not on the township level. On the ways used to disfranchise Negroes in southern states, see U.S. Commission on Civil Rights, 1959 Report, pp. 31–32.

11. See Williamson, *American Suffrage*, p. 244.

12. The story is told in detail by Jacob Frieze, a one-time follower of Dorr, in a pamphlet called *A Concise History of the Efforts to obtain an Extension of Suffrage in Rhode Island from the Year 1811 to 1842* This work went into at least three editions, the last I have seen being 1912.

middle-class agrarian, Protestant, native-born Rhode Islanders." [13] There was probably (I do not say certainly) a vestige of the old feeling that those who do not own property are shiftless and lazy and, what is more serious, uninterested in the welfare of the commonwealth, coupled obviously with anti-Catholic and anti-Negro bias. It was a long way from Roger Williams, who said that no uniformity of religion had been required by God and who declared that the government of his colony was to be a democracy.[14]

The equality that was sought by most egalitarians was to be actualized in universal suffrage. Innate inequalities, those which Rousseau attributed to nature, had to be accepted with resignation. Economic inequalities could be alleviated by self-help, industry, and, later, organization. Religious and racial prejudice might perhaps be diminished, if not eliminated, by education. But the triumph of egalitarianism is still in the future, and our inalienable rights are still to be universally recognized. The question is bound to arise of why anyone should have wanted all men to be equal in view of the obvious inequalities to be seen everywhere and in all ranks of society. No very satisfactory answer can be given to this question but one can suggest certain motivations of a literary sort.

To begin with there was the biblical text that proclaimed mankind to have been created in the image and likeness of God. This seemed to hold good of all men, regardless of race or social mark. If one actually believed this text, surely one's attitude toward one's fellowmen would have to be one of respect. Then there was the doctrine of the brotherhood of man, accompanied by the command to love one's neighbor as oneself. The early

13. See Williamson, *American Suffrage*, p. 255.
14. See Williams' *Bloudy Tenant*, in his *Works*, Vol. 3, pp. 3 and 249. I use a reprint of the Narragansett Club Publications.

Christian communities seem to have made an effort to practice charity, and charity as brotherly love made no distinction of persons. During the Middle Ages, even when slavery was accepted, the clergy tried to emphasize this.[15] Furthermore, there was that strange tradition of the natural light, the *lumen naturale*, which even Descartes did not doubt, and which granted to all men equal intelligence in rational matters. One of the most compendious statements of this position, as far as America goes, is that of John Wise in his *Vindication of the Government of the New England Churches* (1717). He says,

> [A democracy] is a form of government which the light of nature does highly value and often directs as most agreeable to the just and natural prerogatives of human beings. This was of great account in the early times of the world. And not only so, but upon the experience of several thousand years, after the world had been tumbled and tossed from one species of government to another, at a great expense of blood and treasure, many of the wise nations of the world have sheltered themselves under it again; or at least have blendished and balanced their governments with it. . . . The natural equality of men amongst men must be duly favored; in that government was never established by God or nature to give one man a prerogative to insult over another. . . . Honor all men.[16]

Here one finds a recognition of the natural light, of democracy in church government as a consequence, of social equality, and of general respect for humankind.

Over a hundred years later Channing was to say very much the same thing.

> It is because I have learned the essential equality of men before the common Father, that I cannot endure to see one man establishing his arbitrary will over another by fraud, or force, or wealth, or rank, or superstitious claims. . . . It is because I see in him a great nature, the divine image, and vast capacities, that I demand for him means of self-development, spheres for free action—that I call society not to fetter, but to aid his growth.[17]

15. See A. J. Carlyle, *History of Mediaeval Political Theory*, passim.
16. From the facsimile edition of 1958, pp. 60–61.
17. Quoted by Vernon Parrington in his *Main Currents of American Thought*, Vol. 2, p. 334. Parrington used the 1844 Glasgow edition of Channing's works. The quotation is from the preface to Volume 6.

But here the plea for equality is based on man's common likeness to God. Since God is self-ruled, so must His image be. This should have led Channing into the perfectionism of John Humphrey Noyes, but he stopped short of that. It was apparently enough for him that we all accept our common brotherhood. Channing forgot that the first pair of brothers known to history was broken by murder. Nevertheless, the religious motivation persisted in the United States. One has but to remember the various communities that were founded—Brook Farm, Oneida, the Shaker villages, and for that matter, Deseret—to see how prevalent the religious stimulus was. And what other motive can one attribute to people like Jane Addams, to the preaching of a man like Jacob Riis, or to the sympathy of Dreiser, Sandburg, and Masters, "with their lost and buffeted characters"? [18] Social service could be explained, I imagine, on economic grounds, just as it was criticized as paternalism. But though boys' clubs, settlement houses, public libraries, free schools, and playgrounds are not a solution of economic inequalities, the question might be asked whether that is their purpose. There was of course a good bit of sentimental talk about social service, as when George D. Herron announced that "the Sermon on the Mount is the science of society." [19] But in spite of that, the supporters of the various humanitarian movements were engaged in a religious enterprise. One could hardly be criticized for satisfying one's sense of charity.[20]

Along with this there was a regard for the individual as such, as having a right—and perhaps a duty—to be himself. Emerson, who was the most influential spokesman for this point of view, in

18. Quoted from the unsigned "Postscript at Midcentury," in the *Literary History of the United States*, ed. Robert E. Spiller, Willard Thorpe, Henry Seidel Canby, Thomas H. Johnson (New York, 1953), p. 1398.

19. Quoted by Henry Nash Smith, *ibid.*, p. 795.

20. The influence of the pulpit on the growth of "republican" sentiment as early as the seventeenth century has been beautifully shown in Alan Heimert's *Religion and the American Mind*, esp. chapter 10.

his speech on "The Young American," [21] given on February 7, 1844, recognized and insisted upon differences in ability. "In every society," he said, "some men are born to rule and some to advise." Each shade of character has its place in the whole and presumably each man can discover for himself what that place is and proceed to fill it. He says nothing here about the pressures of school, custom, the family, the neighbors, but perhaps he thinks that will power can resist them. Emerson had so high a regard for particularity that he said in "Self-Reliance," "I would write on the lintels of my door-post, Whim." In short, like Walt Whitman, he felt that no man was obliged to be even consistent. One had a right to change from moment to moment in spite of hitching one's wagon to a star. "Nothing," he said, again in "Self-Reliance," "is at last sacred but the integrity of your own mind. . . . No law can be sacred to me but that of my own nature. . . . The only right is what is after my constitution; the only wrong what is against it." This is atomizing society into its individual members and, consistent with this extremism, Emerson recognized no obligation to the poor.

> There is a class of persons to whom by all spiritual affinity I am bought and sold; for them I will go to prison if need be; but your miscellaneous popular charities; the education at college of fools; the building of meeting-houses to the vain end to which many now stand; alms to sots; the thousand-fold Relief Societies;—though I confess with shame I sometimes succumb and give the dollar, it is a wicked dollar, by and by I shall have the manhood to withhold.[22]

It may well have been Emerson's affection for the particular that led him in "The American Scholar" to emphasize cultural nationalism. The emphasis goes back to Herder who, for analogous reasons, tried to liberate Germany from Mediterranean civilization. The People now, as among the lovers of ballads, folk songs, folklore, were not the totality of human beings, but were fragmented

21. Riverside edition of the Works.
22. Ibid., Vol. II, p. 52, and pp. 53–54.

into nations. Each nation, like each type of individual, had a right to be itself, regardless of its previous condition or general history. And just as every character was to all intents and purposes as worthy of respect as every other, so there was no esteeming one national culture above any other. European culture as a whole, it was usually agreed, derived from Judea and Greece. But during the nineteenth century local differences were becoming respectable and there was apparently no longer a single Occident. More and more Americans were to accentuate their differences from Europeans. Such phrases as "the American dream," "the American way of life," "Americanism," plus "Americanization" and "manifest destiny," all indicated that somehow or other a new kind of civilization, not just another example of the old kind, would evolve. The supposed crudities, the materialism, the comic accents, were to be embraced and not repudiated. Europeans might not like it all, and few of them did, but that was of no importance. Proponents of this point of view asserted the equality of kinds and transcended individuals. It was the sort of formula that justified, when necessary, regionalism, states' rights, religious sectarianism, in fact all forms of collective particularism. But, ironically enough, as the twentieth century developed, conscription in two wars, a national press stifling all local papers, syndicated editorial opinion, communication networks, and national advertising, helped to unify mores and tastes, to say nothing of ideas, and the struggle for individual self-assertion had to be begun all over again.

With the election of Jefferson egalitarianism as a slogan, if not as a program, was reinforced. From 1801 to 1841 all presidents with the exception of John Quincy Adams were Democrats, and of them Andrew Jackson became a symbol of the rough, honest, intuitively wise son of the soil, presumably superior to the sons of landed proprietors. Even Emerson, that fastidious scholar, was able to "embrace the common," "explore and sit at the feet of the familiar, the low." In this he joined ranks with Walt Whitman, with the crackerbox philosophers, and furthered the tradition which had gained popular support through Tom Paine's *Common Sense* and the *Rights of Man*. These men wanted full political equality, at least for whites, if not for Negroes and Indians, but they also wanted social equality. It was all very well for John Adams to speak of the "rude man" as "shiftless, ignorant, spendthrift," [23] the swinish multitude was asserting itself and losing all sense of inferiority, if indeed it ever had had any. It was this self-assertion that shocked visitors like Mrs. Trollope and gave an air of crudity to American manners. The lampoons even of Jefferson show that the feeling was not confined to Europeans.

The myth of Andrew Jackson as a farmer working his own land was a concentrated emblem of this spirit.[24] Here the distinction between the educated and the uneducated man was done away with. The old cultural primitivism that made innate wisdom superior to acquired, implied that lack of schooling was not identical with lack of brains. The Germans had made a distinction between *Verstand* and *Vernunft*, a distinction that in America was sometimes labeled the head and the heart, and the wisdom of the heart, or *Vernunft*, was the better.[25] The philosophers who played upon this were far from being of the crackerbox genus and would have been astonished to see what use had been made of their doctrines. But they would have had no right to be astonished. One of the strongest threads of the Protestant tradition was the irrelevance of schooling to religious understanding, and even popes, for that matter, had been known to depreciate scholarship.[26] Alan Heimert has shown how the anti-intellectualistic strain had appeared in the colonies as early as the middle eighteenth century.[27] And though the more refined members of the clergy objected to

23. See Parrington, *Main Currents of American Thought*, Vol. 1, p. 313. Also Adams' letter to John Taylor in *Works*, Vol. 6, p. 516.

24. See John William Ward, *Andrew Jackson: Symbol for an Age*, chapter 3.

25. How this was utilized in argument is clearly expounded in Arthur O. Lovejoy, *The Reason, the Understanding, and Time*.

26. See Boas, *Essays on Primitivism . . . in the Middle Ages*, p. 122.

27. *Religion and the American Mind*, pp. 164 ff., 188 ff., 212 ff.

the hysteria stirred up by evangelists like Whitefield, they had to admit that the Spirit of the Lord was in such preachers. A moment's reflection will show that this type of anti-intellectualism has never died out in the United States. The professor is still an object of ridicule, and it is still customary to prefer practice to theory, as if the two could actually be separated.

In describing Jackson as the type of self-made man, Professor Ward has said, "For the early nineteenth century Jackson objectified the belief that a man could overcome all obstacles and rise from obscurity to greatness." [28] The greatness of Jackson was proved not only by the Battle of New Orleans but also by his having been elected to the presidency. All this was political, not moral or intellectual, greatness. The slogan "From Log Cabin to White House" became in time a program for every American boy. To be president was an ideal. But it was not the only ideal. There was also the ideal of commercial and industrial eminence. There was the ideal preached by R. H. Conwell in his sermon "Acres of Diamonds": "I say you ought to get rich, and it is your duty to get rich. . . . There is not a poor person in the United States who was not made poor by his own shortcomings, or by the shortcomings of someone else. It is all wrong to be poor, anyhow." [29] This was not very different from the moral of the Horatio Alger stories. Alger's poor boys, often the sons of widows, make good by their own efforts. Character, persistence, industriousness, these were the qualities by means of which a man might make himself.

But while one group was putting the onus of success on the

28. *Andrew Jackson*, p. 123.

29. "Acres of Diamonds," pp. 18, 21. This point of view was anticipated by the Rev. Thomas P. Hunt in *The Book of Wealth; in which it is Proved from the Bible that it is the Duty of Every Man to become Rich*. Later, in 1910, Lyman Abbott in an article called "Righteousness" (*Outlook*, March 12, p. 576) wrote that the Parable of the Talents proved that "Jesus Christ was one of the men who think that it is right to be rich." See Irvin Gordon Wyllie, *The Cult of the Self-Made Man, 1830–1910*, unpublished doctoral dissertation for the University of Wisconsin.

individual alone, another was organizing to give the individual the means essential to making the effort. I am not speaking here of settlement houses and social service, but of the very large program of free education running from the first grade in primary school through the university, supplemented by generous scholarships, fellowships, and grants in aid of research. It has been this movement, along with the labor movement, that has put most members of American society on the same level. There is still plenty of inequality to be eliminated if one wishes to do so. But at least one can say that the Welfare State has made it an avowed purpose to eliminate inequality, whether political, economic, social, or intellectual. How far it will succeed is another question, for those natural inequalities of which Rousseau was aware will probably always exist, and it need not be forgotten that among such is the desire to obey rather than to command. The submissive individual, humble, self-effacing, shunning responsibility, has something of the quality of the saint. He finds his place in the Church, for there he is honored. But in the world he is doomed to be the burden bearer, and he wears no halo. He may not starve, for someone or some institution will feed him; he will vote but vote a straight ticket; he will read but will guide his choice of books by the book reviews. A new myth will be developed to justify his existence and give him a feeling of security. We see it emerging in the pride we take in being "common men."

To be a common man, to be a 100 per cent American, or to be a perfect example of any other category, is an ideal. But ideals of that sort have a power that is as strong as that of anything concrete. And during the last three quarters of the nineteenth century it became an important political as well as social slogan. So far as its embodiment in action is concerned, however, the seeds of its decay were planted while it was at its point of greatest influence.

After the Industrial Revolution got under way, class warfare and, naturally, class consciousness arose and there was an uneasy balance in the minds of the working class between devotion to the nation and devotion to one's fellow workers. It was part of the propaganda of the popular leaders to play down nationalism and to accentuate the common interests of the "workers of the world." It was even hoped before the opening of World War I that the representatives of the working class would refuse to vote credits for armaments and thus would prevent the outbreak of that catastrophe. But that hope came to nothing. German workers shot at French and English workers just as the sons of the nobility did. And though there were plenty of writers to declare that World War II was a civil war, that declaration was as futile as earlier slogans had been. The outstanding exceptions—there were conscientious objectors in both wars—were members of the various communist parties who until the Soviet Union was attacked by Hitler were vociferous in their objections to what they termed an imperialists' war. But once the situation changed they became as nationalistic as their bourgeois brethren. The war was then a People's War against Fascist tyrants.

We have seen in these essays how the term, "The People," has fluctuated in its denotation, being at times the *Plebs*, the mob, male citizens of voting age and with the proper amount of real estate, and at one time even the princes of the empire.[30] During all these changes few writers had anything good to say of the

30. Cf. Michael Wilks, *The Problem of Sovereignty in the Later Middle Ages*: "When the fourteenth century writer [Marsilius of Padua] spoke of the *populus* he was thinking only of its *senior pars*, the princes and magnates who were held to represent the whole community" (p. 196). And again: "The people can act only with and through the magnates, not against them. The *communitas imperii* therefore comes to mean nothing but the princes, forming an autonomous body" (p. 198). And finally: "Princely liberty meant what it said: complete freedom of action for the princes and for nobody else, whilst popular movements came automatically under the heading of sedition and subversion" (p. 199).

People, and popular taste, like popular opinion, was identified with bad taste and thoughtless opinion. One might grant political power to an individual or social class without on that account endowing it with intellectual, moral, or aesthetic insight. But it is clear, I hope, that this is precisely what was granted to the People when the People became the Masses or the Working Class, and esteem for their wisdom increased as their political power increased.

When one begins to speculate on how this came about, one first thinks of the relatively novel notion of the dignity of labor. In the book of Genesis, 3:19, labor is a punishment for Adam's sin, though in chapter 2 he had been put in the Garden to tend it. On the whole men thought of work as unpleasant, if not downright painful. Aristotle had already laid it down as a principle that manual labor was degrading, and in Latin literature manual arts were inherently lower than liberal arts. In fact, in ancient times most manual labor was performed by slaves. Men have generally sought a life of leisure as their goal, and the only hard work which was considered worthy of a gentleman was warfare. Warfare was of course extolled and, though the actual fighting involved as much sweat and muscle as farming or carpentry, the sanction of its being self-protection seems to have given it a place in a class by itself.

In the monasteries a certain amount of labor was prescribed, field work for the most part. But the idea that the monks spent their time at hard labor is erroneous; they spent their time at various things, and the orders themselves varied in what they demanded of their members. When a monastery owned slaves, the monks did little work, and some monks, the mendicants, did none at all. Nevertheless, the tradition developed that the monastic life was one of penance, and that part of the penance consisted in labor. After the Gothic Revival of the early nineteenth century, monastic life was glamorized and one had a picture of the monks engaged in painting pictures, making stained glass, putting frescoes on the walls of churches, and doing it *ad majorem Dei gloriam*. Coulton has shown how exaggerated this picture is. But the fact remains that it led directly to a cult of handicraft and, in men like William Morris and later Eric Gill, to work with one's hands became almost a religious duty. Thus a sentimental regard for the manual laborer appeared along with depreciation of the machine. That it was the machine which gave men time for manual labor was usually forgotten.[31] Work now took on a new aspect, and it was logical enough for Morris to preach a brand of socialism, for he made no distinction between the labor of the artisan and the labor of the mill hand. And since the lot of the laboring man was incontestably bad and humanitarianism was on the increase, since political economists began to see that individual charity would never succeed in giving the laborer the decency his human nature deserved, to invest labor itself with dignity was a natural enough outcome. There was nothing dignified in the life of the English mill hand, man, woman, or child, and one suspects that the attribution was a sort of sop to the working man to give him the impression that he too had a place in the social hierarchy, and a necessary place. But when a man feels that he is necessary, he will demand recognition of his contribution to the body politic. It was to be expected that political democracy would spread, and before many years were past social democracy was to be added to political.

This evolution was not inevitable. It was made possible by the organization of labor into unions which demanded and got compensation in the form of higher wages, shorter hours, and finally various fringe benefits. There was a recognition on the part of those immediately concerned of the interdependence of capital and labor. This was so obvious that it might have been recognized somewhat earlier, but since labor had no means of making its demands felt, the obvious interdependence had no effect on changing

31. Morris, of course, did not invent the Gospel of Work. That originated as far as literature goes in Carlyle's *Past and Present*.

the social order. It was the idea of the class war that turned the trick. And whatever one may think of the desirability and justice of strikes, one had to admit that as the years advanced strikes produced the results that labor wanted. The laboring class found that its standard of living was steadily rising and, as of today and in the United States, it has become absurd to speak of the working man in terms that were current in the eighteenth century. Such terms are obsolete. One might object to the word "dignity" as applied to the conduct of some labor leaders, but dignity is obsolescent also and it is rather social rank that is in question.

In the United States, except in the South, everyone is supposed to "do" something. The leisure class as a class is so tiny that it has no effect on the general level of taste and morals. It is taken for granted that everyone, even men of wealth, has some sort of job, and, since the enfranchisement of women, almost the entire adult population has been at work. The demand for manual labor has decreased noticeably as work is being done more and more by machines. It has become almost impossible to find individuals willing to undertake jobs that were formerly common, such as domestic service, gardening, driving cars, and the like. Work is not only easier than it used to be, but pleasanter, and the average American takes it for granted that when he reaches a certain age he will go to work. As a working man he is no longer isolated from his fellow citizens. He has all the advantages of everyone else and there seems to be little effort made to deprive him of them. What effort is made in that direction is exerted to prevent the Negro from living the life of other citizens. But even in that area history is moving fast.

Industrialization has fused large numbers of individuals into groups conscious that they have a common interest. As soon as industry left the cottage for the factory, this change began. But cottage industry was gone for good since it could not possibly turn out enough products for the demands of the consumers. This might not have been true if England, for example, had remained without colonies, but the colonies were a market for English goods and a market that was to be respected. The entrepreneur found himself caught in his own devices. On the one hand he had to produce large quantities of goods, and on the other he could do so only by recognizing his dependence on labor. As soon as labor, for its part, recognized this simple truth, it used its power; and now in every industrialized society it wields a power which a hundred years ago was only a dream.

As industry has evolved it has utilized technological innovations which have moved the laborer towards the so-called white-collar status. To symbolize modern labor by a hammer and sickle is anachronistic. Push buttons and switches would be more to the point. There is nothing grimy about the modern factory. It is clean and orderly and the machines work under the supervision of only a few men and women. The main annoyance is the noise, but since the noise is no worse in the factory than in the home, where nine times out of ten a radio or television set is turned on, no one is in a state of acute suffering when at work. It is of course true that not all workingmen are in so delightful a situation. There are still women on their feet for eight hours a day in the large retail stores, builders high on their scaffolds in cold or heat, road builders operating heavy machinery. None of this is idyllic. But on the whole the working class, as a class, is in a position of control. The strike is no longer merely a threat to management; it is a weapon used more against the consumer, who is powerless to grant the demands of the worker. It is thus anachronistic too, for since industry is now country-wide, and labor is industry-wide, the consumer cannot refuse to buy from producers who are being closed down by strikers and buy elsewhere. There is no elsewhere. If there is a strike in the steel industry, building halts. If there is a strike in the telephone network, communication halts. In such cases it is not management that suffers, but the public. And since the public includes both members of the managing and of the working class, everyone suffers at the same time. Hence the next step—and I am not alone in prophesying this—will be the participation of labor in management, the frank admission that both parties are in partnership.

It is clear that we are seeing the People transformed into Labor. In some countries there are Labor parties, but in the United States there is no need for one. Both parties recognize the power of organized labor and unorganized labor hardly exists. Moreover, in the United States one is used to invisible parties, or power groups, lobbies of all sorts which constitute a fourth power in the government. This is deplored by some, but their criticisms have had no effect. Churches, military organizations, patriotic societies, veterans associations, industrial groups, almost any interest that can be organized is organized and acts as a lobby to bring pressure on Congress to pass the kind of legislation that will satisfy it. The only thing that is new about this is our frank admission that it exists. In the Old Regime the Court, the Clergy, and probably the Bank, always had power and used it. But their power was exercised in the dark. Moreover, lobbies were not so numerous, since the number of interests that were recognized as worthy of satisfaction was smaller. It is the United States which has brought the lobby to fulfillment. Whereas on the continent of Europe (though not in Great Britain) there are political parties by the dozen to take care of special interests, in the United States it is preferred to keep the two-party system on the surface and allow the other parties to operate as lobbies.

When the People are identified with Labor, as when they might be with management or the clergy or the armed services, the individuals who are not of the laboring class, for there is always some degree of heterogeneity in every society, are almost without political power. They can, of course, vote, but they have to vote for those candidates who are agreeable to the dominant social class. It is unlikely, as a factual matter, that any candidate proposed by a minority group, if elected to a major office, would be able to carry out legislation that ran counter to the interests of the dominant group.[32] One observes this when an intellectual, a university professor, is elected to Congress. He gets elected by obeisance to the machine or never gets re-elected. There are occasionally individuals, like Woodrow Wilson, who become a sort of Third Force. He was elected because the Republican Party was split. His opponents, Roosevelt and Taft, polled almost a million and a half votes more than he did. He was the choice of a minority, though the candidate of a major party. But once in office, he was shrewd enough to speak for a group whose power was growing. And in his second campaign his slogan was, "He kept us out of war," a slogan which was rejected a month after his inauguration.

The notion of a two-party system includes the objection to a third party. No one objects to the idea of a loyal opposition, except those to whom it is opposed, but there is no reason why a third party, if it actually represents interests that can be satisfied by legislation, should be silenced. Yet no third party has ever succeeded in becoming an important force in American national elections. I assume, but can hardly prove, that this is because there are no deeply felt political sentiments among Americans. It has often been remarked that there are no differences between the platforms of the major parties. This may be because Americans satisfy their needs nonpolitically; the tradition of individualism is too strong for there to be any deeply rooted class-consciousness. There is group-consciousness aplenty. Social bonds are firmest in churches, then in the various societies, clubs, associations, fraternities, to which individuals belong. But there is little evidence that such membership is admitted to be a social tag. And since everyone works, and the combined AFL-CIO has more political power

32. The irony of the situation is brought out by G. William Domhoff in *Who Rules America?*, which shows how national, but not local, problems are settled by a minority.

than any other organization, and since its members traverse parties, its pressure on Congress is strong enough to make the possibility of a Labor Party nil.

There is another feature of American culture which is relevant —that is, urbanization. The urban population of the United States, according to the 1960 census, was 69.9 per cent, and varied from 80.2 per cent in the northeast to 58.5 per cent in the South. The tradition of the village lingered on in the northeast and was carried into the Middle West and the Northwest by the settlers who came, on the whole, from upper New York State and New England. There was and is plenty of snobbery in urban areas, but there are no landed proprietors, owners or descendants of former owners of plantations. Hence distinctions of social class, as distinguished from economic class, are vague, and the dream of rising from rags to riches is realized frequently enough to become folklore. It is hard to keep a person in his place in a city; he has any place he can afford to occupy. And though the corner grocer, where he still exists, or the barber, may not be thought of as the cream of the cream, he is not educated to think of himself as lower in any sense of the word than anyone else. I doubt that any American would be capable of thinking of himself as "not quite top drawer," as so many characters in English novels do.

The point is that the city is taking the place of both the village and the plantation but the transition is not yet completed. The individualism of the town meeting has become as obsolete as cottage industry, but the feeling of being any man's equal is far from obsolescent. Urbanization forces the individual into the mass, compresses him into social solidarity. The very fact that everything he does is now done by large numbers of his associates might be thought to overcome every shred of personal difference. The congregations of churches are no longer two or three gathered together in His name; they are hordes. The media of entertainment cater to millions, not to scores. Two or three newspapers at a maximum, and in some cities only one, peddle the same news and the same editorial opinions to all readers alike. The shops all sell the same goods and the goods themselves are manufactured for all parts of the country. Even the gladiatorial combats on the baseball diamond or the football gridiron belong, so to speak, to the City. They belong in the sense that they symbolize the athletic interests of the community as a whole. When the Orioles win the pennant, it is the city of Baltimore that wins, and everyone, except a handful of "loners," is excited and proud. The inhabitants of the city are supposed to support their team as if some deeply seated interest of each man were bound up in the team's success. So important is this that the President of the United States has to throw the first ball of the season in the capital. If we Americans had a Pindar, he would write odes to celebrate the Giants, the Dodgers, the Orioles, and so on. But our Pindars write for TV and radio.

This ought to lead to the utter suppression of the individual. But it has not done so. For there are so many subsocial groups with which a man can be identified that he may be at one with his neighbor as far as the city's baseball team is concerned but at odds with him as far as his lodge, his church, his service club are concerned. Christian sects, which might seem to be the easiest to amalgamate, proliferate in the United States. There are two hundred and forty-six religious sects exclusive of Roman Catholics and Jews. If we derive all these from the Reformation, we may surmise that religious individualism has survived in America because of the ingrained notion of freedom of conscience. Actually there is very little religious prejudice, and there seems to be a tacit understanding that any kind of theist is to be tolerated. The only restriction is that he share his religious beliefs with others; he must not be so free in his thinking that he is a solitary worshiper. That is, he must belong to some church; any church will do. One thus has individualism within corporate solidarity. And it is this that probably lies at the root of our striving for leadership. One can be an individualist in the sense that one searches for autarky in its ancient sense of complete independence of all externals, people as well as things. But one can also be an individualist in the sense of being the head man, the leader, the man with initiative, the captain, the inventor. It is this latter type who would seem to be more typical of the American urban man, for the former scarcely exists. Sometimes this passion for outstanding importance takes on a ludicrous aspect, when the mere mention of one's name in the local newspaper suffices to confer distinction. If the name is accompanied by a photograph, so much the better. But I have probably said enough to make my point, and should I go further it would land me in a bog of coarse satire.

The Voice of the People, then, in a typically urban culture is no more strictly described than in any other. But there are two more comments that may be useful in discussing it. First, the Voice of God has tended to be de-emphasized. The Voice of the People is not so much justified by its relation to a divine source as by its inherent rightness. Whether this is because one hesitates to identify certain popular decisions with divine decrees in view of their weakness, or because God has lost the prestige He used to have, I do not know. In any event majority rule is seldom if ever disputed. It is held to be self-justified. Second, the technique of inducing the People to say what you want them to say has been developed to a point beyond which it would seem impossible to advance. Advertising or psychological warfare or brain-washing, whichever name is the most pleasing, has caused large numbers of individuals to accept as their own opinions ideas that originate in small offices or committees. The technique is sometimes that of mob rule, based on turning every issue into a crusade against a hidden enemy. The hidden enemy is usually some subsocial group easily identified by color or race, accused of all the crimes in the calendar. Hatred is the most cohesive social cement, and apparently it can be whipped up without too much effort into something approaching frenzy. When one has heard people who are apparently sane accusing the Chief Justice of the Supreme

Court of treason because of his respect for the Bill of Rights, one realizes how irresponsible such accusations can become. And when one overlooks the definition of treason as clearly stated in the Constitution and finds that the accusation is based on the Justice's strict interpretation of the Fifth Amendment, one wonders what influence American education has had upon its pupils. But this is only one example among many. Works of art and styles of art, educational fads, medical nostrums, philosophic fashions, no matter what, can be popularized by the well-known tricks of advertising. The American love of belonging to societies is of course a great help. One's mail is heavy with appeals to join groups—upon payment of dues—whose purposes turn out to be support of the group regardless of its efficacy. The average American seems to enjoy merging his psyche into a collective psyche. This seems to be enough. There is no need to argue that one must fight for popular opinion because it emanates from God. The fact that it is popular suffices. But the added fact that it is made popular by individuals whose business is precisely to make it popular, that is never emphasized.

It is possible that the acclamations of the crowd that aided in the election of bishops, or the *suffragia* of the *Comitia*, were spontaneous and unsolicited, though I doubt it. But in our own times that which takes the place of such outbursts of enthusiasm is surely not the spontaneous expression of any sentiment or idea, but simply results from the manipulation of a mass of human beings made to believe that they are acting freely. It is known that the very phrasing of a question will determine the kind of answer that will be given to it. A small committee which is expert in posing the right questions can determine the People's Voice without any help from God. One turns back to the first Book of Samuel and one realizes that collective opinion will always overcome reason and common sense, in the future as it has now for some 2500 years. *Vox populi vox signiferi.*

BIBLIOGRAPHY

This bibliography contains the editions of books and articles that I have actually quoted or referred to, and only those. It does not aim to be a complete list of all the possible sources of material pertinent to our subject. Moreover, some of the editions, especially of the ancient classics and of standard English poets, are those that go back to my college days and that therefore obviated my traveling to a large library to get later editions. Scholars may disapprove of this but the usual changes in such texts are trivial.

I have used the following abbreviations:

CSEL—Corpus Scriptorum Ecclesiasticorum Latinorum
DNB—Dictionary of National Biography
JHI—Journal of the History of Ideas
MGH—Monumenta Germaniae historica
PG—Patrologia Graeca
PL—Patrologia Latina

Adams, John. Works. Boston, 1850–56.
Alain of Lille (Alanus de Insulis). Summa de arte praedicatoria, PL, 210.
Alciphron. Epistolae. Leipzig, 1856.
Alcuin. Letter 132, Epistolae Karolini Aevi. MGH, Epistolae, Vol. 4. Berlin, 1895.
Ambrose. De officiis ministrorum, PL, 16.
Anon. The Deluge. In Everyman and Other Interludes. London (Everyman edition), 1909.
Apocryphal Gospels. Translated by B. Harris Cowper. 7th ed. London, 1910.
Arendt, Hannah. On Revolution. New York, 1963.
Aristophanes. The Knights. Translated by Benjamin Bickley Rogers. Loeb Classical Library. London and Cambridge, Mass., 1960.
Aristotle. Athenian Constitutions. Translated by Frederic G. Kenyon. Oxford, 1920.
———. Politics. Translated by Benjamin Jowett. Oxford, 1921.
Athanasius. Apologia contra Arianum, St. Athanasius's Four Orations against the Arians. Translated by Samuel Parker. London, 1713.
Augustine. City of God. CSEL, 40.
———. De Genesi contra Manicheos, PL, 34.
Bacon, Francis. "Expostulations to the Lord Chief Justice Coke," The Works of Francis Bacon. New edition by Basil Montague. London, 1827.

Baillet, Adrien. *Jugemens des Sçavans*. Paris, 1722.

Baker, John Tull. "The Precursors of Naturalism." In *Courbet and the Naturalistic Movement*. Baltimore, 1938.

Beaumarchais, P. A. Caron de. *La Folle Journée, ou le Mariage de Figaro*. Paris, 1785.

Beecher, Henry Ward. Speech on the Puritans and Art. *New York Times*, December 22, 1860.

The Holy Bible.

Boas, George. *Essays on Primitivism and Related Ideas in the Middle Ages*. Baltimore, 1948.

————. *The Cult of Childhood*. Studies of the Warburg Institute, Vol. 29. London, 1966.

————. Introduction to *The Hieroglyphics of Horapollo*, Bollingen Series XXIII. New York, 1950.

Bonaventura. *Itinerarium Mentis in Deum, Opera Omnia*, Vol. 5. Claras Aquas, 1891.

Bowen, Catherine Drinker. *Miracle at Philadelphia*. Boston, 1966.

Brandt, Paul. *Schaffende Arbeit und Bildende Kunst*. 2 vols. Leipzig, 1927–28.

Briggs, Wallace Alvin. *Great Poems of the English Language*, New York, 1935.

Browne, Sir Thomas. *Pseudodoxia Epidemica, Works*. Edited by Geoffrey Keynes. Chicago, 1964.

Burchardus of Worms. *Decretals, PL*, 140.

Burns, C. Delisle. *The Principles of Revolution*. London, 1920.

Cahill, Holger. *American Folk Art: The Art of the Common Man in America, 1750–1900*. (Museum of Modern Art catalogue of exhibition.) New York, n.d.

Campanella, Tommaso. *Poesie*. In *Scrittori d'Italia*, Vol. 70. Edited by Giovanni Gentile. Bari, 1915.

Calman, A. R. *Ledru-Rollin après 1848*. Paris, 1921.

Carlyle, R. W., and A. J. *A History of Mediaeval Political Theory in the West*, Vol. 1. New York, n.d.

Carlyle, Thomas. *Past and Present*. London (Everyman edition), n.d.

Charlemagne. *Capitularia, PL*, 97.

Charron, Pierre. *De la Sagesse*. Paris, 1630.

Chaucer, *The Canterbury Tales*. In *The Student's Chaucer*. Edited by Walter W. Skeat. New York, 1894.

Chicchetti, Emilio. *La Filosofia di Giambattista Vico*. Milan, 1935.

Child, Francis James. *The English and Scottish Popular Ballads*. Boston, ca. 1882–94.

Cicero. *De legibus; De republica; De finibus; Tusculans*. Loeb Classical Library. London and Cambridge, 1950, 1951, 1959.

————. *Pro L. Murena*. Edited by W. E. Heitland. Cambridge, 1886.

Commynes, Philippe de. *Mémoires*. Edited by Joseph Calmette. Paris, 1925.
Claudian. *De consulatu Stilichonis; In Rufinum; In Eutropium*. Loeb Classical Library. London and Cambridge, 1956.
Comte, Auguste. *Politique positive*. Paris, 1912.
Constitution of the United States.
Conwell, R. H. *Acres of Diamonds*. New York [1915].
Coulton, G. G. *Medieval Panorama*. New York and London, 1938.
Crabbe, George. *The Village*. Edited by Adolphus William Ward. Cambridge, 1905.
Dahlmann-Waitz. *Quellenkunde*, no. 5723. Leipzig, 1912.
Denziger, H., ed. *Enchiridion symbolorum*. Fribourg, 1921.
De Turk, D. A., and Poulin, A., Jr. *The American Folk Scene: Dimensions of the Folksong Revival*. New York, 1967.
Dickens, A. G. *The English Reformation*. Reprint. New York, 1964.
Duine, F. *La Mennais*. Paris, 1922.
Dumhof, G. William. *Who Rules America?* Englewood Cliffs, N.J., 1967.
Duverger, Maurice. *Les Constitutions de la France*. Paris, 1961.
Einhard. *Vita Caroli Imperatoris, PL*, 7.
Emerson, Ralph Waldo. *Essays*. Riverside edition of the *Works*. Boston, 1883.
Emerton, Ephraim. *The Correspondence of Pope Gregory VII*. New York, 1932.
Encyclopedia of World Art. s.v. "Folk Art." New York, Toronto, and London, 1961.
Escholier, Raymond. *Daumier*. Paris, 1930.
Faral, Edmond. *Les jongleurs en France au Moyen-Age*. Paris, 1910.
Farrand, Max, ed. *The Records of the Federal Convention*. New Haven, 1911.
Finkelstein, Sidney. *Art and Society*. New York, 1947.
———. *How Music Expresses Ideas*. New York, 1950.
———. *Composer and Nation: The Folk Heritage of Music*. New York, 1960.
Foss, Hubert. *Ralph Vaughan Williams*. London, 1950.
Francorum regum capitularia, PL, 138.
Frank, Grace. *The Medieval French Drama*. Oxford, 1954.
Frank, Tenney. *A History of Rome*. New York, 1923.
Friedländer, Walter. *Caraveggio Studies*. Princeton, 1955.
Friedman, Albert B. *The Ballad Revival*. Chicago, 1961.
Frieze, Jacob. *A Concise History of the efforts to Obtain an Extension of Suffrage in Rhode Island from the Year 1811 to 1842*. (1st edition, 1842.) Providence, 1912.
Furnivall, F. J. *Bishop Percy's Folio Manuscript*. London, 1868 (privately printed).

Gallacher, S. A. "Vox Populi Vox Dei." *Philological Quarterly*, Vol. 24 (January, 1945).

Gascoigne, George. *Posies*, in the *Complete Works of George Gascoigne*. Edited by John W. Cunliffe. Cambridge, 1907.

Gauthier, Maximilien. In *Les Maîtres Populaires de la Réalité*. (Catalogue to exhibition of paintings.) Paris, 1937.

Gellius Aulus. *Noctes Atticae*. Edited by Hertz. Leipzig, 1886.

Gerbi, A. *La Disputa del Nuovo Mondo*. Milan and Naples, 1955.

Gibbon, Edward. *History of the Decline and Fall of the Roman Empire*. London (Everyman edition), 1910.

Gierke, Otto. *Political Theories of the Middle Ages*. Translated by F. W. Maitland. Cambridge, 1900.

Gilson, Etienne, ed. *The Church Speaks to the Modern World*. Garden City, N.Y., 1954.

Glinka, Mikhail Ivanovich. *Memoirs*. Translated by Richard B. Mudge. Norman, Okla., 1963.

Gobineau, Comte Joseph Arthur de. *L'Inégalité des races*. Paris, 1853–55.

Gombrich, E. H. *Art and Illusion*. New York, 1960.

Goncourt, Edmond. *Germinie Lacerteux*. New edition. Paris, 1911.

Gower, John. *Mirour de l'Omme*, in *The Complete Works of John Gower*. Edited by G. C. Macaulay. Oxford, 1899.

Green, J. R. *History of the English People*. New York, 1880.

Grosskurth, Phyllis. *John Addington Symonds*. London, 1964.

Guicciardini, Francesco. *Ricordi*. Translated by Mario Domandi as *Maxims and Reflections of a Renaissance Statesman*. New York, 1965.

Gummere, Francis B. *The Popular Ballad*. New York (Dover Reprint), 1959.

Hall, Henry Marion. *Idylls of Fishermen*. New York, 1914.

Hamann, J. G. *Aesthetica in Nuce*. Translated by Ronald Gregor Smith in *J. G. Hamann: A Study in Christian Existence*. London, 1960.

Hauser, Arnold. *The Social History of Art*. New York, 1951.

Heimert, Alan. *Religion and the American Mind*. Cambridge, Mass., 1966.

Heine, Heinrich. *Geständnisse*, in *Werke und Briefe*. Berlin, 1962.

Held, Julius S. "Edward Hicks and the Tradition." *Art Quarterly*, Vol. 14 (1951).

Herder, J. G. *Auch eine Philosophie der Geschichte zur Bildung der Menschheit*, in *Werke, Suphan*, Vol. 5, 503.

———. *Auszug aus einem Briefwechsel über Ossian und die Lieder alter Völker*, in *Werke*, Vol. 5.

———. *Vom Geist der Ebräischen Poesie*, in *Werke*, Vol. 2.

Hinks, Roger. *Michelangelo Merisi da Caravaggio*. New York, 1953.

Hoccleve, Thomas. *Regement of Princes*. Edited by F. J. Furnivall. Early English Text Society, extra series, Vol. 72. London, 1897.
Hoch, G. P. W. A. *Manegold von Lauterbach und die Lehre von der Volksouveräntat unter Heinrich IV*. Berlin, 1902.
Hoffmeister, Karel. *Anton Dvořak*. Translated by Rosa Newmarch. London, 1928.
Holt, Elizabeth Gilmore. *Literary Sources of Art History*. Princeton, 1947.
Horace. Odes, Book III, 1. Edited by E. C. Wickham, Oxford, 1881.
Hortus deliciarum. (Facsimile reproduction.) Strasbourg, 1901 (?).
Hugo, Victor. *Actes et Paroles, in Oeuvres complètes*. Paris, 1882.
————. *Les Châtiments*. Geneva and New York, 1853.
Hunt, Thomas P. *The Book of Wealth*. . . . New York, 1836.
Hunt, William. "Odo" in *DNB*.
Isidore of Seville. *Etymologiae*. Edited by W. M. Lindsay. Oxford, 1911.
Jamot, Paul. *Les LeNain*. Paris, 1929.
————. *La Peinture en France*. Paris, 1934.
Jouffroy, Théodore. *Mélanges Philosophiques*. Paris, 1833.
Kent, James. "Remarks to the New York Constitutional Convention, 1821," in *Report of the Proceedings . . . of the Convention of 1821, etc.* Albany, N.Y., 1821. Pp. 220–21.
Kleinclausz, A. *Charlemagne*. Paris, 1934.
La Bruyère, Jean de. *Les Caractères ou Moeurs de ce Siècle*. Edited by Gaston Cayrou. Paris, 1913.
La Fontaine, Jean de. *Oeuvres*. Paris, 1883–97.
Lamennais, F. de. *Paroles d'un Croyant*. Paris, 1937.
————. *Le Livre du Peuple*. Paris, 1866.
Lang, Paul Henry. *Music in Western Civilization*. New York, 1941.
Le Grant Kalendrier et Compost des Bergiers. (Facsimile reprint.) Paris, 1924.
Libelli de Lite, MGH. Hanover, 1891–97.
Lipman, Jean. *American Primitive Painting*. New York, 1942.
Livy. *Ab urbe condita libri*. . . . Edited by G. Weissenborn and M. Müller. Berlin, 1885.
Lloyd, A. L. *Folk Song in England*. London, 1967.
Lord, Russell, ed. *Voices from the Fields*. Boston, 1937.
Lovejoy, A. O. *The Reason, the Understanding, and Time*. Baltimore, 1961.
————. *Reflections on Human Nature*. Baltimore, 1961.
————, and Boas, George. *Primitivism and Related Ideas in Antiquity*. Baltimore, 1935.
Lucan. *Pharsalia [de Bello civili]*. Edited by J. P. Postgate. Cambridge, 1896.

Machiavelli, Niccolò. *Discorsi*. Translated by Allan Gilbert. Durham, N.C., 1965.

Mackinnon, James. *The History of Edward III (1327–1377)*. London, 1900.

Mâle, Emile. *L'Art religieux du XIIIe siècle*. Paris, 1919.

Mandeville, Bernard. *The Fable of the Bees*. Edited by F. B. Kaye. Oxford, 1924.

Manegold. *Ad Gebehardum Liber; Liber de Lite*. MGH.

Manly, John Matthews. *Specimens of the Pre-Shaksperean Drama*. Boston, 1897.

Manning, William. *Key of Liberty, Shewing Why a Free Government has Always Failed*. 1798. Edited by Samuel Eliot Morison. Billerica, Mass., 1922.

Martial. *Epigrams*. Edited by W. M. Lindsay. Oxford, n.d. [1902 ?]

Maupertuis, Pierre Lewis Moreau de. *Venus Physique*, in *Les Oeuvres de Maupertuis*, Vol. 2. Berlin and Lyon, 1753.

Mazzini, Giuseppe. *Life and Writings*. London, 1866.

Mélanges H. Fitting, Montpellier, 1907.

Mellers, Wilfred. *Man and His Music: Romanticism and the Twentieth Century*. London, 1957.

Michelet, Jules. *Le Peuple*. Edited by Lucien Refort. Paris, 1946.

Moniteur Universel. Vol. 4 (reprint). Paris, 1790.

Monrad-Johansen, David. *Edvard Grieg*. Translated by Madge Robertson. Princeton, 1938.

Montaigne. *Essays*. Translated by John Florio. London (Everyman edition), 1898.

Moore, George. *Esther Waters*. London, 1894.

Münz, Ludwig. *Bruegel, the Drawings*. Translated by Luke Hermann. Greenwich, Conn., 1961.

Murimuth, Adam. *Continuatio Chronicarum*. London, 1889.

Parrington, Vernon. *Main Currents of American Thought*. (Reprint in one volume.) New York, 1930.

Pascal, Blaise. *Pensées*. Paris, Pléiade edition), 1954.

Percy, Thomas. *Reliques of Ancient English Poetry*. London and New York (Everyman edition), n.d.

Petronius. *Satyricon*. Edited by Buecheler. Berlin, 1882.

Pinto, Vivian de Sola, and Radway, Allan Edwin. *The Common Muse*. New York, 1957.

Plautus. *Comoediae*. Edited by Fleckeisen. Leipzig, 1850–51.

Pope, Alexander. *Epistles and Satires of Horace Imitated*. Epistle I, in *Works*. London, 1822.

Porter, Kirk Harold. *A History of Suffrage in the United States*. Chicago, 1918.

Praz, Mario. *The Hero in Eclipse*. Translated by Angus Davidson. London and New York, 1956.

Puttenham, George. *The Arte of English Poesie.* Edited by Gladys Doidge Willcock and Alice Walker. Cambridge, 1936.

Raffin, Léonie. *Saint-Julien de Balleure.* Paris, 1926.

Ramsay, James H. *Genesis of Lancaster.* Oxford, 1913.

Ramsay, F., Jr., and Smith, C. E., eds. *Jazzmen.* London, 1957.

Rappard, William. "Les Etats-Unis et l'Europe," in *Le Nouveau Monde et l'Europe.* Neuchatel, 1954.

Réau, Louis. *Iconographie de l'Art Chrétien.* Paris, 1958.

Records of the Federal Convention. Edited by Max Farrand. New Haven, 1911.

Rolland, Romain. *Le Théâtre du Peuple.* Paris, 1903.

Rousseau, Jean Jacques. *Social Contract,* in *The Political Writings of Jean Jacques Rousseau.* 2 vols. Edited by C. E. Vaughan. Cambridge, 1915.

——. *Discourse on Inequality* in *The Political Writings of Jean Jacques Rousseau.* Edited by C. E. Vaughan. Cambridge, 1915.

Russell, Frances Theresa. *Satire in the Victorian Novel.* New York, 1964. Reprint, originally published in 1920.

Sainct-Julien, Pierre de. *Meslanges historiques et Recueils de Diverses matieres pour la plupart Paradoxales, et neantmoins vrayes.* Lyon, 1589.

Sawyer, Charles H. "Naturalism in America," in *Courbet and the Naturalistic Movement.* Baltimore, 1938.

Scaliger, Julius Caesar. *Poetics.* Translated by F. M. Padelford. In *The Great Critics,* edited by James Harry Smith and Edd Winfield Parks. New York, 1932.

Schenk, H. G. *The Mind of the European Romantics.* London, 1966.

Schlauch, Margaret. *English Medieval Literature and Its Social Foundations.* Warsaw, 1956.

Schlegel, A. W. *Geschichte der romantischen Literatur,* in *Kritische Schriften und Briefe.* hrsg. Edgar Lohner. Stuttgart, 1962.

Schwob, Marcel. *Parnasse Satyrique.* Paris, 1905.

Sensier, Alfred. *La Vie et l'Oeuvre de J.-F. Millet.* Edited by Paul Mantz. Paris, 1881.

Shakespeare, William. *The Complete Works.* Edited by George Lyman Kittredge. Boston (*et alibi*), 1936.

Sidney, Sir Philip, *Defence of Poetry.* Boston, N.Y., *et alibi*, 1890.

Sinclair, Upton. *Mammonart.* Pasadena, 1925.

Slonimsky, Nicolas. *Lexicon of Musical Invective.* New York, 1953.

Smith, A. L. in *Traill's Social England.* Vol. 2. London, 1894–97.

Smith, Page. *John Adams.* Garden City, N.Y., 1962.

Sorel, A. *L'Europe et la Révolution Française.* Paris, 1885.

Spenser, Edmund. *The Faerie Queene.* In the Globe Edition of the *Works,* ed. R. Morris, London, 1907.

Spiller, Robert E., Willard Thorpe, Henry Seidel Canby, Thomas H. Johnson, et al. *Literary History of the United States.* New York, 1953.

Symonds, John Addington. *Sonnets of Michael Angelo Buonarrotti and Tommaso Campanella.* London, 1878.

Taylor, Lily Ross. *Roman Voting Assemblies.* Ann Arbor, 1966.

Thomas, Jean. *Ballad Makin' in the Mountains of Kentucky.* New York, 1939.

Thomson, James. "The Poems of William Blake." In *The Speedy Extinction of Evil and Misery.* Edited by William David Schaefer. Berkeley and Los Angeles, 1967.

Tibullus. *Elegies.* Edited by Postgate. Oxford [1905 ?].

Tolnay, Charles de. *Pierre Bruegel l'Ancien.* Brussels, 1935.

Trench, Richard Chenevix. *Proverbs and their Lessons.* 7th ed. London, 1879.

Trevelyan, G. M. *England in the Age of Wycliffe.* London, 1935.

The Twenty-Four Books of the Holy Scriptures . . . According to the Massoretic Text. Translated by Isaac Keeser. New York and Cincinnati, 1901.

Uhland, J. L. *Alte hoch-und niederdeutsche Volkslieder,* in *Schriften,* Vol. 3. Stuttgart, 1866.

Unwin, Rayner. *The Rural Muse.* London, 1954.

Vaughan Williams, Ralph. *National Music.* London, 1934.

Vaughan Williams, Ursula. *R.V.W.* London, 1964.

Vergil. *Georgics.* Edited by T. L. Papillon and A. E. Haigh. Oxford, 1892.

Vico, Giambattista. *Scienza Nuova.* Edited by Paolo Rossi. Milan, 1959.

Volney, C. F. *Tableau du climat et du sol des Estats-Unis,* in *Oeuvres de C. F. Volney,* Vol. 4. 2d ed. Paris, 1825.

―――. *Voyage en Égypte,* in *Oeuvres de C. F. Volney.* Paris, 1825.

Walsingham. *Chronicon Angliae.* Rolls Series. London, 1874.

―――. *Historia Anglicana.* Edited by H. T. Riley. London, 1863.

Walter, Gérard. *Histoire des Paysans de France.* Paris, 1963.

Ward, John William. *Andrew Jackson: Symbol for an Age.* New York, 1955.

Warner, W. L., and Lunt, P. S. *The Social Life of a Modern Community.* New Haven, 1941.

Webster, Daniel. "Second Speech on Foot's Resolution," in *Works,* Vol. 3. Boston, 1854.

Weigert, Roger-Armand. *French Tapestry.* Translated by Donald and Monique King. Newton, Mass., 1956.

Welsford, Enid. *The Fool: His Social and Literary History.* London, 1935.

Wescher, Paul. *Jean Fouquet and His Time*. New York, 1947.
Wesley, John. *Primitive Physic*. 21st ed. (First edition, 1747.) London, 1785.
Wido, Bishop of Ferrar. *De Schismate Hildebrandi; Liber de Lite*. MGH.
Wilks, Michael. *The Problem of Sovereignty in the Later Middle Ages*. Cambridge, 1963.
William of Malmesbury. *De gestis pontificorum Anglorum, PL*, 179.
Williams, Roger. *Bloudy Tenant*, in *Works*, Vol. 3. Reprint of the Narragansett Club Publications. New York, 1963.
Williamson, Chilton. *American Suffrage, from Property to Democracy, 1760–1860*. Princeton, 1960.
Willoughby, L. A. *The Romantic Movement in Germany*. Oxford, 1930.
Winthrop, John. *Model of Christianity*, in Perry Miller, ed., *The American Puritans*. Garden City, N.Y., 1956.
Wise, John. *Vindication of the Government of the New England Churches* (1717). Facsimile edition. Gainesville, Fla., 1958.
Woermann, Karl. *Geschichte der Kunst aller Zeiten und Völker*. Leipzig and Vienna, 1911.
Wordsworth, William. Preface to the *Lyrical Ballads*. Edited by George Sampson. London, 1914.
Wright, Thomas, ed. *Anecdota Literaria*. London, 1844.
———. *Political Poems and Songs*. London, 1861.
Würtembeyer, Franzepp. *Mannerism*. Translated by Michael Heron. New York, 1963.
Wyllie, Irvin Gordon. "The Cult of the Self-Made Man, 1830–1910." Ph.D. dissertation, University of Wisconsin, 1949.
Zborowski, Mark, and Herzog, Elizabeth. *Life Is with People: The Culture of the Shtetl*. Schocken Paperback. (Original edition, 1952.) New York, 1962.
Zeeveld, W. Gordon. "Social Equalitarianism in a Tudor Crisis," *JHI*, vol. 7, no. 1, 1946.
Zola, Emile, Preface to *l'Assomoir*, 1877. Paris (Pléiade edition).

INDEX

In many cases discussion of a subject extends over several pages. Only the first page on which the subject is referred to is cited here.

Designed by Edward King

Composed in Linotype Electra by The Colonial Press Inc.

Printed offset on P&S Old Forge by The Colonial Press Inc.

Bound in paper and cloth editions by The Colonial Press Inc.